D1824845

Helping Children of Troubled Parents

A Guidebook

Helping Children
with Feelings

Helping Children of Troubled Parents

Monica Plum's
Horrid Problem

Margot Sunderland

Illustrated by
Nicky Armstrong

A Guidebook

Margot Sunderland

Illustrated by

Nicky Armstrong

Speechmark

www.speechmark.net

Note on the text

For the sake of clarity alone, throughout the text the child has been referred to as 'he' and the parent as 'she'.

Unless otherwise stated, for clarity alone, where 'mummy', 'mother' or 'mother figure' is used, this refers to either parent or other primary caretaker.

Confidentiality

Where appropriate, full permission has been granted by adults, or children and their parents, to use clinical material. Other illustrations comprise synthesised and disguised examples to ensure anonymity.

Published by
Speechmark Publishing Ltd
Sunningdale House, 43 Caldecotte Lake Drive, Milton Keynes MK7 8LF, United Kingdom
Tel: +44 (0)1908 277177   Fax: +44 (0)1908 278297
www.speechmark.net

First published 2013

Text copyright © Margot Sunderland, 2013
Illustrations copyright © Nicky Armstrong, 2013

All rights reserved. The whole of this work, including all text and illustrations, is protected by copyright. No part of it may be copied, altered, adapted or otherwise exploited in any way without express prior permission, unless it is in accordance with the provisions of the Copyright Designs and Patents Act 1988 or in order to photocopy or make duplicating masters of those pages so indicated, without alteration and including copyright notices, for the express purposes of instruction and examination. No parts of this work may otherwise be loaded, stored, manipulated, reproduced, or transmitted in any form or by any means, electronic or mechanical, including photocopying and recording, or by any information storage and retrieval system without prior written permission from the publisher, on behalf of the copyright owner.

002-5686 / Printed in the United Kingdom by CMP (uk) Ltd

British Library Cataloguing in Publication Data
A catalogue record for this book is available from the British Library

ISBN 978 0 86388 800 7

Contents

ABOUT THE BOOK   1

HOW TO USE THE BOOK   2

INTRODUCTION   3

PART ONE

HOW PARENTS' TROUBLES CAN AFFECT THEIR PARENTING   13

CHILDREN WITH AN ANXIOUS PARENT   21

CHILDREN WITH AN ANGRY PARENT   41

CHILDREN WITH A DEPRESSED PARENT   59

CHILDREN WITH PARENTS WHO FIGHT   79

CHILDREN WITH PARENTS WHO ARE SEPARATING, SEPARATED OR DIVORCED   93

CHILDREN WITH PARENTS ADDICTED TO DRUGS, ALCOHOL OR SOLVENTS   107

CHILDREN WITH A PARENT WHO IS ILL OR DYING AND THE PLIGHT OF THE YOUNG CARER   129

PART TWO

OBJECTIVE/INSTRUCTIONS/DEVELOPMENT   151

MY FEELINGS ABOUT MUM OR DAD   159

THE WORRY MOUNTAIN   162

THE 'IT'S ALL TOO MUCH' FEELING   166

LOSS AND LONGINGS   169

SHOCK   174

MUSEUM OF RESENTMENTS   178

THE CLOUD WE LIVE UNDER   184

WHAT I WANT FOR ME AND MY LIFE   189

MUM/DAD: THE ROCK BOTTOM AND THE BEST BITS   194

SEPARATION AND DIVORCE   198

PARENTS FIGHTING   204

LOVING SOMEONE WHO ISN'T GOOD AT LOVING BACK   209

FACILITATING A HEALING CONVERSATION BETWEEN PARENT AND CHILD/TEENAGER   212

REFERENCES   219

ABOUT THE BOOK

This book is designed to enable adults to help children whose emotional well-being is being adversely affected by troubled parents. These are children who live with the burden of having to navigate their parents' raw or tormented emotional states, often leaving them with a mass of painful feelings and a chaotic disturbing world. When parents are preoccupied with their own troubles, they are often unable to address effectively their child's relational and emotional needs – for example, soothing, validating, attunement, co-adventure and interactive play. As a result, children are left self-helping, which all too often means drugs, drink, self-harm, depression, anxiety, eating disorders or problems with anger in the teenage years.

This book offers readers a wealth of vital theory and effective interventions for their work with these children:

✧ Children of mentally or physically unwell parents.

✧ Children of alcohol or drug-addicted parents.

✧ Children of clinically depressed or anxious parents.

✧ Children of chronically under-supported parents.

✧ Children stuck in the middle between two warring parents.

Particular focus is given to the effects on children of witnessing parents fighting, family breakdown, separation and divorce.

Readers will learn:

✧ The complexity of children's feelings about troubled parents.

✧ Common physical, emotional and behavioural symptoms.

✧ How to enable children to address their unspoken hurt, fear, shock, grief, rage, resentment or guilt about their troubled parent in order to move forward in their lives.

✧ How to empower children to find their voice when they have been left in the role of impotent bystander.

✧ Key tools for effective parent–child communication when parental troubles are adversely affecting the child.

✧ How to help a parent and child 'find' each other again.

✰ How to empower the troubled parents who are willing and able to process their emotional pain so they can address their child's unmet psychological needs.

This book is for any adult who wants to help:

✰ Young carers – children who look after their troubled parents.

✰ Children whose parents inflict domestic violence.

✰ Children of abusive parents.

✰ Children whose parents are suffering from ongoing stress and anxiety (eg financial worries).

HOW TO USE THE BOOK

The book is divided into two sections:

Part one: This part is all about developing an understanding of what it is like for a child to live with a troubled parent. It also covers the latest research in terms of common effects, short and long term, and what can be done to help.

Part two: This part is the practical intervention section. It provides a wealth of exercises, drawing worksheets and tasks to support therapeutic conversations with children. These conversations can enable children to reflect on their lives and find ways of being, doing and thinking which enable them to thrive.

The book also includes an accompanying story for children:

Monica Plum's Horrid Problem

This is a story for children with troubled parents. Monica has a horrid problem. It gets everywhere: into her schoolwork, her dreams, and her ability to make friends. People keep telling her to cheer up. She can't. She feels as if she is carrying around some very heavy luggage. Then one day, a helpful teacher sees how miserable Monica is, and tells her about the knights in the world, who are posing as people. In a whispering wood, Monica finds some of these knights. They teach her how to make her problem far less horrid. In particular, they show her how to cope when other people's problems weigh you down and make you feel miserable. Most importantly, they show her how to do life well. Monica leaves the whispering wood feeling empowered and ready to face what she was finding too difficult to face before.

INTRODUCTION

... If we fail to help these children it should be never said that we didn't know what they were going through.

(Channel 4, *Dispatches*, 3 November 2008)

It's shocking, the impact that troubled parents can have on their children, when there is no intervention or support for parent or child.

The famous Adverse Childhood Experience (ACE) studies (Felitti *et al*, 2003) involving over 17,000 people over three generations, found that you have a very high risk of physical and mental health problems, including drug, alcohol or nicotine addiction and then early death, if you grow up as a child:

✫ with someone in the household who is in prison

✫ where the mother was treated violently

✫ with an alcoholic or a drug user

✫ where someone is chronically depressed, mentally ill, or suicidal.

We also know now that parents troubled by anger are part of this list: parents who shout, scold, humiliate and constantly criticise a child (Teicher *et al*, 2006).

If you have six or more adverse childhood experiences involving troubled parents there is on average a nearly 20-year reduction in life span (Brown *et al*, 2009).

So when people glibly say, 'but children are resilient', they are very wrong. We often assume the most resilience when the child's brain is at its most vulnerable: namely over the childhood years when the brain is still forming itself in ways that makes it extremely susceptible to being adversely altered by the chronic stress of living with a troubled parent. In fact, research also shows that early adverse childhood experiences are responsible for:

✫ 50 per cent of all drug abuse

✫ 54 per cent of all depression

✫ 65 per cent of all alcoholism

✫ 67 per cent of all suicide attempts.

(Felitti *et al*, 2003)

Despite these shocking statistics, we are still putting in massive financial resources in terms of picking up the pieces after a troubled parent leads to a troubled child. The result is health care costs, youth offending costs, child welfare costs, medical costs and juvenile justice costs. Far less money is spent on prevention (known as 'invest to save'). Yet, with far more therapeutic and supportive intervention for parents and children, an enormous amount of suffering could be prevented and massive financial savings could be made. Massive savings have been quantified by world leading financiers such as James Heckman (2011), if we only invest in child well-being. Moreover, the resilience studies show again that what is needed is intervention by thoughtful caring adults.

Researchers analysing resilience in teenagers dealing well with painful life events found that connectedness to at least one adult was a key factor in developing resilient behaviour and it was equally valuable whether it happened in the family, in the community or at school (Howard and Johnson, 2000). Then, The Minnesota Study of Risk and Adaptation (Sroufe *et al*, 2005) followed 180 infants born in poverty from birth to age 30, focusing on risk factors for abuse and neglect. The key factor for non-perpetuation of maltreatment was relationship – an alternative, non-abusive adult during childhood or the teenage years, and/or for the child or teenager to have participated in a therapy experience for at least six months during some period. Virtually none of the parents who perpetuated the cycle of abuse had experienced any of these forms of relationship.

So this book hopes to support those intent on prevention and who want to have interventions which will support social change and the alleviation of suffering of children and teenagers.

So what is a troubled parent?

Of course it is normal and entirely understandable for all parents to feel very stressed from time to time, with all the demands of bringing up a child. Parenting in so many ways is a Herculean task! But this book is not about that. It is about parents who are troubled in ways that mean it is difficult for them to respond well enough to all the emotional and relational needs of their children. That said, it must be emphasised from the start that this book is not about criticising parents who are struggling. It is about empowering them to change in ways that will benefit children and to get the support for their children when they feel unable to change. So to suggest that all parents who have a problem with alcohol, depression, mental illness or anxiety, or who suffer from domestic violence, are bad parents or dangerous to their children is often absolutely not true.

Research shows that with good support, 'parents who are experiencing a single disorder are often able to be effective and loving parents and present little risk of significant harm to children' (Cleaver *et al*, 2007).

When parents are troubled, they can find many or all of the key components of good parenting difficult – for example, playing, talking with the child, going out to the park and other child-focused activities, taking an interest in their child's interests, keeping to routines (bedtimes, mealtimes, etc) and repeating family rituals. As a drug-using parent once said, 'Probably the only routine they had was my drug use and me getting my drugs; that was the only routine' (Barnard, 2007).

This often leaves the child suffering from emotional and relational impoverishment. Even birthdays can get forgotten and looked-forward-to holidays or outings aborted. So there can be endless losses and disappointments for the child and often a real sense of betrayal. 'But Mum, you promised…'

Kesha, aged 17: 'A couple of Christmases ago, she was sober from the 18th to the 26th … And we went out shopping and we been skating. We done a lot within those days. But then she went back to the drink' (Bancroft *et al*, 2004).

With some troubled parents, children are under-supervised, left for far too long on their own, and their physical need for safety, warm clothing, changed nappies, and so on are not met. Parents are often only too aware of how their 'troubles' leave them unable or not wanting to relate to their children in the way they would like to. This can leave them with acutely painful feelings of guilt, inadequacy and failure.

The different ways in which parents are troubled

Ashley's mother could not act as a protective parent because she had convinced herself as a child that there were no protective parents.

It is clear from the research (Cleaver *et al*, 2011) that one key factor, such as depression, or alcohol abuse, or domestic violence, puts the child at risk of long-term mental health problems, but not always. What is far more concerning for the child are multiple factors, for example, the parent who is being hit uses alcohol to deal with her feelings and suffers depression.

We will look at this in more depth throughout the book. In the meantime, here are specific ways that parents are troubled:

✩ Some parents are troubled because they never received enough emotional regulation and empathic listening when they were children.

✩ Some parents are troubled because they are battling with unworked-through trauma or loss in their own lives for which they have not sought professional help or talking therapy. They mistakenly think that things will just get better. This flies in the face of all the latest trauma research which shows continued emotional fallout adversely affecting parenting, with unprocessed trauma and loss (Wickes, 1988; Hunter, 2001; Cooper *et al*, 2003).

✩ Some parents are troubled because they are desperately unsupported. They are overwhelmed and isolated, suffering from a profound lack of emotional support and people in their lives to emotionally regulate them. In other words, a parent can be suffering from all manner of horrible events in their life, but if someone – a therapist, sibling, spouse or friend – is really helping that parent with all her feelings, she can still be a good parent. It's quite simple. If she is being regularly emotionally regulated, she can then be an emotional regulator for her child.

Darren, aged six

Darren's Mum, Sally, was a single parent. She had no real support from any adult. Darren had two siblings who were under five years of age. This would be a Herculean task even for the most supported parent. One day Darren was arguing with his little sister. Something snapped in his Mum. She held a knife to his throat and said 'this is arguing'. She realised things had crossed a line. She rang ChildLine and said 'if I don't get help I am worried I will kill them'. Some very sensitive social workers were called in who realised that Sally was basically a good Mum who was just desperately under-supported. They helped her set up a programme of things to do with her children and got her some support. Sally started to enjoy her children and her anger subsided.

☆ Some parents are troubled because of threat of future losses – for example, the threat of bailiffs, not having enough money to pay the mortgage, living in fear of losing their job or the death of a parent.

☆ Some parents are troubled by family breakdown or other conflicts within the family, such as domestic violence or constant arguing with a partner or relatives.

☆ Some parents are troubled by drug or alcohol abuse.

☆ Some parents are troubled with a physical or mental illness, such as clinical depression, problems with anxiety or anger, or battling with cancer or other debilitating or frightening illness.

☆ Sometimes the partner walks out because the other is so troubled, but that leaves the child dealing with the troubled parent on their own.

☆ Troubled parents can be found in all social strata.

When addressing the emotional state of the child, people often forget to ask about the emotional state of the parent

Just as a tree is affected by the quality of air, water and soil in its environment, the emotional health of children is determined by the quality of intimate relationships that surround them.
(Gottman and DeClaire, 1998)

There is a common misassumption that whenever a child has challenging or concerning behaviour, what is needed is simply better discipline, clearer boundaries, or classes in parenting skills. For some children such interventions are effective, but for others it is totally missing the point. As we know, humans are very complex creatures and so are the causes of their troubled behaviour. When looking to address a child's emotional or behavioural problems, therefore, we need to think multi-causally as in the table on the next page.

KEY UNDERLYING CAUSES OF CHALLENGING BEHAVIOUR
REASON ONE UNDER-DEVELOPED FRONTAL LOBES/DYSREGULATED BODILY AROUSAL STATES (From lack of emotional regulation)
REASON TWO INSECURE ATTACHMENT
REASON THREE UNWORKED-THROUGH TRAUMA/LOSS
REASON FOUR UNMET STIMULATION HUNGER/RECOGNITION HUNGER/STRUCTURE HUNGER
REASON FIVE LACK OF EFFECTIVE PARENTING SKILLS (eg discipline)
REASON SIX STRESSFUL FAMILY CULTURES
REASON SEVEN TROUBLED PARENTS
REASON EIGHT TROUBLED PARENT–CHILD RELATIONSHIPS

Table 1 *Key underlying causes of challenging behaviour*

This book will focus on the last three underlying causes for a child being troubled:

Reason six – Stressful family cultures

Reason seven – Troubled parents

Reason eight – Troubled parent–child relationships.

Many parents don't appreciate just how much their emotional state and physiological arousal levels affect their child

If, when faced with a child's troubled behaviour, we only think in terms of discipline, or parenting classes (as lots of popular parenting books and TV programmes do), we are failing to address the other ways that children can be affected.

One of the key causes of a child's troubled behaviour is living with a parent who is troubled. In other words, a child's troubled behaviour is so often a barometer for the parent's emotional states, for parental stress, parental unprocessed trauma and loss, feelings brushed under the carpet, and the emotional atmospheres in the home. Out of awareness, the child discharges the tension from their parent's painful emotional states. The tension comes out in challenging behaviour and/or neurotic symptoms.

Research shows that the level of family stress is an excellent predictor of child behaviour problems in the preschool period (Egeland and Kreutzner, 1991, cited in Sroufe *et al*, 1990). In short, troubled parents so often equals troubled children, and if it doesn't come out in childhood it will in the teenage years.

Yet all too often the child is treated as an island, labelled with ADHD for example, and even given drugs for problematic behaviour, without anyone asking, 'How is the child being affected by their parent's emotional states?'

Helping Children of
Troubled Parents

PART ONE

HOW PARENTS' TROUBLES CAN AFFECT THEIR PARENTING

Troubled parents often find it difficult to be an emotional regulator for their child

All children need their parents to be 'emotional regulators'. This means that they need their parents to help them with big feelings such as rage, frustration, separation distress. They need their parents to soothe their distress, to provide empathic listening when needed, to help the child make sense of what is happening and has happened to them in their lives for better or worse and to enable them to manage conflict with siblings and peers well. In other words, a key parental role is to help the child in states of intense emotional dysregulation to move back to emotional regulation and so a feeling of well-being.

Freud knew that all children need emotional regulation. 'The child is really not equipped to master psychically the large sums of excitation that reach him whether from without or from within' (Freud, 1926).

> Their self-confidence as they carried us when we were babies, their security when they allowed us to merge our anxious selves with their tranquility – via calm voices or closeness with their relaxed bodies as they held us. [All this] will be retained by us as the calmness we experience as we live our lives.
> (Kohut and Wolf, 1978)

When the child is being infuriating, irritating, relentlessly demanding, parents who are effective emotional regulators will stay stable under stress, calm and reflective rather than shouty, angry, controlling or critical, or becoming like a toddler themselves.

Emotional regulation not only develops the child's mind but also their brain. It sets up stress regulatory systems in the brain, enabling good handling of life's inevitable stressors and knocks (Cozolino, 2006; Schore, 1999, 2003a, 2003b). In other words, when we are consistently and repeatedly emotionally responsive to children then top-down brain pathways naturally inhibit primitive impulses to lash out or run away. When this doesn't happen, life becomes very difficult and minor stressors can be experienced as major emergencies. This leaves the parent vulnerable to developing mental health problems with anxiety, aggression or depression.

To be an emotional regulator for a child you need the space in your mind to be able to think into and feel into your child's pain. Troubled parents don't have this space due to their own mind being full of their own distress, which they are finding it difficult to deal with. It takes up all their time to try to emotionally regulate themselves.

Troubled parents often don't have the patience to respond to the infant's incessant (but entirely developmentally appropriate) needs

Behavioural psychologists have observed that preschoolers typically demand that their parents deal with some kind of desire or need every 20 seconds. So if you have more than one preschooler it's a need every 10 seconds (Gottman and DeClaire, 1998). Under ideal circumstances, a parent can respond cheerfully, with interest and attunement, but when a parent is troubled, a child's incessant, and sometimes irrational, demands can drive parents wild.

Example
Amelie's (aged two) needs, which come every 20 seconds:
- to show you her plastic dinosaur for the fifth time
- to separate the sweetcorn from the ham on her dinner plate
- to help lift her up to see what is on the top shelf
- to pick her up and give her a cuddle when she hurts her knee on the toy car
- to be the one who switches off the cold tap when you brush your teeth
- to get your help in trying to turn a key in the front door lock
- to get you to comment for the sixth time on the spider crawling up the bathroom wall
- to listen to her story for the umpteenth time about how the naughty puddle made her slip that morning.

Troubled parents affect the child's behaviour

Troubled parents, distracted by their own problems, have less quality time and quality attention for their children, so children can move into more disturbed or troubled behaviour. The parent's emotional dysregulation is very dysregulating for the child. In other words, the parent's tensions become the child's tensions. The child can end up discharging, or 'acting out' through bad behaviour, the tension from their parent's painful feelings or painful feelings in the parental relationship.

Also, children learn through modelling. If a parent is impulsive, reactive and having angry outbursts, they teach their children to be reactive and impulsive and to have angry outbursts. If a parent is anxious, the child will be anxious. If a parent is warm, kind and gentle, the child will be warm, kind and gentle, and so on.

Troubled parenting affects the child's quality of life

There is no doubt that gross events – such as births, deaths, illnesses and the deaths of siblings, the illnesses and deaths of parents, the breakups of families, the child's prolonged separations from the significant adults, his severe and prolonged illness, and so on – can play an important role in the genetic factors that lead to later psychological illness. But ... experience tells us that in the great majority of cases it is the specific [mental unwellness] of the parent(s) and specific [negative] features of the atmosphere in which the child grows up that account for the mal-developments, fixations and unsolvable inner conflicts characterizing the adult personality. (Kohut, 1977)

The child of troubled parents often has poor quality of life. This is because they are so often deprived of a carefree childhood and live in a family culture where the very atmosphere of relational exchanges is troubled in the way described above. Instead, they are dealing with major existential issues at a very young age, such as:
- how to respond to the emotional needs of an adult
- how to manage adult mental health problems
- how to live with a parent who is clinically depressed or addicted to substances
- how to manage the fallout from parents arguing and family breakdown.

This is so much the case that the troubled parent can become the child's world:

> If Mummy is wobbly, the world is wobbly
> If Mum ain't happy, no one is happy
> If Daddy is frightening the world is frightening
> If Mum is chaotic – the world feels mad
> (Brian Post)

Some children of troubled parents don't realise that there is anything wrong. They don't know any other reality. They had not had another childhood or another set of parents – so unhappiness is just a way of being. Some may never have been close enough to a fortunate child's home life to know there is another very different reality for some children. So they may think, this is what you do as a child: look after your parent, put her in bed when she is drunk, mop up the sick, get the younger children ready for school.

Troubled parenting affects the child's ability to learn

The troubled parent is so much of a worry for so many children that it can be difficult to think of other things, or focus on anything else. Many children are constantly monitoring their parent. For some children all the space in their minds is taken up thinking about their troubled parent and how to get him or her to be happy or well again.

Troubled parenting affects the child's ability to feel

A child with a troubled parent may survive by emotional numbing. Seeing their parent in so much emotional or physical pain is just too much. It's a way of surviving, but surviving is not living. If you cut off pain you can cut off life, in other words, living without the capacity to feel passionate or excited or loving. The lines in Ted Hughes' poem called 'Sheep' offer a poignant portrayal of this numbing process.

> Only slowly their hurt dies, cry by cry
> As they fit themselves to what has happened.
>
> (Ted Hughes, from 'Sheep' (part III), 1995)

I have known many children and adults for whom these two lines are particularly resonant, who have indeed had to 'fit themselves to what has happened', by closing their hearts. The lines describe the gradual building of defences to protect against pain, accompanied by certain loss of aspects of one's very humanity. Some children have learned not to have feelings, so that they don't burden their parents with them. As a six-year-old said to me, 'I keep my feelings in a tunnel'.

Troubled parenting affects the child's mental health now and in the future

A large number of studies link troubled parents to conduct disorders, learning difficulties, mental ill-health in infants, children, and teenagers. The statistics clearly show that chronic distress or stress states in parents appears to be one of the biggest contributory factors to children developing or sustaining emotional problems (Department of Health, 2005).

Some anxious children develop obsessive-compulsive ordering or checking rituals. Sometimes this is due to them trying to 'tidy up' their parent's too messy feelings. Research has shown that having angry or depressed parents is predictive of later aggression in children (Lyons-Ruth, 1996). This is due to the persistent activation of the stress system in the child's brain called the hypothalamus-pituitary-adrenal axis (HPA axis). This 'axis' can become wired for oversensitivity if the child has an alarming parent.

Some children get a double whammy of two emotionally dysregulated parents, such as a depressed mother and a father who experiences angry explosions. This can be a damaging situation for a child to grow up in.

Parental mental health in the first years of life has a significant influence on early brain activity and long-term behavioural outcome (Dawson *et al*, 2000). Biochemical systems activating maternal feelings of protective, warm, tender, compassionate feelings towards her baby can become blocked by high levels of stress hormones. The stress in the parent's own body and brain will result in too high levels of stress chemicals in her child's brain (Schore 2003a, 2003b).

Troubled parenting affects the child's body

With the calm untroubled parent, 'The infant merges with the strength and calm of the mother's body' (Mahler, 1968). Over time, her calmness becomes the child's calmness. When a parent is troubled, there is no merging with anything lovely, only with a body with the tensions and agitations from being anxious, angry or depressed. So a troubled parent's body can become a place of alarm not of calm. Over time, this can then lead to disgust for the mother's body, particularly as the child gets older.

Research shows that children will be reacting to the parent's stress or distress states physiologically as well as psychologically, so children of troubled parents often have sleep, eating or elimination problems. They are far more highly aroused and, during rest periods, far slower to relax, particularly when both parents expressed intense emotions (Hibbs *et al*, 1992).

Children of troubled parents may experience the following physiological problems:
- heart rate (racing – sometimes 140 beats per minute)
- sleep
- eating
- toileting
- immune system.

(Field, 1994; Dawson *et al*, 2000; Hibbs *et al*, 1992)

When emotionally well parents become troubled

When a previously well parent becomes mentally ill or troubled, the child suffers a terrible pain of loss.

These are some of the common losses for the child:
- loss of their parent as an emotional regulator – someone who helps them with their feelings
- loss of their parent as a playmate
- loss of their parent as protector
- loss of their parent as encourager and advocate.

These lost elements make a child feel safe in the world and without them they feel bereft.

Example
Angela, aged eight (whose mother has depression): 'She used to hold me, carry me and now she doesn't.'

The children often don't know what 'normal' is

> She also thought that all her friends' fathers had sex with them –
> until one day she asked her best friend Mitzi. Mitzi acted shocked
> and disgusted, and Janette felt that she had made a terrible mistake
> by asking. She felt betrayed by Mitzi. After all, they had talked
> about everything else.
> (Clayton, 1997)

Many children of troubled parents don't know what normal parenting is or would feel like. Sometimes they 'get it' that their parenting is not normal because it's so different from the parents they read about in nice children's books. But until they actually spend some time in the presence of the parents of other children and see lots of lovely parent–child interactions, they can have little notion of 'normal'. When they do watch other parents being with their children it can be very shocking and sometimes very painful for them – knowing what they have been missing out on.

Teenagers with troubled parents

Troubled parenting not only affects younger children. It also has a big impact on adolescents and young people. The teenager of a troubled parent can be left feeling responsible for the parent that is left behind when they themselves want to move away to leave home or go to university. They can feel responsible, thinking that they are at an age now when they must look after the parent. The guilt can leave no room for their own feelings of grief and loss, while at the same time adding to their feelings of resentment (owned or denied). Furthermore, it is difficult to leave the mother at the appropriate time for them developmentally (eg, aged 16 to 18) if she is at risk of endangering herself or if she has evoked deep anxiety in her teenager.

Also, troubled parents of teenagers must know that they have been role models for their children. This can often result in them having to watch their teenagers make the same mistakes that they did: teenage pregnancy, getting attached to an abusive partner, taking drugs, getting addicted to alcohol, or developing similar problems as their own with aggression, anxiety or depression. So parents with drug or alcohol problems may find it hard to instil restraint in their teenagers, at risk of hypocrisy.

CHILDREN WITH AN ANXIOUS PARENT

SECTION ONE: WHAT LIFE IS LIKE FOR THE CHILD WITH AN ANXIOUS PARENT: THE RESEARCH, THE PSYCHOLOGY AND THE BRAIN SCIENCE

Children talking ...

George, aged eight: 'When my mum wobbles it's like my whole world wobbles.'

Toby, aged seven: 'My worries spoil my happiness.'

Delphine, aged nine: 'Other children like firework night. I stay indoors quaking in my shoes. I am very worried that our house might burn down and that my Mummy will be burnt to death.'

Gemma, aged twelve: 'I don't want to go to the big school next year because I don't know who will keep me safe.'

Rupal, aged ten: 'I never wake up in a good mood, more a sense of dread. I think who will be the frightening people in my life today?'

HOW COMMON IS PARENTAL ANXIETY? THE STATISTICS

- General anxiety disorder (GAD) affects about 1 in 20 adults in Britain. Slightly more women are affected than men, and the condition is most common in people in their twenties (NHS, Generalised Anxiety Disorder, www.nhs.uk/conditions/anxiety/Pages/Introduction.aspx last reviewed April 2012).

- Among people under 65, nearly half of all ill health is mental illness. In other words, nearly as much ill health is mental illness as all physical illnesses put together (LSE and Centre for Economic Performances Mental Health Policy Group, 2012).

- More than 1 in 10 people are likely to have a 'disabling anxiety disorder' at some stage in their life (Ehlers, 1997).

- A recent World Health Organization (WHO) study concluded that the impact of depression is 50 per cent more serious than angina, asthma or diabetes (Mousavi *et al*, 2007).

- The most recent Psychiatric Morbidity Survey indicates that there are approximately 3 million people in the UK with an anxiety disorder (Singleton *et al*, 2000).

- The diagnosis for an anxiety disorder in the UK increased by 800,000 from 1993 to 2007 (Mental Health Foundation, 2009).

- Prevention of childhood anxiety is critical because anxiety disorders affect one in five US children but often go unrecognised. Delays in diagnosis and treatment can lead to depression, substance abuse and poor academic performance throughout childhood and well into adulthood (Budinger *et al*, 2013).

- It often takes between 10 and 15 years for people with obsessive-compulsive disorder (OCD) to seek professional help (Mental Health Foundation, 2007).

About parents who are anxious

When you suffer from neurotic anxiety, then anxiety is part of who you are, part of the absolute fabric of your personality. You wake up with it, go to sleep with it and it is there throughout the day. You are always on the lookout for the next possible threat. You live in a state of being 'on guard', ready for the crash, that unexpected blow of fate. And so it's never safe to really relax, or let go, because that's exactly when things could go wrong. You are never free to just drift or languish, because the present is forever tainted with fear of what might happen in the future. You are never at ease, even if the sword of Damocles never actually falls. You believe from your very soul, that something very bad will happen soon. Your anxiety is ever present.

So, in terms of parenting, it is very difficult to offer soothing and calming to a child, when you cannot soothe yourself! There will be a gap in terms of Margaret Mahler's statement, 'The child needs to merge with the calm and strength of the mother's body' (Mahler, 1968). The constant dwelling in your mind on an endless array of possible catastrophes eclipses any possibility of fully experiencing pleasure with your child on a sustained basis, or really enjoying the fruits of your role as a parent in a peaceful way. This means that there will be many times when there is not space in your mind for your child's emotional needs.

Some parents are anxious because their parents were anxious or fearful when they were little. As a result, their brains never habituated to calming chemicals such as opioids and oxytocin (Panksepp, 1998) and their body never established good vagal tone (a well-balanced autonomic nervous system) (Gottman *et al*, 1996). It is never too late for this to happen, but by and large such parents will have to go for long-term counselling or psychotherapy as a form of re-parenting.

Anxious, uncalm parents are often trying so hard to manage and regulate their own stress states that they misattune to their own child. As a result, sometimes the dance of the dialogue goes wrong between them. The anxious parent, for example, may fail to allow sufficient pauses and standing back in the way they relate to their infant. They may over-stimulate the infant with too much 'in your face' interaction. They can fail to read the infant's cues that the stimulation level is too high and that the infant needs to break contact for a while. Research shows that panic-disordered mothers were less emotionally attuned to their infant (Warren *et al*, 2003). As a result, infants may experience their parent as a source of stress rather than a source of calm.

This can mean that they become avoidant attached – not turning to their parent for solace and comfort – or ambivalent attached – getting anxious and clingy as they learn not to trust that they will get the attuned emotional responsiveness they need. At other times, the child can feel unheld in their mind, as the parent's thoughts focus away from the child onto their own worries and preoccupations. As a result, the infant feels dysregulated and alone, left too often in states of unmanageable relational stress or poverty.

Example

Syreeta was a very anxious person, and so a very anxious mother. She had read that babies need lots of stimulation. As a result, she would fuss her baby, Layla, wiggle her legs, endlessly straighten Layla's clothes, bounce her up and down and shake rattles in her face to try to get Layla to smile at her. Sometimes she put her face very close to Layla's face and kept saying 'googa googa, my little babykins, babyboo' for a very long time. Often Layla would turn away from Syreeta when she did this. After a while, Layla stopped looking at Syreeta altogether. She stopped crying too. People worried that she was autistic. What had happened was that Layla felt very emotionally dysregulated by her mother and over-aroused. The dance between them was no longer a dance, but rather a kind of unintentional assault of endless hyper-joy! Like any human being, Layla needed a break from it, so she had cut off to find refuge in her own world of one.

Worried about Layla's cutting off, Syreeta went into therapy and was able to see how she was over-compensating for her own childhood, in which she was left alone too long with a depressed mother. After therapy, she became an excellent mother, far more sensitive in the parent–infant dance and Layla started to relate to her again.

Example

Millie was age ten when she developed night terrors, a school phobia and checking rituals. Her mother, Maureen, couldn't understand it. It was the GP who asked Maureen what had happened in her own childhood. Maureen told him that her own mother was so phobic of the outside world that she couldn't leave the house. Maureen remembered endless times of collecting her prescriptions for her – valium and sleeping pills. Maureen said she had hated her mother for her depression but also loved her very much. With time to reflect, Maureen admitted that she was terrified that Millie would get run over on the way to school so she would often lecture Millie about how to cross roads even when she was nine or ten. She also realised that she would check up on her all the time: 'Do you need the toilet dear?', 'Are you warm enough?', 'Just one more mouthful please – do it for Mummy.' When Maureen went for counselling and grieved about her own very depressed anxious mother, her parenting of Millie improved dramatically. Millie started wanting to do things with her Mum whereas before she would quickly retreat to her bedroom after meals each evening.

In a very recent study, research shows that parents with social anxiety tend to be less warm and affectionate and have higher levels of criticism towards the child. Such behaviours are well known to result in children suffering from anxiety disorders. Parental social anxiety should be considered a risk factor for childhood anxiety, and physicians who care for parents with this disorder would be wise to discuss that risk with their patients (Budinger *et al*, 2012).

What's going on in the anxious parent's brain?

The essential symptoms of generalised anxiety disorder (GAD) are intrusive worries about everyday life circumstances and social competence, and associated bodily states of hyperarousal. Very anxious parents tend to have too high levels of noradrenaline, adrenaline and cortisol in their body and brain (Charney *et al*, 1990).

The fear system, involving a structure called the amygdala (Panksepp, 1998) in the parent's brain, keeps triggering, as every day of their life, events, people, thoughts and feelings are perceived as threatening when they would not be perceived in this way by another person who is not anxious. The amygdala is the part of the brain that detects threat. (With a non-anxious parent, for the most part, it can be quickly shut down by frontal lobe thinking and reassuring self-talk.) But with the anxious parent, the amygdala activates a cascade of chemicals involving the hypothalamus communicating with the pituitary gland communicating with the adrenal glands (known as the HPA axis). The adrenaline glands then release too high levels of adrenaline and cortisol, which flood the brain and body. This means they will feel highly dysregulated and so they will be in no position to be an emotional regulator for their child.

Panic attacks and social anxiety are marked by chronic bodily states of hyperarousal, often with a resting heart rate of over 100 beats per minute (a healthy resting heart rate is usually between 50 and 90 beats per minute) (George *et al*, 1989). Once again, if you are having a panic attack or worried about having one, you are not in any position to be a soothing, calming presence for your child.

HOW CHILDREN ARE AFFECTED

How a child's developing brain can be affected

Steve Suomi (1995) studied both anxious monkey mothers and confident, calm monkey mothers. The calm monkey mothers had calm monkey children. The anxious mothers had anxious children. But when cross-fostered, meaning the infants of the anxious parents were put with the calm mothers, they grew up to be calm.

With a similar study by Caldji *et al* (2003), so great was nurturing, calm parenting that it positively affected the gene expression of some key calming chemicals in the brain (gamma-aminobutyric acid – GABBA) that make us resilient to stress. In contrast, the non-nurturing, anxious mothers adversely affected the gene expression of these anti-anxiety systems in the brains of their offspring. Without effective activation of GABBA in the brain, we would all be very anxious indeed! In the study, infants of non-nurturing parents were then given to nurturing mothers early in life. In these infants, the actual gene expression of GABBA was positively affected, making a permanent improvement in their ability to be calm in the future. This key brain research underlines the well-established relationship between early parent–child interactions and vulnerability to anxiety disorders in later life.

Research demonstrates that insecure attachment in early life can result in hypersensitivity in the stress response systems in the infant brain. Without sufficiently influential calming and soothing from other adults in the child's life, this can cause vulnerability to depression and other psychiatric disorders in later life (Beatson and Taryan, 2003).

Research shows more hyperactivation of the stress response system in the brain (HPA axis) in shy and inhibited children, in response to novelty, showing that anxious children can be averse to trying new things (Zimmermann and Stansbury, 2004).

Research shows that early relational stress with an anxious parent may alter development of noradrenalin and serotonin systems in the brain, which, without help for the child from other soothing and calming key adults in the child's life, can cause susceptibility to adult anxiety and emotional disorders (Rosenblum *et al*, 1994).

Research also shows that an insecure attachment of infant to mother produces far more cortisol in childhood than with securely attached children. This showed up as social fearfulness in the infant in their second year (Gunnar *et al*, 1996).

That said, with a therapeutic intervention in the teenage years or later life, it is possible to correct these chemical imbalances. But it usually does take in-depth counselling or therapy. Such changes rarely result simply from a good intimate relationship in adult life.

Anxious parents can affect the child's sleep

Research demonstrates that infants of mothers with panic disorders had higher salivary cortisol levels, arousability and more disturbed sleep. Panic-disordered mothers also displayed less sensitivity towards their infants and reported parenting behaviours concerning infant sleep and discipline. Elevated salivary cortisol and disturbed sleep might be important early indicators of risk. Helping panic-disordered mothers parent their more highly aroused/arousable infants could reduce the development of psychopathology (Warren *et al*, 2003).

Anxious children seem to exhibit an altered pattern of night-time cortisol secretion. These findings suggest subtle alterations in HPA axis function in pre-pubertal children with anxiety disorders (Feder *et al*, 2004).

Anxious parents can affect the child's eating habits

You can teach your child to have a problem
(Dr Tanya Byron, House of Tiny Tearaways, BBC, May 2012)

Some children have eating problems because they are anxious. It is impossible to eat and chew if you feel fear or anxiety. Fear also wipes out appetite. Sometimes children start to develop eating problems because they pick up on the high levels of their parent's anxiety around their eating. The parent moves into what is called 'over-watching'. This can mean a running commentary on what the child is doing:

'…Try a bit more. No, do eat this bit, at least this bit. Now hold your fork properly. No, not like that, like this. Now don't mess with your potato. Sit up straight, no I mean it, stop messing about. Now at least eat one of your potatoes. Look, you are just messing with it…'

With infants it can be even worse because while this is going on they are 'strapped in' to a high chair. Now if you were sitting in a restaurant with your friend, partner, or spouse and they did this 'over-watching' you would probably want to throw the food at them! But children tend to internalise their feelings about eating. Food all too easily gets all muddled up in the child's mind with their parent's stress levels and, before you know it, the child has a food phobia!

'Over-wiping' is another invasive behaviour of the over-anxious parent. They come in far too soon to clear up spills and the inevitable mess with a toddler. Sometimes the parent's anxiety is very evident for the attentive observer at mealtimes, as he or she mops away spillages, not letting the smallest drop stay. Over-wiping is a form of parental OCD.

Toby, aged four, has a food phobia

Toby would only eat dry food: bread and biscuits. When he was a baby, his mother, Sheila, would 'over-wipe' whenever Toby got messy. When Toby's mother went to counselling, she talked about her anxiety about mess. It became clear that she had been the child of a very depressed mother. When Sheila came home from school, she often found her mother still sitting at the breakfast table, in front of her uneaten breakfast cereal, rather like Miss Havisham in Great Expectations. The house was a total mess. As a result Sheila had developed a life-long irrational connection between mess and utter desolation, fearing that if she ever let her own house get messy, she would end up like her mother. When Sheila mourned and grieved about her own childhood, and worked on her irrational fears, Toby started eating other foods than just bread and biscuits. He no longer had a food phobia.

HOW A CHILD'S MENTAL HEALTH CAN BE AFFECTED

All too often the parent's anxiety means the child suffers from some sort of anxiety disorder too, for example, phobias, obsessions, panic attacks or chronic shyness. Often children of anxious parents will be insecure attached. This is because when the parent is overcome by anxiety, they will be too dysregulated to offer attuned emotional responsiveness to the child.

Here are some of the key research studies:

- Infants with insecure attachment lack the maternal buffering effect, enjoyed by children with secure attachment (Beatson and Taryan, 2003).

- Children of parents with an anxiety disorder were more fearful (Pine *et al*, 2005).

- A study of preschool children, aged from two to six years, found significant correlation between the children who feared dogs and the mothers who feared dogs, and also between children and mothers who feared insects (Hagman, 1932).

- Infants of mothers with panic disorders had higher salivary cortisol levels, arousability and more disturbed sleep (Warren *et al*, 2003).

In contrast, we know that with a non-anxious parent, who can provide consistent emotional regulation, the child can develop effective stress regulatory systems in the brain which will naturally enable him or her to calm down effectively. Research shows that children who are securely attached have what is known as good vagal tone (Gottman *et al*, 1996). The vagal nerve in the base of the neck plays a part in this regulatory system. It is the tenth cranial nerve. When a parent has been effective over time in calming and soothing a child, then that child will establish good vagal tone. Vagal means 'wandering' and this is just what the nerve does. When you have good vagal tone, the 'wandering nerve' wanders around the body, regulating all the major organs. In other words, it makes them function optimally.

The vagal nerve regulates:
- the digestive system
- ingestion
- the defecating system
- heart rate
- breathing
- the immune system.

Good vagal tone is associated with the ability to calm oneself down well and to regulate strong feelings. It is known that poor vagal tone is a key aspect of anxiety and panic disorders and an incapacity to stop heart palpitations.

Young children are very open and undefended, and hence easily affected by their parent's emotional energies and mood states. If the parent's inner world is full of fear or anxiety, then the child can feel frightened and anxious. Children all too easily pick up on a parent's anxious bodily arousal and feel dysregulated by it. Although these symptoms may never be overtly spoken about, the child picks them up acutely at a subliminal level. Looked at another way, there is commonly an 'underground' communication from the parent's unconscious to the child's. Freud was right that a person's unconscious can speak to another person's unconscious without being consciously thought or spoken about.

> The baby is anxious and the mother experiences a [sense] of the baby's anxiety; she picks up the baby and holds it close. As a result of this sequence, the baby feels simultaneously understood and calmed … If the mother … tends to respond with panic to the baby's anxiety, then [something else happens]. She may wall herself off from the baby, thus depriving him of the beneficial effect of merging with her [calm body]. Alternatively, she may continue to respond with panic, in which case … her child [may suffer] a lifelong propensity for anxiety.
> (Kohut, 1984, p83)

Some anxious children develop obsessive-compulsive rituals because they are sensing some of their parent's raw, undigested, unprocessed feelings. By developing ordering or checking rituals, they are arguably trying to 'tidy up' mother's too-messy feelings.

Pine *et al* (2005) and Van Ijzendoorn *et al* (1999) have shown that anxiety passes from parent to child. As a result, a child can easily end up feeling burdened by the unexpressed anxieties or denied fears of their parent, as well as those that are being overtly expressed. This can come out as free-floating anxiety ready to attach itself to anything in its path.

Example

Tom was referred to CAMHS at the age of twelve because he suffered from phobias, panic attacks and obsessive-compulsive disorder:

Tom's mother was stressed out by a very demanding job, wobbly marriage and another child to look after. She didn't get the emotional support she needed during pregnancy and her anxiety was strong and sustained. She didn't know that her stress chemicals in the third part of pregnancy would directly affect Tom in her womb.

Tom's mother had never mourned the death of her own father, or the miscarriage she had before Tom. She was brought up to brush strong feelings under the carpet and not talk about them. She had no idea that unprocessed trauma or grief in the parent is one of the major causes of anxiety in the child. As a result of her own unworked-through bereavements, she went into 'over-watching' Tom at mealtimes, as she had an underlying anxiety that Tom might die if he didn't eat properly. What is more, her own mother was obsessed about cleanliness, so she moved into 'over-wiping' at mealtimes, whenever Tom was messy. As a result Tom developed a food phobia by the age of three.

Tom's father did the disciplining in the household. Tom's own father had disciplined him through shouting, angry faces and commands. So, as parents often repeat the discipline they have received, Tom's father disciplined Tom the same way. Tom became very compliant as he was very frightened of his father.

Example

Nathan, aged six, whose mother was too anxious to be able to emotionally regulate her son's big feelings:

Nathan was phobic about walking on busy streets. He was certain that a double-decker bus would suddenly lose control, swerve on to the pavement and kill him or his Mummy. Nathan had learned all too early that his rage was dangerous because, from the age of two, whenever he had a temper tantrum his mother threatened to send him away if he didn't stop it at once. So, Nathan did not get angry any more. The problem was that his anger did not disappear; he simply cut off from his strong feelings, so he didn't have any strong feelings any more. His teachers described him as being 'too good'.

Nathan's destructive impulses had become transferred onto double-decker buses. In other words, they symbolised his own dangerous, too-powerful feelings of rage, which he feared would get out of control and make him lose everything (eg his Mummy who had threatened to send him away). This is very common in phobias, where the phobic object often carries an aspect of the feared dangerous self. To Nathan, his fear of the bus getting out of control and killing people symbolised his own wish to charge at the people he was furious with.

In counselling, Nathan was able to get in touch once more with his feelings of rage. As a result, he repeatedly joyfully drove toy double-decker buses in a sandpit over a character he called Mrs Pudding (probably his mother!). He would laugh and laugh with relief, as he was able to feel that his raging impulses, which were squashed in the two-year-old Nathan, were both witnessed and accepted by his counsellor. His counsellor, unlike his mother, enabled him to realise that his feelings were natural and understandable, as opposed to dangerous. His counsellor helped Nathan to reflect on his rage and find words for it. As a result, his phobia stopped.

This example of phobic defence is very understandable in the anxious child. If the child replaces a fear of me with a fear of a danger outside me, he can simply avoid that thing or event (eg stay away from double-decker buses). But if he lets himself know that what really feels frightening and 'attacking' are his own feelings (which in Nathan's case, he believed were so dangerous they could cause his mother to abandon him), then he is helpless and powerless because the danger is him. Children can keep on running from themselves endlessly in this way. But of course, locating the danger outside of himself in the phobic object takes a child ever further from getting help with the fear of his own feelings and finding adults who can both normalise and understand.

Children of anxious parents often bottle things up and move into self-help

Children who suffer from neurotic anxiety often don't tell anyone about their fears and worries. Many think this is just how life is. Many have no concept of help, so it wouldn't even occur to them to turn to Mummy and say, 'I am frightened, can you help me with that?' Many children simply internalise their feelings, which then leak out in one or more of the following symptoms:

- bedwetting (age-inappropriate)
- eating problems
- day soiling
- phobias
- obsessions
- compulsive rituals
- sleeping disorders
- psychosomatic symptoms (aches and pains for which there is no physical cause)
- some learning difficulties
- some self-harm.

Here are some of the debilitating legacies a child can suffer from when their parent is troubled by anxiety:

- fear of new experiences
- fear of social occasions
- avoiding people in case they are angry with you about something
- fear and avoidance of people
- fear of making a mistake
- fear of being found out for something
- fear of being noticed
- fear of being spontaneous
- phone phobias (fear of answering the phone in case someone on the other end is angry with you about something).

Many children of anxious parents suffer from what is know as 'free-floating anxiety', where, as soon as one worry proves unfounded, the anxiety will simply latch on to something else, like a parasite. Sometimes it attaches on to a very little thing, perhaps something someone said, a blemish, a line in a letter, or a squeak in the boiler. This little thing eats away at you, becoming a big preoccupying worry, given far too much of your thought time.

Free-floating anxiety particularly likes to link itself to the body, so a child may suffer from repetitive thoughts that there is something wrong physically. As they move into the teenage years, they may be burdened with frequent preoccupying fears of having a heart attack, of getting cancer, of collapsing in the street. Any small sign feeds their catastrophic imaginings, and if something does actually go wrong, the event can be magnified in their mind out of all proportion. They replay it again and again, re-experiencing the awful feelings that were felt when it happened, over and over. It becomes a preoccupation, an obsession, keeping them awake at night, demanding the same thoughts a thousand times.

SECTION TWO: HOW TO HELP THE CHILD WITH AN ANXIOUS PARENT: WHAT TO DO, HOW TO BE AND WHAT TO SAY

HOW TO HAVE A THERAPEUTIC CONVERSATION WITH THE CHILD

As with all other categories of troubled parents in this book, children of anxious parents need help to talk about their home life and relationships with someone who can really listen and help them process what is happening to them, grieve, protest and express over feelings.

The practitioner needs to be aware of and empathise with the following range of feelings:

Resentful
Here an adult reflects on her childhood with a mother with anxiety problems: Gemma, aged eighteen: 'My childhood was nothing to do with me. It was all about my mother.'

Aware of a lack of sense of self in over-awareness of the anxious parent
Tyler, aged fifteen: 'I often don't know what's in my mind because I am always thinking about what is in my Mummy's mind.'

Repeatedly anxious about a wobbly Mummy
John, aged nine: 'Are you all right Mummy?' (The child is having to continually check.)

Fearful and mistrustful
Daryl, aged four: 'The world is just one big wobbly jelly that I could fall off at any time.'
Daryl feels a lack of trust that there are people in the world who will keep him safe psychologically. The play of children with anxious parents often shows this, but here, with the wobbly jelly, the issue of psychological safety is often represented by the child as an issue of physical safety.

Example

> In his play, people in the boats kept mistaking their enemies ...
> thought them less aggressive or dangerous than they turned out to
> be ... they saw the fin of the big shark ... and they thought it was
> the fin of a dolphin. They got happily into the water to play with the
> dolphin and were torn limb from limb as they were eaten in silence.
> (Hunter, 2001)

The practitioner should help children consider which adults they have in their
life at school or elsewhere who are not troubled and who really like them,
believe in them and want to help. Help them to think how they might 'call'
on these safe adults more, or bring them to mind more often when they are
feeling unhappy.

OTHER INTERVENTIONS TO HELP THE CHILD

The child needs lots of hugs from adults in their lives who are not anxious

Research studies show that:

- High levels of warm, physical affection in childhood positively affect the
  child's capacity to handle stress well in adulthood. Physical affection
  results in long-term changes in brain mechanisms that moderate stress
  reactivity (Francis *et al*, 2002).
- Comforting maternal behaviour has a profound influence on an anti-
  anxiety system in the child's brain called GABBA (see p25), thus enabling
  the child to be less vulnerable to developing anxiety disorders in later life.
  Infants receiving lots of physical affection were less fearful in adulthood.
  The touch altered the development of the neural systems in the brain that
  mediate fearfulness. Low levels of physical affection in childhood resulted
  in increased fearfulness in later life and increased stress reactivity in the
  brain (Caldji, *et al*, 2003).
- Lots of physical affection in childhood activates oxytocin in the brain,
  which reduces stress reactivity and brings the bodily arousal system into
  balance (Uvnas-Moberg and Petersson, 2005; Debiec, 2005). Peptides of
  love and fear, vasopressin and oxytocin, modulate the integration of
  information in the amygdala.

- Reassuring touch will quieten the amygdala and reduce vigilance so there is no longer a sense of threat. When a person's amygdala is quiet, a person does not feel afraid. Touch can calm a child when reassuring words fail (Uvnas-Moberg and Petersson, 2005).

Massage for anxious children

Anxious parents can help their children by ensuring that they get massage. This is because the oxytocin released in the brain as a result of good massage reduces agitation, anxiety and stress hormones. Oxytocin also maintains the sensitivity of the opioid system, a system that, when activated, gives us a real sense of well-being and feeling that all is well in our world (Panksepp, 1998).

This can start by baby massage. Many parents stop after that, but it doesn't need to be like that. Lots of toddlers respond to massage and love it – just on an ad hoc basis, as they are sitting watching TV or being restless in bed. That said, a parent suffering from anxiety may not be a good masseuse if her anxiety is transferred to how she touches her infant. Often it depends on how comfortable she is with massage and touch herself. If she isn't comfortable, it's good to get someone else to massage the child; someone who is calm and who is very comfortable with massage and loves being massaged themselves.

Research evidence

Preschool children who received massage fell asleep sooner, and slept longer during nap time, and had better behaviour ratings (Field *et al*, 1996b).

Infants who received massage from a parent before bed experienced less difficulty falling asleep and better sleep patterns (Field and Hernandez-Reif, 2001).

Parents massaging their asthmatic children resulted in increased peak air flow, improved pulmonary functions, reduced anxiety and stress hormone (cortisol) in the children. Parental anxiety also decreased. Infants showed fewer stress behaviours (eg grimacing and clenched fists) and lower cortisol levels (stress hormones) following massage with oil versus massage without oil (Field *et al*, 1998).

Tai Chi for children of parents troubled with anxiety

Hyperactive teenagers displayed less anxiety, inappropriate emotions and hyperactivity and their conduct improved after participating in Tai Chi classes (Hernandez-Reif *et al*, 2001).

HOW TO HELP THE PARENT TO HELP THEIR CHILD

Parents need to know that they cannot protect their children from their anxious states; the only thing to do is to go into personal counselling or therapy

> The parent cannot keep their child from the truth, only the verbalisation of that truth.
> (Armstrong-Perlman, 1995)

Parents who are suffering financial strain, relationship problems, work problems or emotional baggage often tell themselves they will protect their child from it. The truth is they can't. Although the parent may never have overtly spoken about it, the child senses the parent's emotional states at a subliminal level. The brain picks up emotional atmospheres at 30 milliseconds (Schore, 2001).

Wickes (1988), a Jungian analyst, explains that, 'the child's unconscious may be infected by the fears which the mother refuses to recognise as her own'. In other words, if a parent has a worry, the child can develop a debilitating neurotic symptom or even dream about the issue. When the parent is able to resolve their fears or worries, say by going to counselling, the child can move on in their own development. Jung, the famous psychoanalyst, made the following statement about what he called this 'participation mystique':

> The 'participation mystique', that is, the primitive unconscious identity of the child with its parents, causes the child to feel the conflicts of the parents, and to suffer from them as if they were its own troubles. It is the things vaguely felt by the child, the oppressive atmosphere of apprehension and self-consciousness, that slowly pervade the child's mind like a poisonous vapour and destroy the security.
> (Jung, personal communication with Frances Wickes, cited in Wickes, 1988).

Sometimes a child's persistent angry or distressed outbursts can be the musical score for the anguish in their parent or in their parents' relationship. In effect, the parent is doing their screaming on the inside, but as the child picks this up, they end up doing the parent's screaming on the outside. Parental tensions discharged by a child can be from any parental emotion, for example, depression, anger or bitterness, or even unmourned grief.

Examples

Harpreet, aged seven:
Harpreet's mother was trying to keep from her little girl the fact that she had a serious heart complaint and might die. But Harpreet said to her teacher, 'Look, I've drawn black holes again for the little girl to fall into.' When the teacher asked why she had fallen in, Harpreet said, 'Because she has lost her Mummy. Lost forever, not just for a minute.' Of course, it is totally understandable that a mother would try to protect her child from this horrendous truth, and yet on another level, as we have seen, she cannot protect her. Harpreet's mother could not keep her from the truth, only from the verbally expressed truth. Both Harpreet and her mother need professional help, to enable them to talk through and feel their feelings with each other. Without this, Harpreet is left holding all her fear and sadness all on her own.

Gemma, aged three:
When Gemma was three, her mother, Susan, had a miscarriage. Susan did not grieve, but adopted a 'just better get on with life' mentality. She did not tell Gemma what had happened. Gemma started having nightmares about death, and was obsessed with the dead leaves rotting in the plant pots in the garden. When Susan went into counselling about her miscarriage and started to grieve for the first time, Gemma stopped having nightmares and was no longer obsessed with death.

Tanesha, aged eleven:
At the age of eight, out of the blue, Tanesha, who had been a very happy child, developed a terrible school phobia, started bedwetting and was diagnosed as having depression. When a counsellor asked her mother what had happened to her when she was an eight-year-old child, she said, 'Well, my Dad was killed in a car crash, but I think I quickly adjusted and put it behind me.' Her child was simply picking up on it.

Clara, aged four:
Clara was very wobbly indeed. She could not concentrate on her schoolwork, clung to teachers and was very agitated. She had a bereaved and deeply grieving mother who had too few people in her life to whom she could take her feelings. Eventually, the doctor referred Clara and her mother to family therapy. Clara was asked what she would like from her mother. She replied, 'Mummy, I want you to stop the rain coming through the roof and into my bedroom, it makes me too sad and scared.' There was no actual leak; Clara's statement was simply a metaphor to say that her very self (the image of the house) was not insulated well enough to protect her from the 'rain' of tears of her mother's grief. When Clara's mother started going to a bereavement counsellor, Clara stopped being agitated and her schoolwork improved dramatically.

Mary, aged six:
Mary's nightmares about death walking into her room and eating her all up stopped when her mother got help from a counsellor to deal with her repeated ungrounded fears about having cancer.

Reema, a young mother:
Reema was denying to herself the full extent of her grief at losing her latest boyfriend. She tried to 'put it behind her', and to be 'jolly' in front of her five-year-old son, Billy. She told Billy that she was fine and it was 'good that Jay had gone'. The little boy, who until this time had no problems, started bedwetting and had nightmares of overflowing toilets full of wee and tears. When the mother went into therapy and expressed her grief, Billy was fine again and all his symptoms disappeared.

Therapy or counselling for the anxious parent

Anxious, agitated parents are in need of emotional regulation themselves so they can be effective emotional regulators for their child. If a parent has suffered a trauma, a shocking life event or loss of a loved one, then it is a true gift to their child if they go into therapy or counselling to deal with this.

As with all other categories of troubled parents in this book, children of anxious parents need help to talk about their home life and relationships with someone who can really listen and help them process what is happening to them, grieve, protest and express over feelings (see Part Two of the book as to how).

Remember, research shows it is impossible for a parent to protect their child from their emotional baggage. The child will pick up on it. Also, unprocessed feelings in a parent can leak out in all manner of neurotic symptoms in the child. The research bears this out: fearful or avoidant parents had children with more externalised symptoms (Yoo *et al*, 2006).

The importance of going for family therapy when a parent has anxiety symptoms

In one study by Ginsburg (2009), a third of children of anxious parents got anxiety symptoms themselves. But when the parents of the children were given family therapy, none of the children got anxiety symptoms.

Yoga and meditation for anxious parents

Meditation has wonderful calming effects for people diagnosed with anxiety disorders. Research shows that, if practised on a long-term basis, meditation reduces blood pressure, anxiety and cortisol levels.

Yoga has calming effects. Research shows that people who practised yoga showed decreases in anxiety and cortisol levels, and increases in positive feeling. One research study showed that yoga was more effective than diazepam in alleviating anxiety (Platania-Solazzo *et al*, 1992).

Massage for anxious parents

Research shows that brief sessions of massage therapy and music therapy shifted the EEG (recording of the brain's electrical activity) of depressed mothers from greater relative right frontal activation (a pattern associated with depression) to a more integrated right/left brain activation (non-depressed response to life) (Jones and Field, 1999).

In addition:

- Depressed teenage mothers were less anxious after massage. Their cortisol (stress hormone) levels were lower and serotonin (mood stabiliser) levels were higher (Field *et al*, 1996a).

- Massage reduces psychological distress and brings down blood pressure (Field *et al*, 1999).

- People with severe post-traumatic stress were happier, less anxious and had lower cortisol levels after massage therapy (Field *et al*, 1996a).

CHILDREN WITH AN ANGRY PARENT

No matter how righteous a parent's anger, it is always frightening to the child.
(Lieberman, 1995)

SECTION ONE: WHAT LIFE IS LIKE FOR THE CHILD OF AN ANGRY PARENT: THE RESEARCH, THE PSYCHOLOGY AND THE BRAIN SCIENCE

Children talking ...

Zeinab, aged 10. Her parents have used fear to discipline her:
Zeinab told her teacher, 'I can never look forward to a new day, because it might have frightening people in it.'

Tommy, aged six. His mother disciplined him through screaming, shouting and hitting:
When his mother came to school to meet Tommy, the teachers felt frightened too. They talked of the level of hate in her eyes. One day, Tommy went on a school trip to the museum. He rushed out in terror. When asked what had happened, he said, 'The eyes, they might have eaten me all up.'

Rashida, aged eight. Her father was often extremely angry:
'It's difficult to have my feelings when Daddy is having his all the time.'

Woman with a social phobia. She was disciplined through anger as a child:

'My memories of my father from when I was a little girl are so strong that they colour how I see people in my life now. I am often too scared to answer the phone, or go into new situations, in case someone gets angry with me.'

Cai, aged thirteen. His father often flew into a temper:

'When Dad came home I would hide under the bed. I had been doing it for years. When I was little I remember wetting myself on several occasions when he got angry with me. His voice and face when he was angry was far more scary then any monster I've seen in a book or on TV.'

HOW COMMON IS PARENTAL ANGER? THE STATISTICS

- 87 per cent of parents in the UK shout at their children (ChildLine, 2008).

- One in five parents thinks it is OK to smack a toddler for throwing a tantrum.

- One in 10 parents think it is OK to smack a toddler for refusing to get into their buggy.

- Infants under one are more at risk of being killed at the hands of another person than any other single year age group in England and Wales (Brookman and Maguire, 2003).

- Every 10 days in the UK a child is killed by their parent (Smith *et al*, 2012).

- A 2001 study in the *American Journal of Psychiatry* found that yelling and other forms of emotional abuse were a more significant predictor of mental illness than sexual and physical abuse (Simeon *et al*, 2001).

About parents who frequently get angry

I knew my tantrums were bad for my children ... but I didn't know how to stop. It was like I had two speeds – nice and mean – and I didn't have any control over the switch.
(Gottman and DeClaire, 1998)

Of course, every parent will express hot anger at times towards their children. This is perfectly natural and understandable. A child's frontal lobes are not developed enough for capacities for concern, and social sensitivities, so they can at times be infuriating, loud, crass, totally egocentric, with all the overlays of 'naughty behaviour'. In addition, where a child's safety is concerned, such as when a child runs into the road, momentary shouting can be vital. But this chapter is not about occasional angry moments between parent and child. It is about parental anger that frightens, shames or humiliates a child. It is about the parent who, regardless of how much they love their child, repeatedly expresses anger and/or irritation with them. These negative interactions happen frequently, and form a major part of the family culture, which is usually devoid of laughter, mutual play, spontaneity and warmth. The atmosphere at home feels heavy and far too serious. In fact, research shows that when parents troubled with anger related to their children, there was far less mutual positive emotion, more mutual anger, and more emotional mismatches (Cole *et al*, 2003).

Example

I recently recorded every transaction between a clearly angry mother and a five-year-old in a café. It went like this:

Mother: 'Now are you going to be quiet so that Mum and I can talk.'
Mother: 'Don't do that.'
Mother: 'Don't do that.'
Mother: 'You'll break the glass if you do that.'
Mother: 'Just stop that now.'
Mother: 'If you do that I'll put you outside.'
Mother: 'Now put that down; how many times do I have to tell you?'

There was not one moment of joy or playful interaction during this meal and the child did not speak a word.

Anger can be expressed loudly through shouting, or expressed quietly through cold, silent withdrawal, turning away, not listening. In such a family culture there will be far more harshly toned commands and criticisms than expressions of warmth, praise and affection. In assessing one parent–child couple who were having difficulties, I asked the parent and the six-year-old girl to play together for 15 minutes. In that time the parent gave 35 negative interactions such as 'don't do that', 'no, do it like this', 'not like that', and so on. There was not one positive relational moment at all. This lack of positive interaction with a parent can be lethal for the child's developing brain.

Parents can be frequently angry for so many reasons. Sometimes it's because of conflict in the parent-to-parent relationship. Sometimes it's modelled behaviour. Their own parents were like this. Sometimes it's due to unresolved trauma or loss in their own childhood. Sometimes it's because of financial strain, unemployment, frustrated aspirations, fear of illness. Sometimes it's displaced anger: this means they are angry towards someone else, for example, their employer or own parent, so the child gets angry feelings which are about others. Sometimes it's because the parent is not getting enough warmth and support from the people in their life and so are emotionally depleted.

How the trouble can begin after babyhood

Some parents show great loving tenderness towards their babies, and then, around the 'terrible twos', they change as the infant develops a separate mind and a strong will. The parent's previously tender loving can become persistently angry or irritated. Sometimes this happens because the toddler triggers the parent's unresolved feelings about controlling relationships in the past, so the toddler's battle of wills is seen as far more than it is, a challenge to their authority that cannot be tolerated. The terrible twos in their child can be taken very personally by the parent, with the defiant infant triggering painful memories of being controlled by their own parent.

Angry parents often discipline their children through anger

It's very easy to discipline children through shame and fear. It can get really quick results. In fact child-rearing books for centuries have advocated breaking the child's will. As in this key text written in 1748: 'If parents are fortunate enough to drive out willfulness from the very beginning by means of scolding and the rod, they will have obedient, docile and good children whom they can later provide with a good education' (Sulzer, 1748).
For all too many adults the temptation can be to teach the child, once and for

all, who's the boss. They do this through shouting and scaring the child in some way, or through cold silences, shaming or contemptuous withdrawal. The problem is that disciplining a child through anger, shame and fear will trigger the primitive fear and rage systems deep in the old mammalian and reptilian parts of the brain and not the higher social brain (frontal lobes). This leaves a child vulnerable to problems with anxiety, depression and aggression in the childhood and teenage years and in adulthood (Zolotor *et al*, 2011; Ateah *et al*, 2003; Straus, 1980). One study found that when a three-year-old child is smacked more than twice a month, there is a marked risk of problems with aggression at age five (Taylor *et al*, 2010).

What's going on in the parent's brain when they are angry?

Parents troubled with frequent angry outbursts usually have problems regulating their emotional states. So, all too easily, they move into primitive fight reactions deep in the reptilian and mammalian parts of the brain. Of course, anger is often not the only feeling that is expressed and experienced in such a dysregulating way. Research shows that women with high levels of anger tend also to suffer from depression and anxiety (Field *et al*, 2002).

Many parents are frequently angry because they never developed effective stress-regulating systems in their brains. This is because their own parents were too anxious, depressed, angry or busy to be effective emotional regulators for them when they were children. It is only with endless repeated parent–child interactions of soothing, calming and reflecting together that effective stress regulating pathways are established in the brain. Without these systems in place, an adult can have the emotional volatility of a two-year-old. They then 'sweat the small stuff' (Tremblay, 2005). A gas bill coming through the letter box, for example, can be enough for a man to hit his wife or shout at his children.

In addition, if the parents have been brought up in a home with lots of conflict, research shows that serotonin levels tend to be low in family members (Raine and Yang, 2006). Serotonin is a mood stabiliser, so if a parent has low serotonin levels they will feel far more irritable with their tantruming teenager or toddler and so far more likely to get angry or critical (Dolan *et al*, 2002).

Parents who are troubled with anger often carry a legacy of insecure attachment from their own childhood. Secure attachment, on the other hand, activates anti-aggression chemicals – namely optimal levels of opioids and oxytocin (Panksepp, 1998; Panksepp and Biven, 2012). The brain habituates to these chemicals, so the person grows up with a disposition, which means that as a parent they rarely lose their temper. In contrast, high levels of stress hormones are the biochemical profile of insecure attachment leading to emotional volatility.

HOW CHILDREN ARE AFFECTED

If the demand is made by a witch or giant whose features are distorted with rage, whose voice smashes through all the defences of the child's mind, and whose hand is ever ready to strike humiliation and terror into his face and head, it requires enormous therapeutic power to neutralise this programming.
(Berne, 1979)

Angry parents can affect the foetus

In research studies, the foetuses of high-anger women in the second trimester onwards were more active and tended to experience growth delays. The high-anger women had high scores in depression and anxiety. They also had a biochemical profile of high levels of cortisol and adrenaline and low levels of dopamine and serotonin, and, extraordinarily, the babies were born with the same biochemical profile. This means that the babies will be born very emotionally volatile. As a result, things can go from bad to worse as the high-anger parent can find the baby unrewarding or even move into 'my baby hates me' (Field *et al*, 2002).

Angry parents can leave a child insecurely attached

Children are often frightened of an angry parent, the noise and intensity of their anger or rage. For others, it's not shouting and hitting that cause fear and toxic levels of stress hormones, it's the silent angry glare, which can feel far worse. Such children often learn to skilfully navigate the angry parent. They know how to behave around them, learn how to 'walk on eggshells'. But when they learn this so young, in adult intimate relationships they can still over-adapt to the needs and feelings of the other. In contrast, they have little or no idea what they themselves want from a relationship.

It is not usually possible as a child to truly love someone they deeply fear. As we will see, many children give up loving their angry parent. That said, they can still connect, but it's from a place of need, not from a place of love. The parent can confuse this with love and not realise that there is a grave problem in their relationship.

Some parents think their child will automatically love them no matter how they behave. And yet, just as we cannot command the clouds to move so the sun will shine, parents cannot command love from their child. As a child psychotherapist, I have seen many children who have been on the receiving end of just too much parental anger. As a result, I have met many versions of the following statement: 'I don't have a Mummy. My Mummy is dead. Will you be my Mummy?' They did have a Mummy. It was just that their love for that Mummy had been eroded by too much parental anger. Sometimes it is one angry outburst or criticism too many that causes an attachment rupture and means a shift in the child from loving to hating or cold contempt. The latter is often cleverly disguised by the child, so the parent has no idea what has happened between them. Despite the fact that children are often so ready to forgive, to wipe the slate clean, to start again, there can come a day when their love dies. When this happens it often needs professional intervention – for example, counselling, family therapy – if there is to be any chance of healing the parent–child relationship.

Children with frightening, angry parents can form a 'disorganised attachment'

Disorganised attachment in the child results from having a parent who is frightened or frightening. Without therapeutic intervention, research shows that many disorganised attachment children grow up to have all manner of mental health problems, depression and/or antisocial behaviour, conduct disorder, poor stress management (Van IJzendoorn *et al*, 1999). In addition, they usually suffer a string of troubled relationships. They avoid seeking solace and use self-help when life gets tough. This often means some form of drug or alcohol abuse or self-harm. Some move, quite unconsciously, into re-victimisation. This commonly shows itself as bullying: 'I frighten you just as my parent frightened me.' Without therapy, the child is usually unaware of this process of passing on to others what he himself has suffered.

The disorganised attached child builds up an internal template of adults as unsafe and/or scary, cruel and unfeeling. So when the child meets a kind, warm adult (eg a teacher) their internal template is easily reactivated. This means that the child doesn't want to connect with that adult and can suffer a deep level of mistrust. The warm, friendly adult can then feel disheartened and so moves away. This just reinforces the child's feeling that they are living in an unfriendly, cold world. This awful pattern is very prevalent with children in the care system, with foster and adoptive parents feeling deeply rejected and that their warmth and concern are worth nothing to the child.

Example

Saleem, aged fourteen:
For many years Saleem adored his father, despite the fact that his father would have regular angry outbursts and give harsh punishments. One day, when Saleem was twelve, he dropped a plate of food by mistake. His father hit Saleem across the face with a shoe. This event broke something for Saleem. At that moment, all the injustice and betrayal of so many other such relational events with his father constellated in his mind. When his father moved out two years later, Saleem did not cry. For some children, their parent is just too angry, too emotionally volatile, so the child's love either never really gets established in the first place or gets badly broken along the way.

Angry parents can affect the child's capacity for fulfilling relationships

Research shows how children under the age of five, who have experienced relationships at home as being based on power and control, are already acting out victim persecutor scenes in their play (Troy and Sroufe, 1987). Some of these children can then grow up to abuse or put up with abuse in their intimate relationships. It's what they have known. Others become phobic about healthy angry expressions in intimate relationships. So any minor disagreement, clash of views or expression of anger in a relationship can feel catastrophic. As a result, they may keep their intimate relationships 'very nice' or 'too nice'. They are convinced that anger destroys, because for them in childhood it may have destroyed a bond with their parent. But 'nice relationships' inevitably become flat and empty. Intimacy is lost.

Angry parents can affect the child's bodily processes

Research shows that newborns of high-anger mothers often have sleep problems, disorganised sleep patterns and poorer motor maturity (Field *et al*, 2002).

The other symptoms of high-anger parenting on children are:
* bedwetting
* eating problems
* phobias
* obsessions
* learning difficulties
* self-harm.

Angry parents can affect the child's ability to play, laugh and have fun

Research showed that when a tuft of cat hair was placed near to some rats, which were playing, the rat play ceased totally. The animals continued without playing for up to five successive days – even when the cat fur had been taken away (Panksepp, 1998). This is how powerful the brain's mammalian fear system is once triggered. Similarly, when children are frightened, they also lose their capacity to play. All humour and fun and laughter stops. They often become withdrawn, losing their spontaneity, just trying to get through. But play, of course, is key for a child's development, of mind and of brain (Panksepp, 1998), which is why this is such a major concern.

Angry parents can affect the child's behaviour, often leading to conduct disorders

In studies of preschool children in the 1970s, Baumrind found that:
* Children of authoritarian parents were conflicted and irritable. In contrast, children of untroubled parents were most consistently cooperative, self-reliant, energetic, friendly, and achievement-oriented.

* The child can identify with the aggressor and become aggressive like their parent. This leads to all manner of problems with conduct disorder and oppositional defiance (Gottman and DeClaire, 1998).

* Research found that parental anger predicted antisocial behaviour and other behaviour problems in children (Denham *et al*, 2000).

* Troubled mother–preschooler angry exchanges predicted conduct problems, particularly in boys (Cole *et al*, 2003).

Angry parents can affect the child's developing brain

When a child too often feels alarmed by a parent due to their frequent explosive and/or hostile outbursts, rather than experiencing them as a place of safety and solace, high levels of stress hormones will be released in the child's brain. These are not dangerous per se but become so if the child suffers from prolonged uncomforted stress states. Too high levels of stress hormones for a duration can cause actual cell death in parts of the brain, particularly those vital for memory and social and emotional intelligence.

> Through advancements in brain scanning technology we can now see how some forms of disciplining a child through anger can actually damage the child's developing emotional brain:
> * cell death in the corpus callosum (Teicher *et al*, 2006)
> * adverse changes to the stress response system in the brain (HPA axis)
> * adverse changes to the dopamine systems in the brain – resulting in particular vulnerability to substance abuse in later life (Andersen and Teicher, 2004; Alyahri and Goodman, 2008; Bugental *et al*, 2003; Teicher *et al*, 2010; Zolotor *et al*, 2011).
>
> **Cell death in the hippocampus**
> Repeated episodes of excessive release of stress chemicals can cause cell death in one of the child's major memory systems, called the hippocampus. On brain scans, when a child has suffered the severe stress of parents who are verbally or physically angry (Teicher *et al*, 2006) this part of the brain shows up as shrunken. The hippocampus does restore some cells, but scientists have found that this is only a small proportion. This may pose a serious problem for a child's ability to learn, as the hippocampus is key for short-term memory. Scientists don't yet know to what extent this may affect a child's ability to learn in the longer term (Teicher *et al*, 2006).

At the moment the science is so new that there is disagreement as to how much of this can be repaired. That said, there is hope as the young brain is far more able to change and to repair the damage than the adult brain. We know this because Howard Dully was aged twelve when given a lobotomy. Adults were all severely incapacitated when given a lobotomy, but because of his young age, Howard is now fully functioning. His brain had successfully re-formed itself to repair much of the damage from the large holes in his brain caused by the lobotomy (Dully and Fleming, 2009).

In addition, when a parent is repeatedly angry, the stress systems in the child's developing brain can become hypersensitive. High levels of stress hormones block the mood-stabilising chemicals in the brain, such as serotonin and anti-anxiety chemicals (Watamura, 2003; Warren *et al*, 2003). This means that minor stressors are experienced as major emergencies, leaving the child in frequent states of high anxiety, anger or distress with things that are not actually dangerous at all.

The child can also suffer from an overactive fear system in the old mammalian part of the brain. This can result in all manner of social phobias in later life. The frightening parent is generalised to other people everywhere. Without child counselling, we can't stop the brain from generalising in this way.

Children with overactive fear systems can:
- fear new experiences in case someone shames them
- fear social occasions
- avoid people in case they are angry
- fear making a mistake
- fear being found out for something
- fear being seen, noticed or feeling too visible
- fear being spontaneous.

Post-traumatic stress disorder (PTSD)

Just like Vietnam veterans, and people who have experienced war, some children who have been frightened in the name of discipline end up with post-traumatic stress. In post-traumatic stress, chemical messages from the old mammalian and reptilian parts of the brain will overwhelm the frontal lobes (higher thinking part of the brain) and derail the child's capacity to think about what is happening rationally. PTSD also causes significant cell death in the hippocampus (see above).

SECTION TWO: HOW TO HELP THE CHILD WITH AN ANGRY PARENT: WHAT TO DO, HOW TO BE AND WHAT TO SAY

HOW TO HAVE A THERAPEUTIC CONVERSATION WITH THE CHILD

The practitioner needs to be aware of and empathise with the following range of feelings:

Unsafe
'I always ran and hid under the bed when Dad came home, because I never knew if he was going to be in one of his cross moods or not.'

Emotionally numb
There is so much painful raw emotion in the house, the child just cuts off. Nothing shocks any more. In this way they are the opposite of their raging parent and as a result often feel deeply alienated from that parent.

Hate
'My father thought the word father was enough. It wasn't' (*Nil by Mouth*, film, Dir. Gary Oldman).

Many parents assume they always have 'credit in the bank', so to speak, with their children. In other words, that somehow whatever they do to them, their children are genetically programmed to love them. So many parents like this are mistaken. That first smack, that first hit with the shoe, can be experienced by the child as a shocking betrayal. This is made all the worse if there is no apology but rather a repeat of the angry attack. Some children move into hate that does not move back to love.

Betrayal
As above, children often feel totally shocked when their warm, loving parent loses their temper in a way that is extremely frightening. They can feel a deep betrayal of their trust.

Agitated/hyperarousal/attention deficit
When a child is hit they can experience an unbearable level of bodily

arousal. This can leave the child vulnerable, agitated, hyperactive and hyperaroused.

Fear and sometimes terror

'You don't have to frighten a human being very much at all for them to establish an anxious attitude for the rest of his life' (Adamec, 1994; Adamec and Shallow, 1993.

> When a parent has out-of-control anger it can be terrifying. The days that Dillon's (age nine) Mum screamed at him at the school gates, 'And ye'r better do well at school today', were the days that Dillon could not learn anything. He would lie on the classroom floor and hum all day like a wounded animal. It is in this sense that Acquarone is so right when she says, 'Dysregulated parents can become "scare-givers" rather than care-givers' (Acquarone, 2004).

As with all other categories of troubled parents in this book, children of angry parents need help to talk about their home life and relationships with someone who can really listen and help them process what is happening to them, grieve, protest and express over feelings. They need to find their own anger about their parent's anger. They need help and modelling about healthy anger and how it differs from unhealthy anger. They need information about how unhealthy anger, as in the table below, is usually fuelled by old hurts from someone's past. All this should support the child in not taking it so personally when the parent gets angry with them. See Part Two of the book as to how to help with this.

The practitioner must be sensitive as to whether the child is idealising the parent, and, if this is the case, to respect this. In such an event, the problem with parental anger can be addressed indirectly through therapeutic story.

If you are seeing a child troubled by an angry parent, it is good to assess whether the child would benefit from putting down a boundary with their parent in face-to-face time. If the child wants the opportunity to talk to their parent with the help of the third party adult (eg teacher, counsellor) it is vital to assess, before agreeing to this, whether the parent has enough self-awareness not to get defensive and go into blaming the child, and also has a good capacity to listen. If this is the case, you can always ring the parent beforehand and establish a working alliance. This will be an agreement that the parent will listen to what the child says without contradicting or going into telling the child off again.

HEALTHY AND UNHEALTHY ANGER

CHARACTERISTICS OF UNHEALTHY ANGER (fuelled by past hurt, anger, resentment)
Intensity and volume – ie the event has triggered hurt, rage, shame, feelings of betrayal, fantasies (from your past).
A wish for vindictive triumph over the other; preoccupation with revenge – eg a wish to hurt, smash, damage, spoil, destroy.
A desire to find the words/actions that will really hurt.
The same angry, indignant or hating thoughts going round and round in your head, like a stuck record.
In-depth post-mortem in your head of the anger-inducing events, going over and over what happened, and what you could have done/said but didn't.
Lingering angry feelings – you still feel angry even if what made you angry has stopped. **Feeling really bad for hours** after the row/confrontation/ negative exchange.
Apologies or attempts to make amends from the other person can count for nothing – you go on hating and attacking as if nothing had been said.
On some level you know you are overreacting and that the row has triggered pain from the past – eg not being responded to, rejection, abandonment, submission, shame, jealousy, not being understood.
You experience some relief at having a core belief about self or others confirmed – eg 'See, this proves how unlovable I am', 'See, this proves that you can't ever really trust anyone', 'See, this proves that everyone is really out to get you.'
You have difficulty remembering what you were angry about after the period of anger is over.

CHARACTERISTICS OF HEALTHY HERE-AND-NOW ANGER
Healthy anger is focused on the resolution of the problem as opposed to wanting to hurt the other person: 'We have a problem, a difference of opinion here – so how can we resolve it?' This is completely different in tone and energy from: 'You are to blame because…', 'You are x/y/z and I am furious with you about it', 'It's all your fault.'
Healthy anger is often vibrant, active and soon over – some people call it 'warm anger'. There is a 'clean' feel to it. Although it can still be loud and passionate.
Ordinary language about the offending other, rather than the very bad/wicked language of extremes of archaic anger – eg 'You are evil/ an abuser/a psychopath' – in the expression of anger.
Little or no evidence of vindictiveness, sadism or vengeful purpose.
Healthy anger is finite – it will not go on and on. When communicated and understood, it is over.
The rows or arguments do not feel like a catastrophic or dangerous event – it just feels like part of life.
You don't carry on thinking about the incident afterwards.
Healthy anger leaves you feeling OK about yourself and the other person.

Table 2
Healthy and unhealthy anger

Example: Parent–child counselling

Donal, aged nine:
Mummy smacked Donal repeatedly. One day Donal said to his school counsellor, 'Will you be my Mummy? I don't want my one anymore.' When asked why, he said, 'She could use words, not hands to tell me what I'm doing wrong.' So, with Donal's agreement, the counsellor called in his mother and said to her, 'I will be quite frank with you, I think your child's love for you is dying.' The mother was relieved, not offended. She had thought the same. In a parent–child therapy session, Donal was able to tell his mother how deeply hurt he had felt when she smacked him. They repaired their relationship, just in time. Donal's mother never smacked him again. The counsellor gave her other ways of establishing boundaries with her son.

Always consider if you need to make a referral to social services. This is if you feel the child is at risk and/or the parent needs help from a social worker.

HOW TO HELP THE PARENTS TO HELP THEIR CHILDREN

So many parents who move into frequent anger and/or over-the-top anger with their children hate themselves when they lose it. The parenting practitioner needs to empathise with how being an emotional regulator for a child who is in a dysregulated state can be hugely challenging. But then the parent needs to be given strategies and information so they can act differently when they feel they are ready to blow.

The parenting practitioner needs first to clarify underlying causes of the parent's too-frequent and/or frightening angry outbursts.

- Is the parent under-supported? In other words, who is emotionally regulating the emotional regulator (the parent)?

- Are the parents victims themselves of too much relational stress or relational poverty in their own childhood? If they haven't been for therapy or counselling, this can leave them with poor stress regulatory systems in the brain.

- Are they suffering from an unprocessed trauma or unmourned loss? The chemical imbalance in the brain resulting from this can make the parent persistently angry or irritable.

The message is that it's never too late to form better relationships with your child or indeed to repair troubled parent–child relationships. That said, if the parent is suffering from their own unprocessed traumatic life experiences from their own childhood, they may need to go into psychotherapy or counselling. The counsellor/therapist can then become the effective emotional regulator the parent never had as a child. As a result of good therapy, people can change the biochemical profile in their brain from repeated activation of too high levels of stress hormones (triggering all that anger) to optimal levels of opioids, oxytocin and prolactin (Panksepp, 1998). These are anti-aggression, anti-anxiety chemicals, so, when optimally activated in the brain, the parent will then not feel angry or want to fight with their child.

If the parent thinks that it's OK to shout at a child as part of discipline, they need to be given the information about the psychological damage that this can cause – for example, low self-esteem, shame issues, problems with anger. They also need to know about the research, which shows that disciplining a child through shame or fear can damage the child's relationship with their parent, preventing or curtailing secure attachment (Schore, 2001; Posada and Pratt, 2008; Bugental *et al*, 2003). In addition, in order to make an informed decision, they can also be given the research findings that shouting and using words as missiles is as damaging to the brain as hitting a child, in terms of causing cell death (Teicher *et al*, 2006). In short, they need to be helped to find other ways to socialise their child; ways that do not include anger.

What parenting practitioners can do

Parents who keep getting angry with their children need to know about the research that shows that the more commands you give a child – for example, 'Don't do that', 'Stop doing this' – the more naughty and oppositional your child is likely to be. It's quantifiable! (Forehand and Scarboro, 1975). They would be well advised to read easily accessible books such as *How to Talk So Kids Will Listen* and *Listen So Kids Will Talk* (Faber and Mazlish, 2013) or *Discipline with Love and Logic* (Cline and Fay, 2006). These great books give handouts, tools and techniques for disciplining a child in ways that never includes anger but rather uses consequences, delivered in a matter-of-fact, calm-voiced way. Research shows that this means the child does not experience shame or fear but rather learns to reflect about good and bad choices. Foster Cline has found that, as a result, children respected in this way then make far better choices in the teenage years (Cline and Facy, 2009).

It is often said that the best form or discipline is praise. There is much truth in this; lots of parent–child play and praise and 'ask to play' activates those opioids and oxytocin in the child's brain so that they don't feel aggressive.

CHILDREN WITH A DEPRESSED PARENT

SECTION ONE: WHAT LIFE CAN BE LIKE FOR THE CHILD WITH A DEPRESSED PARENT: THE RESEARCH, THE PSYCHOLOGY AND THE BRAIN SCIENCE

Children talking ...

Paulette, aged seven: 'In this place, dead might take over completely...'

Simon, aged six: 'I drank from my mother and emptied her. There was no milk left.'

Chantal, aged nine: 'Why are the wolves howling? I think they are howling for their mother.'

Ben, aged ten: 'When women are old, when they are about thirty, they don't want to play with you anymore.'

Jordan, aged four: 'I don't need my Mummy very much. It's easier to need my Thomas Tank.'

Hitesh, aged eight: 'So you see, Mum and I don't really talk. I want to say to Mum, "please don't sleep all the time".'

HOW COMMON IS PARENTAL DEPRESSION? THE STATISTICS

- At least one-third of people experience a major depressive episode during their lifetime, and for many individuals the experience reoccurs. Mixed anxiety and depression is the most common mental health disorder in the UK (Mental Health Foundation, 2007).
- It is very rare to experience depression without anxiety. Only 2 per cent of the population experience a depressive episode without anxiety occurring at the same time (Mental Health Foundation, 2007).
- Mental health problems are among the most common health conditions, directly affecting about a quarter of the population in any one year. Depression and anxiety are the most widespread conditions. One in four families worldwide is likely to have at least one member with a behavioural or mental disorder (Mental Health Foundation, 2007).
- The World Health Organization forecasts that by 2020 depression will be the second leading contributor to the global burden of disease (World Health Organization, 2001).
- Between 8 and 12 per cent of the population experience depression in any year (Singleton *et al*, 2000).
- About one in 10 women will suffer from prenatal or postnatal depression. The latter statistic rises to five per cent with twins (Green and Thachil, 2010).

About parents who are depressed

Of course, we all feel fed up and anxious from time to time. But we are not talking here about a passing bad mood, or feeling of hopelessness, but rather when a parent is in a persistently low state. Depression as a mood is transitory and you can do lots of things to adjust the biochemical imbalance in your brain to increase feel-good chemicals. You can see a friend, be with nature, do some exercise, listen to music, go to a lovely coffee bar, have a massage. You will feel better.

Depression as an illness, rather than just a passing mood, is a truly awful affliction. It is called clinical depression. Clinical depression is when the brain keeps triggering the pumping out of more and more stress chemicals and you can't turn the pump off. If a parent suffers from clinical depression, all their emotional and mental energy is taken up in managing their own feelings. There is not one moment of joy, as the release of pleasure chemicals in the brain is blocked. Therefore, with the resulting acute levels of anxiety, angst, paranoia and anhedonia (an inability to experience pleasure) it is like living in a kind of hell with not a moment of relief. This also means that parents don't have the mental space in their mind to manage the feelings of their child, let alone enjoy him or her. The child is then deprived of all that emotional regulation which they so desperately need for their developing physical and mental systems that are key to managing stress well and ultimately to living a fulfilling life.

The high level of stress hormones in clinical depression block parental feelings of empathy for their child, and any desire to play. It is known as 'blocked care'. In other words, the last thing the parent feels like doing is interacting with their child in warm, loving or playful ways. Instead, the parent's high levels of stress hormones can make them experience the infant's natural emotional volatility and intense feelings of excitement and distress as unbearable. This can lead some clinically depressed parents to lash out in anger, hit and smack or switch off from the child emotionally. A recent study (Davis *et al*, 2011), for example, found that depressed fathers were nearly four times more likely to smack their children as non-depressed fathers and far less likely to read to them.

Here are the telling signs of clinical depression:
- not one moment of pleasure in the day
- very low self-esteem or self-loathing
- guilt
- anxiety/agitation/panic attacks/unable to be still and relax
- exhaustion
- feeling like you are a bad parent/repeated self-criticism
- lack of energy
- wanting to withdraw from most people
- problems with eating and/or sleeping
- inability to be soothed by the comforting of others
- anger/irritation
- being very affected by even minor stressors
- tearfulness
- possibly wanting to harm yourself and your baby.

Depression can make you feel suicidal, not look after yourself properly, not eat properly, drink a lot, smoke and self-harm, all of which are bad for children to be around. Some parents who are clinically depressed can still be good-enough parents, although it can be a huge strain. But for the most part, clinical depression badly affects parents, making them insensitive and intrusive, unempathic, unplayful, misattuning and angry with their child.

When parents are suffering from mild depression, as opposed to clinical depression, they can feel pretty low, lethargic, lacking in joy and enthusiasm for some of the time. However, unlike clinical depression, there are times when they don't feel like this and can be present, attuned and emotionally responsive to their child.

Parents with mild depression can feel like they:
- can't enthuse over things
- can't find enough passion
- can't find enough enthusiasm to follow a dream
- find nothing interesting any more
- can't think outside of the limited tasks of the day
- can't find the joy in life any more.

About parents with postnatal depression

This is how it works: the trouble is that the high levels of stress hormones triggered in postnatal depression block the brain chemicals oxytocin, opioids and prolactin, which are responsible for all that beatific bliss and deep love the parent feels when the baby is born. If this happens, it's time to get counselling/therapy and maybe antidepressants in order to be a good-enough carer to the baby.

Which parents are particularly vulnerable to becoming depressed?

Causes of depression in parents are thought to include the huge change in the hormones that occur before, during and after birth, exhaustion, lack of support and strain in partner relationship. When a woman has a history of loss, which she has not properly grieved for, recent research shows this can make her vulnerable to developing depression before or after giving birth. The other major factor triggering postnatal depression is stress and conflict in the woman's relationship with her husband or partner (Panksepp and Watt, 2011). In fact, research shows that over 60 per cent of couples say they experience relationship difficulties after the birth of their first child (Relate, 2012). Such parents need to be supported to get counselling and couple therapy to deal with their relationship problems and emotional baggage. This is a real gift for any child.

HOW CHILDREN ARE AFFECTED

Research shows that children are deeply affected by the depressed state of a parent. It is shocking how early this starts, from babies turning away from the expressionless face of a depressed parent or showing high levels of cortisol in response to a depressed voice (Ham and Tronick, 2006).

A tragic outcome for some children is when, after years of trying to please the parent, to be their resident joker, soother and helper, the parent then kills themselves. It can be experienced as the ultimate betrayal, leaving the child in desperate need of professional help to manage their rage and their grief. If this child doesn't get help, their life can be utterly troubled with their own depression and misplaced guilt at not being able to save Mummy. Without help, the child may never feel safe enough to properly attach or love again.

Common effects of prenatal depression on the foetus

'One of the times when we are most susceptible to the influences of our surrounding environment is when we are developing as a foetus' (Sarkar *et al*, 2008).

A mother's depression can affect an unborn baby as early as 17 weeks after conception, with potentially harmful effects on the brain and development. This is because in the first trimester the baby's organs are still forming (Sarkar *et al*, 2008).

In addition, research shows that prenatal depression can result in:
- excessive activity in the foetus

- growth delays in the foetus

- more labour pain

- strong risk of prematurity and low birth rate

- greater incidence of infants born with difficult temperament, sleep problems, or that are more fearful; later problems with attention, concentration, emotional and behavioural problems in childhood and teenage years; chronic illnesses in adulthood

- lower cognitive ability at 19 months (often 10 points below)
- babies born with poorer vagal tone (good vagal tone is vital to regulate digestion, breathing and immune system)
- an association with lowered IQ in the baby and adverse effects on the baby's stress response systems.

> The above will be worse if the mother is not only depressed but suffers from problems with anxiety, anger and stressful life events. Prenatal depression is also a strong predictor of postpartum depression (Bergman et al, 2007; Li *et al*, 2008; Field *et al*, 2002; Sarker *et al*, 2008).

> Half of the parents whose babies cried more than six hours a day had experienced severe psychosocial stress in pregnancy. None of the women whose babies cried very little described social pressures of this kind in their pregnancies (Kitzinger, 2005).

In the third trimester, the prenatally depressed mother will have high levels of stress hormones in her brain and low levels of the mood-stabilising chemical serotonin and the feel-good chemical dopamine. Amazingly, the baby is born with the same biochemical profile, high levels of stress hormones and low levels of serotonin and dopamine (Field *et al*, 2002). This will make the baby emotionally volatile and easily distressed. They will be hypersensitive to minor stressors or misattunements from the mother or father. This can make that baby very unrewarding to a parent. High cortisol levels in the mother in late pregnancy are related to the baby having a more difficult temperament, and more crying, distress and negative facial expressions. When the mother supports to soothe and calm her infant all will be well. When this doesn't happen it can lead to persistent states of hyperarousal (Glover *et al*, 2009) and the common downward spiral of mothers who then believe that their baby doesn't like them. In other words, a mother who doesn't know the science can take the baby's distress personally and think that the baby doesn't like her or that she is a bad mother. Such thoughts can be a major contributing factor to her developing postnatal depression (Field *et al*, 2002).

Stress response systems in the child's brain may be adversely affected

Maternal stress and depression during critical periods of foetal brain development can re-programme the child's stress response system, in such a way that they are vulnerable to developing problems with anxiety or depression later in life. This means that the child can be hypersensitive to stressors and react to minor stressors as major emergencies, which is exhausting for them and the people around them (Ashman *et al*, 2002).

Stress in pregnancy may, in some cases, feminise the brain of boy babies

Too much stress in the mother has also been shown sometimes to affect the genetic unfolding of some very key emotion chemical systems. In other words, certain vital genes don't move to the place in the brain they are supposed to move to. This disruption can have life-long adverse effects. In studies with other mammals, it was found that prenatal stress can feminise the brain of the male foetus. Too high levels of stress in the mother changed the impulses of the hormones testosterone and oestrogen in the male foetus. As a result some male infants were born with a somewhat feminised brain, causing feminised behaviour in later life (Panksepp, 1998).

So, just as the foetal brain is vulnerable to alcohol, nicotine and other drugs, it is also vulnerable to too high levels of cortisol. Most parents wouldn't dream of subjecting their unborn baby to cigarette smoke, alcohol or toxic environmental fumes, but by not addressing the fact that they are prenatally depressed and not getting help they may be subjecting their infant to other toxic chemicals (Field, 2006).

Common effects of postnatal depression on the child

Everything the mother does with her baby has a specific energetic charge; how she changes his nappies, picks him up, feeds him. Her energies are with him all the time. If his mother's energies are calm, they can become his calm energies. He can feel deeply soothed by them, sometimes even reaching intense states of bliss or peace. Her calm energies can transport him out of the most unmanageable states of inner tension into a place of peace again. If, however, her energies are not calm, but rather anxious, fraught or irritated for too much of the time, he can feel very disturbed. He may experience her jarring energies at a worse intensity than she does herself. This is because the baby's right brain (the deeply feeling part of the brain with strong links to the limbic system – the emotional brain and the body) is far more advanced that the logical verbal left brain (with weak links to body and limbic system). So, infants feel things very deeply and very painfully without the ability to defend.

One study with over 3,412 mothers who had been depressed for the first four months of their child's life found that:

- they talked less with their two-and-a-half-year-old

- the parent was less likely to limit TV or video watching with their two-and-a-half-year-old

- the parent was less likely to follow daily routines

- the parent was less playful and nurturing with their two-and-a-half-year-old

- the parent was more likely to use harsh punishment with their two-and-a-half-year-old.
(McLearn *et al*, 2006)

In addition:

- Children showed less distress during maternal separation (Dawson *et al*, 1992).

- Mothers were less emotionally attuned to their infants and the way they talked to their infant was not attuned to the age of the infant. This resulted in the infants developing a negative mood, which affected their interactions with other people and sometimes led to emotional problems (Stanley *et al*, 2004; Herrera *et al*, 2004).

- The part of the brain activated in approach emotions was not activated in 11- to 17-month-old infants during playful interactions with their mothers. So they didn't seek their parent's attention very much (Tronick, 2004).

- Mothers touched their infants more negatively and in an intrusive way (Herrera *et al*, 2004; Malphurs *et al*, 1996).

- Half of women with postnatal depression have thoughts about harming themselves or their baby, but it is very rare for either mother or baby to be harmed (Murray *et al*, 2011).

Long-term effects on the child of maternal postnatal depression

- After birth, the baby's brain is still in the process of forming itself and some key genes for anti-anxiety are still expressing themselves. Research shows that maternal depression may disturb vital brain organisational processes at this stage, leaving the infant vulnerable to developing problems with depression in later life (Panskepp and Watt, 2011).
- Maternal depression during the child's first two years of life was still showing up as elevated salivary cortisol when the child was four and then again at seven. These high cortisol levels exhibited greater mental health symptoms in the first grade. Children had more internalising symptoms (Ashman *et al*, 2002).
- Some teenagers were still being affected by maternal postnatal depression as they suffered from higher cortisol levels (a predictor of depression) (Halligan *et al*, 2006).
- Maternal prenatal and maternal postnatal depressive symptoms were associated with externalising problems and lower social competence in teenagers, particularly boys (Korhonen *et al*, 2012).
- The children of mothers who suffer postnatal depression are nearly four times as likely to suffer from depression themselves compared with their peers at 16. This is even long after the mothers have recovered from their depression. This is due in part to sensitising of the stress response systems in the brain (HPA axis) to later stressors. This can lead to vulnerability to problems with anxiety, anger or depression. However, this need not be their destiny. A great deal can be done with really good parenting and/or counselling in later life (Murray *et al*, 2011).

Hence, in light of all of the above, once again we see just how vital it is to support a parent with postnatal depression and to encourage them to get help.

The loss or lack of an enlivened mother

Children can be affected when parental depression means they suffer the lack and/or loss of an enlivened mother. Imagine this from the child's point of view: 'Before your mother got depressed, her face lit up with delight because of you. You were filled with a delicious glow and sense of well-being. You adore her. But over time something happens to that light. It became too precarious, too on-off, too unreliable, too temporary. The world starts to grow darker. You feel somehow that you've fallen out of her mind and are no longer a delight for her and you may not understand why.'

When parents repeatedly fail to light up in response to their child or the expression of their child's love and affection towards them, research shows that this can result in their child's brain habituating to low levels of positive arousal chemicals and high levels of stress hormones. Furthermore, children of persistently depressed parents also showed reduced left frontal lobe activity in a key area responsible for social approach behaviour (Dawson *et al*, 1999; Ashman *et al*, 2002). This means the child is more likely to be withdrawn and reluctant to approach other children to make friends with them, or to warmly approach the familiar adults in their lives. Sometimes this is mistakenly seen as a genetically programmed shyness.

We know that relational play is so key for the psychological and brain development of a child (Gordon *et al*, 2003). Some children who have had insufficient relational play with parents who are too depressed to play with them show developmental delay in language, motor skills, and ability to concentrate and attend. This is often exacerbated by the fact that the depressed parent, finding relating to their child such an effort, puts the child in front of the TV for too much of the time. Interestingly, one research study found that children watching so-called educational videos had fewer words in their vocabulary than children who had not watched them. This is contributed to by the fact that watching TV, even educational videos, takes away from the best brain-developing activity there is – namely, one-to-one relational time, reading together time and relational play with a parent.

One research study showed that during play (with six-month-olds) depressed mothers touched their infants more negatively and their voice was often misattuning, with far less emotion. The infants spent greater periods of time in touching themselves rather than their mother, perhaps compensating for the lack of positive touch from their mothers (Herrera *et al*, 2004).

The loss for the child of a parent as vital limit-setter

Sometimes the parent is too depressed to set down boundaries and so the child becomes what is known as a 'limit-deprived' child. Research shows that this can result in the child developing challenging behaviour patterns, such as conduct disorder or oppositional defiance. The worry is that some of these children don't grow out of such problems and so grow up to be adults who lack social and emotional intelligence and suffer from poor impulse control.

SECTION TWO: HOW TO HELP THE CHILD WITH A DEPRESSED PARENT: WHAT TO DO, HOW TO BE AND WHAT TO SAY

HOW TO HAVE A THERAPEUTIC CONVERSATION WITH THE CHILD

The practitioner needs to be aware of and empathise with the following range of feelings:

Low self-esteem

'I'm not interesting enough for Mum to play with me.'

'My Mum doesn't like kids.'

The play story of an eight-year-old girl with a depressed mum: 'The little girl drowned. Her Mum could have saved her but she didn't because she wasn't pretty enough...'

'I'm rubbish. I've always known it.' He then made up a song called 'I am really awful'.

Emotionally cut off

'It hurts too much to feel sad.'

Desolate, alone, empty

'I need help with being lost.'

Sad, lonely and depressed themselves

Jay, aged eight: 'I sometimes get buried in quicksand. I struggle and struggle to get out. The trouble is Mum gets stuck under the quicksand too. When I go home I just go to bed. Sad is lonely. Sad has got to be black, black, black, and a bit scary too. I need a deeper, much deeper blue for lonely. 'So you see, Mum and I don't really talk. I want to say to Mum "please don't sleep all the time". The sea is tidal and takes me from the beach and puts me on the ugly island.' When Jay was asked what he'd like to say to the sea, he said, 'Don't take me away from my happiness – you wouldn't like it.'

All the following were said while children were playing or drawing.

'In this world there are vases with no flowers, houses with no windows, people with no smiles.'

'Sad is lonely. Lonely is fog and fog is too still.' The little six-year-old also made up a story about a blob called 'What's the point?'.
'There was nothing the tortoise could do but die.'
'Someone in the sand has given up.'
'Why do wolves howl? I think they are howling for their mother.'
'I've drawn a road going nowhere.'
'In this place, dead might take over completely.'

Worry and anxiety about their depressed parent

Millie, aged four, asked her teacher, 'Can you die from getting upset all the time?'

Guilt

For many children the belief that 'my Mum's unhappiness is all my fault' can be difficult to overcome.

Mixed up hate and love

Tina, aged ten: 'I love my Mum but I hate her sadness.'
Children need to know that they can feel love and hate and love and anger and love and frustration all at the same time.

Loss, yearning

Sam's (aged fourteen) mother suffered from repeated bouts of depressed mood. Sam told his counsellor how one minute she would be lovely and warm to him and the next he would experience the 'death' of her love. He talked of desperately trying to find the 'alive Mum' again, but he just kept finding a 'dead one' whom he could not resurrect. He said it was like trying to search in a hall of mirrors for his alive mother, but he just kept finding illusions of her, deadened, jarring versions of her; her face, tired, lifeless, and staring into space.

There is often a household devoid of fun and laughter

The attachment theorist Patricia Crittenden defined a household of what she called 'depressed neglect'. In such a household:
- everyone is just sitting there
- the atmosphere in the house is flat
- children are not offered stimulating relational activities with their parent, but rather are often found plopped in front of the TV or sitting on the floor doing nothing. When these children go to nurseries or children centres they often don't know what to do. They don't know how to play, they just sit there.

OTHER INTERVENTIONS TO HELP THE CHILD WITH A DEPRESSED PARENT

Baby massage classes

Baby massage classes are excellent for babies who are born stressed out due to the anxiety or depression in their mother. The right pressure in massage will activate the baby's vagal nerve, which calms their body down, in particular, their digestive, elimination, breathing and immune systems. Research has also shown that the infant massage group (as opposed to the control group) resulted in a reduction in postnatal depression in the mothers. When the babies were one year old, the mothers who had attended infant massage also had far more sensitive interactions with their babies (O'Higgins *et al*, 2008). After massaging their babies, mothers had lower depression and anxiety scores (Feijo *et al*, 2006).

It is important that the children of depressed parents are provided with an enriched environment in the early years

Research shows also that an 'enriched environment' can reverse the effects of prenatal chronic stress in the mother. This means offering the child optimal nutrition (which dramatically affects brain chemistry) and optimal levels of stimulation and relational play in particular. This means ensuring that someone in the child's life is engaging the child in lovely one-to-one interactions, relating to them while they engage with age-appropriate toys, taking the child to playgroups, baby massage classes, sing and sign classes, and so on, as opposed to the infant being stuck at home or put in front of the TV for hours with a depressed or isolated parent.

Koo and associates have demonstrated that reduced spatial learning produced by prenatal stress can be greatly reversed by an enriched postnatal environment (Koo *et al*, 2003). 'The evidence that postnatal environment (ie maternal care) can mitigate or reverse the cognitive alterations induced by gestational stress reveals the high plasticity of the neonatal brain that can be correctly reprogrammed, when appropriately manipulated.' (Koo *et al*, 2003).

What schools or nurseries can do to help children of depressed parents

Where a mother is very depressed and without people in her life to relate well to her child, a nursery would be better than staying at home with Mum. But when a mother is not depressed, research shows that going to a nursery for long hours, for under-threes, elevates stress hormones to a concerning level (Watamura *et al*, 2002, 2003).

If school or nursery is to be a real second chance for children who live with depressed parents, then teachers must take up the task of offering the child enlivened, warm interactions with that child on a regular basis. The 'lit-up face' of teacher, showing genuine warmth and delight in response to the child, takes on crucial significance. Herein lies one of the very foundation stones of self-esteem. 'If I do not see myself as lovely in my mother's eyes, how can I learn to love myself?' The moving paper entitled 'The Importance of Beauty in the Psychoanalytic Experience' (1990), written by the psychoanalytic child psychotherapist Sue Reid, is a true testimony to this. It tells of a two-year-old whose psychotic mother carried him around in a plastic bag. The child was both physically and psychologically dying. There were concerns that he had moved into autistic withdrawal. In the therapy, he saw Reid's face light up because of him. So powerful was this, coupled with her adept therapeutic interventions, that his inner world was gradually transformed into a warm place. He thrived.

Ensure the child has significant adults in their life who are not depressed

As with all other categories of troubled parents in this book, children of depressed parents need to talk about their home life and relationships with someone who can really listen and help them process what is happening to them, grieve, protest and express other feelings (see Part Two of this book to find out how).

So, when working with a child whose parent is depressed, it is important to consider the people in the child's life who are not depressed and ensure that they know how important they are in terms of offering the child secure attachment and vital emotional regulation for their developing brain. To reiterate, this means adults who can meet the child's needs by amplifying their joy states and soothing their distress and stress states.

Encourage the parent and child to take fish oil

Docosahexaenoic acid (DHA) from fish oil is a very powerful player in brain chemistry. It has been shown to improve mood by boosting serotonin levels. DHA is only obtained from your diet. Research on fish oil consumption in different countries has shown that as fish oil consumption goes up, depression rates go down. In fact, the lower your DHA level, the more severe your depression may be. Many people's diets are badly lacking in DHA. So when you eat oily fish or take DHA supplements, the brain is likely to grab most or all of it (Carper, 2000).

So, it is good to give infants, toddlers and children fish oil supplements if there is not enough oily fish or other sources of DHA in their diet.

Help parents to be resourced in relational play

Relational play (eg 'theraplay', see Booth and Jerberg, 2010) will help the parent to relate to their infant and child in ways that naturally activate the wonderful brain chemical oxytocin. If the parent cannot provide lots of warm physical contact, other adults in the child's life should step in.
- 'We can choose activities and pursuits that release the oxytocin stored in our own inner medical cabinet … We have this wonderful healing substance inside us and need only to learn the many ways we can draw upon it' (Uvnas-Moberg and Petersson, 2005; Uvnas-Moberg, 2012).
- 'If other mammals were injected with oxytocin for 7 days after birth they grew up to be less stressed as adults' (Uvnas-Moberg and Petersson, 2005; Uvnas-Moberg, 2012).

Skin-to-skin contact after birth will release optimal levels of oxytocin in the infant brain. It's best if it is between mother and child but, if not, with another calm, relaxed adult such as the father or other relative would be great. With skin-to-skin contact, the mother's oxytocin levels go up as well as their baby's.

Other benefits of skin-to-skin contact are:
- growth-promoting effects
- the infant's temperature and heart rate stabilise
- their bodily systems are calmed

- mothers who were in skin-to-skin contact with their infants were more sensitive in their interactions skin-to-skin contact promoted attachment, babies felt more secure and were less anxious. It is not just mothers who can provide skin-to-skin contact: there was a rise in father's and infant's oxytocin levels too in skin-to-skin contact after birth. (Uvnas-Moberg, 2012)

In addition, research with humans and other mammals, shows that:
- high levels of physical affection throughout childhood can positively affect anti-anxiety chemical systems in the brain; positively affect the child's capacity to handle stress well in adulthood; result in a far less fearful response in later life
- reassuring touch will quieten the amygdala and reduce hypervigilance so there is no longer a sense of threat; when a person's amygdala is quiet, they do not feel afraid
- lots of physical affection in childhood activates oxytocin in the brain, which reduces stress reactivity and brings the bodily arousal system into balance.
(Caldji *et al*, 2003)

In contrast, low levels of touch in childhood resulted in increased fearfulness in later life and increased stress reactivity. Lots of warm physical contact can positively affect gene expression of GABBA receptors. So infants who received a lot of comfort were less vulnerable to developing anxiety disorders in later life. These are responsible for key calming chemicals in the brain (Caldji *et al*, 2003).

Always consider if you need to make a referral to social services. This is if you feel the child is at risk and/or the parent needs help from a social worker.

HOW TO HELP THE PARENTS TO HELP THEIR CHILDREN

Parent talking ...

'I was anxious about everything. People said I would feel better if I joined playgroups where I would meet other Mums. But I just didn't. I thought they might be judging me as a bad Mum. My baby cries so much. I hated myself, thought I was a terrible Mum. I couldn't stop all those negative thoughts about myself going round and round in my head. Sometimes, when my baby cried, I wanted to scream or just leave him and run away. I often just cried and cried, even at the slightest little thing. I wanted to be dead. Then, one day, a friend advised me to go to the doctor and he gave me antidepressants and referred me to a counsellor. It changed everything. After about a month on antidepressants and talking with my lovely counsellor, I felt normal again. Look, I wish I could tell every depressed mum – don't suffer for one more day – know the symptoms of prenatal and postnatal depression. If you think you've got it, get help now. I wish I had gone for help before.'

Don't tell the parents to 'pull themselves together' or 'think positive'

When a parent suffers from clinical depression, the best thing to do is to help them with their guilt and never to tell them or imply that they just need to 'pull themselves together' or 'think positive'. These are suggestions made by people who don't know about brain biochemistry. Parents can alleviate guilt by knowing that depression is biochemically based and that the stress hormones of depression block a parent's warm playful feelings towards their child. The parent needs professional help and often medication for a time. Antidepressants will address the biochemical imbalances in the brain.

Encourage parents to get professional help – the doctor/referral to a counsellor

It is vital for parents who are depressed to acknowledge that, even with the best will in the world, it can be very difficult, if not impossible, to protect their children from their own painful mental states. They need to get professional help. So encourage the parent to go into therapy to deal with their emotional baggage and unmourned loss and unprocessed trauma. If they do, tell them, it's a massive gift to their child. When parents went to some form of counselling when they were postnatally depressed, they were more sensitive in their interactions with their infants at 18 months (Cooper *et al*, 2003).

Support parents to consider antidepressants in combination with talking therapy

Research shows that with the most debilitating depression, the best treatment is a combination of antidepressants and talking therapy. Antidepressants work by disrupting the 'stubborn [narrow and dominant] constellation of neurons' [in the frontal lobes] (Greenfield, 2000). This accounts for all the repeated negative self-talk – for example, 'I am such a rubbish Mum' – that often drives close relatives of the depressed mother crazy. This is because they have so little impact on the depressed person who is suffering from such a powerful brain biochemical imbalance. Antidepressants help to activate mood-stabilising chemicals such as serotonin, which block these too-high levels of stress hormones that so distort perception and derail good thinking and appropriate action.

The adverse effects of prenatal depression should be weighed up against the possible adverse effects to the foetus and then the infant. At the moment, antidepressants in the first trimester of pregnancy have only showed up as a less than 1 per cent chance of increase of heart defects in the baby. Lars Perdersen, who led the research, said 'Even if SSRI use is causally related to septal heart defects, these heart defects might not necessarily require treatment and some might resolve spontaneously.' No other malformations were associated with use of antidepressants. There is also a slightly higher risk of miscarriage if antidepressants are taken in the first trimester. Usually about 9 per cent of pregnancies end in miscarriage. With antidepressants it can go up to 12 per cent (Pedersen *et al*, 2009). The exposure of the infant to antidepressants through breastfeeding is far lower than during pregnancy, with less than 5 per cent of selective serotonin reuptake inhibitors (SSRIs) passing into the breast milk. This is generally too low to be of clinical significance and many women who have chosen to breastfeed while taking antidepressant medication have not reported any adverse effects. A small number of studies available to date suggest that antidepressant use while breastfeeding is not harmful in terms of the baby's developmental milestones and preschool performance.

If the parent can afford it, support them to get a doula from the third trimester or/and straight after birth

A doula is a trained professional who touches, holds and supports a woman (physically and mentally) in labour and is there emotionally and in a totally supportive role for the mother in the first days or weeks after birth. This role can, of course, be played by a relative, such as a mother or aunt, or a very close friend.

With this type of support it has been shown that:
- women give birth more quickly
- the need for Caesarean section and pain relief is significantly reduced
- two months after birth, mothers who have been helped by a doula during labour have been shown to have better relationships with their children and also with their partners, when compared to those who did not have this type of support
- mothers are less depressed.
(Hofmeyr *et al*, 1991; Landry *et al*, 1998)

Support the parent to get massage before birth, after birth and throughout the early years

Research shows that massage in pregnancy significantly decreases parents' anxiety and stress. It shows that parents who had massage prenatally had:
- fewer prenatal complications
- decreased excessive foetal movement (a feature of prenatal depression)
- 75 per cent lower prematurity rate
- 80 per cent lower incidence of low birth weight
- decreased depression, anxiety and back pain
- decreased cortisol levels
- babies with lower cortisol levels when born
- babies that performed better on the Brazelton Neonatal Behavioral Assessment
- better bonding with their babies.

But research shows that massage needs to be moderate pressure, not light touch or deep tissue massage (Field *et al*, 2009).

In addition, massage releases oxytocin. Research shows that oxytocin can have the following effects:

- it reduces anxiety, depression and agitation and induces calmness
- it has anti-stress effects (it blocks stress hormones)
- it increases social interaction, more social sensitivity and eye gaze
- it increases trust
- it increases sociability
- it lowers heart rate
- it lowers blood pressure
- it aids better digestion
- it improves learning capacity
- it reduces sensitivity to pain
- it promotes the healing of wounds (often half the time)
- it promotes bonding between baby and parent
- mother will experience herself as less anxious
- it reduces stress hormone activity in the hypothalamo-pituitary-adrenal (HPA) axis and the sympathetic nervous system; it increases vagal activity. (Uvnas-Moberg, 2012; Uvnas-Moberg and Magnusson 2005)

Research shows that very good mothering early on, once the infant is born, can help to undo some of the possible damage that might have been caused through the depression during the foetal period. It is possible to reverse the effects of prenatal stress and bring stress reactivity back to normal. The main thing is to be as calm and physically comforting with the stressed-out infant or child. Of course, their crying and agitation can be extremely stressful, like living with a burglar alarm going off a lot of the time. So it's vital that someone is soothing the parent enough so they can soothe their infant.

Encourage breastfeeding

Each time a mother breastfeeds, it is common for their blood pressure and stress hormone levels to fall. Breastfeeding stimulates the sensory nerves in the nipple, which activates the release of prolactin and oxytocin. These then trigger the production and ejection of milk. Breastfeeding triggers the vagal nerve which makes digestion more efficient, which in turn helps milk production. For all this to happen, however, the mother needs to be breastfeeding in a place where they feel psychologically safe. This is because oxytocin release is very affected by feelings of lack of safety. When cows were moved to an unfamiliar stable, for example, their milk dried up, until they felt safe again. One wonders, therefore, about cold, clinical hospital environments (Uvnas-Moberg, 2012).

CHILDREN WITH PARENTS WHO FIGHT

Please note: many examples in this section are about men abusing women, based on the fact that this is the overwhelming trend. We are aware, however, that female-to-male domestic violence is also an issue and something that is growing in public awareness as a taboo is being lifted.

SECTION ONE: WHAT LIFE CAN BE LIKE FOR THE CHILD OF PARENTS WHO FIGHT: THE RESEARCH, THE PSYCHOLOGY AND THE BRAIN SCIENCE

Children talking ...

Girl, aged fifteen: 'My Mum and Dad were always fighting but I didn't know why. I was sometimes in the room but it was like I wasn't there. I was completely shut out. I didn't know what was going on. I used to get really worried. I was gutted. It was really horrible. My sister never did nothing, so it was down to me. But I didn't know what to do' (Butler and Williamson, 1994).

Lacey, aged nine: 'One night I was in bed and heard Dad and Mum arguing. Then it went into lots of shouting and crying. I went downstairs and Dad was hitting Mum. I said, 'Stop, please stop' but my Dad yelled and said it was between him and my Mum and shouted 'go back to bed'. He looked so mad, I was really scared so I went back to bed. But the sounds of all the hurting and hating went on like forever, I just cried and cried. It was like the end of everything good and the beginning of the bad things I knew I would never forget.'

Ben, aged ten: 'One day I got up and went downstairs. My Mum was crying – I wanted to scream when she looked up. She had a bruise on her face, her hair looked like a mad person and her front tooth was broken. My world ended that day.'

Jakob, aged thirteen: 'People just don't get it. You go to school but you can't concentrate because in your heart and your head you are with your Mum. I keep picturing her crying and hurting all alone at home.'

Pippa, aged twelve: 'Once I was at home and my Dad came home in a foul mood. He hit my Mum. I felt so mad inside. I screamed for him to stop but he just threw me off. My love for him died that day. I thought I had a Dad, not a monster. Guess I was wrong.'

Terri, aged eleven: 'It started about two years ago, my stepfather's constant putdowns of my Mum, being called 'useless, stupid, a whore', then told all the time what she must do, not do, and then to see her getting hit if she does not obey him. He's gone now but she's not my Mum anymore – she's gone weird in the head – all jumpy and angry herself. I swear if I had had a gun I would have shot him.'

HOW COMMON IS IT? THE STATISTICS

- The 2010/11 British Crime Survey found that 27 per cent of women and 17 per cent of men had experienced partner abuse during their lifetime, with women experiencing more repeated and severe violence than men.
- From March 2013, the Home Office will be amending its definition of domestic violence to include sixteen- and seventeen-year-olds, and it will be defined as 'any incident or pattern of incidents of controlling, coercive or threatening behaviour, violence or abuse between those who are or have been intimate partners or family members. This can encompass psychological, physical, sexual, financial or emotional abuse.'
- At least 750,000 children a year witness domestic violence (Department for Education, 2010).
- One in 10 women in the UK suffer domestic violence. In 90 per cent of cases the children are in the same or the next room (Home Office, 1992).
- Half of the 160 child-killings over the last five years have come from a house of domestic violence. Many of the children killed were not on the At Risk Register (*Dispatches*, Channel 4, 13 July 2009).

- Between 30 per cent and 66 per cent of those children who live with domestic violence also suffer direct abuse (Cawson, 2002).
- 42 per cent of murder and manslaughter cases involve a domestic dispute and one third of domestic violence victims are children (The WAVE Trust Report, 2005).
- 60 per cent of the children on the At Risk Register have witnessed domestic violence (Department for Education, 2010).
- Studies show clear linking between domestic violence and child abuse (Appel and Holden, 1998). 'Among parents who engaged in serious spouse abuse, half of the fathers and a quarter of the mothers said they had also engaged in serious child abuse' (Moffitt and Caspi, 1998). In backgrounds of child neglect and abuse, parents fighting is a very common element (Cawson, 2002).
- While many couples believe that having a baby will bring them closer together, most research suggests that couples become less satisfied with their relationship after having children (Belsky and Pensky, 1988). For many couples having a baby means less positive interactions between parents (Belsky *et al*, 1983) while levels of conflict increase (Cowan and Cowan, 1988, 1995).

About parents who fight

Of course, all parents will argue from time to time and it's far more healthy than storing up resentments. This is because the latter, which is often known as stamp collecting, can result in the 'cashing in of their stamps', so to speak, by one of the partners leaving, having an affair, or moving into some form of emotional withdrawal. When a child witnesses a parental argument that is resolved, it can be a really good learning experience that anger and resentment is not a big deal and can be resolved. But what we are talking about here is intense and frequent fighting, verbal or physical, which involves cutting put-downs, ridicule, constant blame, contemptuous attacks where there is real hurt, physical and/or emotional. There is no healthy resolution or making up. It's known as 'low warmth/high hostility' (Howe, 2005). Research shows that the combination of attack and then emotional withdrawal, such as cold silences lasting hours or days, is what is so lethal for the children. If a parent is fearful, they can't be an emotional regulator for the child.

Research shows that people who have mental health problems are far more likely to experience domestic violence than those who don't. The author Professor Louise Howard *et al* (2012) carried out a meta-analysis of over 40 studies. She states, 'The evidence suggests that there are two things happening: domestic violence can often lead to victims developing mental health problems, and people with mental health problems are more likely to experience domestic violence.'

HOW CHILDREN ARE AFFECTED

How parents fighting can affect the foetus and the newborn child

Children of mothers who experience prenatal physical domestic violence are at an increased risk of exhibiting aggressive, anxious, depressed or hyperactive behaviour (Whitaker *et al*, 2006).

At 12 weeks old, babies are using the information not just directly from mother or from father but from what's going on between mother and father, so the behaviour of parents who are 'in sync' or 'out of sync' with each other is reflected in the infant's behaviour (McHale and Fivaz-Depeursinge, 1999).

At six months, babies who heard verbal aggression between parents were recorded as having a higher heart rate (Howe, 2005).

Children suffer from problems with anger, anxiety and depression

Radke-Yarrow *et al* (1985) looked at two-year-olds' reactions to simulated aggression between two female actors. The children became distressed and aggressive in response. Children can become angry, anxious, depressed and may present at school with emotional outbursts. Some do to other children in the school what they have seen their parents do to each other. This is totally understandable for anyone living with a terrifying experience that no one has helped them to make sense of.

Many children grow up to become violent themselves

Children who witness domestic violence are often called secondary victims. Research shows that they are more likely to become violent themselves, having watched the violence, than if they were the primary victims themselves (Holmes, 2000). They can be particularly violent to siblings.

In addition, parents fighting has been associated with:

• emotional and physical problems in the child

- poor peer interaction, more negative and far less cooperative interactions (Gottman and DeClaire, 1998)
- conduct problems
- tantrums
- restlessness and agitation
- problems with sleeping, eating, elimination
- depression and anxiety
- low self-esteem
- poor attachment (all McHale and Fivaz-Depeursinge 1999)
- poor school achievement
- increased susceptibility to illness (Gottman and Declaire, 1998).

Girls who are exposed to their parents' domestic violence as adolescents are significantly more likely to become victims of dating violence than daughters of nonviolent parents (Noland *et al*, 2004).

Children witnessing incidents of domestic violence are at a greater risk of having serious adult health problems, including tobacco use, substance abuse, obesity, cancer, heart disease, depression and a higher risk of unintended pregnancy (Felitti *et al*, 2003).

Graham-Bermann and Seng (2005) also found symptoms of post-traumatic stress disorder, such as bedwetting or nightmares, and that children ran a greater risk of having allergies, asthma, gastrointestinal problems, headaches and flu.

Children can become hyperactive and anxious. They can then be misdiagnosed as suffering from ADHD or conduct disorders.

Jayden, aged nine, had frequently watched his parents fighting when he was a little boy. At six his father left. The school reported that Jayden was unable to sit still for any length of time. He always seemed agitated. He was also obsessed with locks and at home would check that the locks worked on the doors and was never convinced they did work. 'Anyone could come in at night' he repeatedly told his mother, 'Even monsters.' Initially Jayden was labelled as having ADHD. This is a very common misdiagnosis with children who have experienced domestic violence. The child can become hyperactive and then be given Ritalin, no one thinking that maybe the child's behaviour is telling us something about deep underlying conflict in the family home.

SECTION TWO: WHAT TO DO, HOW TO BE AND WHAT TO SAY TO CHILDREN WHOSE PARENTS FIGHT

HOW TO HAVE A THERAPEUTIC CONVERSATION WITH THE CHILD

The practitioner needs to be aware of and empathise with the following range of feelings:
(There is obviously no one way that children feel about witnessing domestic violence, but these are some of the most common emotional responses.)

Terrible emotional pain
Abdul, aged seven: 'What hurts her, hurts me...'

Desperate for the nightmare to stop
When Mum has a partner to whom the child is not attached, then the child can be:
• desperate to get Mum to leave the abuser
• pleading with her to leave him – again and again – but often feeling hopeless and helpless when she doesn't.

Sam, aged nine, screamed in panic in the hope that the neighbours would hear, but it didn't work as the violent partner just turned the music up and threatened the child (Brandon and Lewis, 1996).

Confusion about why Mum puts up with it and doesn't leave
'I don't understand that he is still with her ... He says, "I hate you" and "You are a slag" and "You are a bitch". And I am thinking, "Why are you still with her if you are thinking all this about her", but I think he is just scared to be on his own' (Barter *et al*, 2009).

Horror and terror
Thirteen-year-old girl: 'I've seen him kick and punch, and pull her hair. Once he threw petrol over her. I remember him cutting my Mum's lips' (Humphreys and Stanley, 2006).

Fear

Children are often too frightened to tell anyone about what's going on at home, for fear of being taken into care. The nightmare in its present form can feel the lesser hell in terms of a possibility of losing their beloved parent/s.

Fear for their mother's safety – worried she might die at the hands of the violent partner.

Fear of all men (where the abuser is the male parent).

Feeling crazy with ambivalent feelings – loving and hating a violent father all at the same time.

The confusion and mixed-up feelings of loving your Dad who hurts your Mum can feel maddening.

Tim, aged ten: 'I live in a crazy world – I love Daddy, he plays with us so well, and then he goes and hits Mum. I feel mad.'

Denial, desensitising and emotional numbing

Feeling nothing and not caring. The child may think it's normal to hit and hurt people. This enables the child to feel that they can cope with the unbearable, especially when no one is helping them with what they are feeling.

Anger and hate

Tara, aged eight: 'I feel like killing my Dad for hurting my Mum – I am that angry with him.'

John, aged eleven: 'When my Dad hit Mum I wanted him to hurt him real bad. In fact, I began to hate him so much I never wanted to see him anymore.'

'He … headbutted my Mum and cracked her nose there. He smashed her mobile phone … and she dropped to the floor … I am just thinking all this is for nothing and my Mum has tried to leave him how many times but she just keep coming back and … my Mum's like, "I know it's upsetting for you to see but at the end of the day it's my relationship" … Yeah right, I understand that … but at the end of the day I have to sit here and listen to you arguing and all that crap throughout the whole night and stuff' (Barter *et al*, 2009).

Grief and loss

If the parents split up as a result of the violence there can be utter relief but it is often mixed with missing or yearning for the violent father – if he was loved, of course. The child can either tolerate his love and hate for his father or justify his father's actions – it wasn't that bad, or she deserved it, and so on.

Loss from losing their mother to a depression about her abuse: 'The violence was draining her … she had no personality … she just wasn't happy' (Child quoted in 'NCH Action for Children', 1994).

Helplessness

Research shows that the majority of children felt they have little choice but to endure the violence.

Ruby, aged seven: 'Sometimes I just go and run and hide in the toilet it's so frightening.'

'[My daughter] would just sit there frozen, I mean, she didn't know what to do because if she got up to move … he would maybe have gone for her. So she was just, like, sitting there, trembling and crying and stuff' (NCH Action for Children, 1994).

As with all other categories of troubled parents in this book, children with parents who fight need help to talk about what they have seen and heard with someone who can really listen and help them grieve, protest and express their feelings. (See Part Two of the book in terms of more ways to do this).

Empathise with the child

Watching parents fighting can be devastating for a child, as we have seen. First and foremost, the child needs to be empathised with. This will re-establish a sense of human connectedness so they no longer feel alone with their memories of the awful experiences. Empathise with what it can feel like to be stuck in the middle of two warring parents, perhaps feeling desperate for it to stop. Empathise with the fact that when the fighting is happening, the very person who is there to protect you, that is, your Mum, can't because she can't protect herself. Empathise with the horror and terror and all the other feelings detailed above.

Empathic responses: What many children who have witnessed domestic violence need to hear

- It must have been really frightening.
- I am so sorry you had to see and hear what you saw and heard.
- We need to look at how to make you safe if there is fighting again.
- If you feel hate, that's understandable.
- It would be normal to hate your Mum for not leaving.
- It would be normal to hate your Dad for hurting your Mum.
- It is understandable if you feel love and angry at the same time.

Example

A sixteen-year-old boy was hit and shouted at by his father from a baby to the age of eight. Now, he has no contact with his father at all. He worries that he has been 'cursed' and is obsessively cleaning. He is using the obsession as he tries to assert control when he feels he is spiralling out of control.

Acknowledge the child's probable shock

Most children usually need us to bring the word 'shock' into a conversation about seeing their parents physically and/or emotionally hurting each other. If you don't, shock often remains in the child's mind as an 'unthought known' (Bollas, 1987). This means that the child knows it but has not had a thought about it, thus the experience is not properly processed. The word 'shock' helps the child then properly locate and label his feeling in a way that helps him work through and make sense of the painful experience.

When a child has moved into a helpless withdrawal, denial or emotional numbing, support them to find their voice, their protest and their letting go into crying. Provide the child with a language-appropriate version of the following two quotations:

> When the energy [about a traumatic experience] is not fully discharged, it does not simply go away; instead it stays trapped, creating the potential for traumatic symptoms. The likelihood of developing traumatic symptoms is related to the level of undischarged survival energy ... Children need support to release this highly charged state.
> (Levine, 2006)

> It is of great consequence whether there was an energetic reaction to the [emotional] experience. By reaction we here understand a whole series of voluntary or involuntary reflexes [eg crying/shaking] through which, according to experience, affects are discharged. If the success of the reaction is of sufficient strength it results in the disappearance of a great part of the affect. [In other words, the child doesn't suffer mental ill-health.] Language attests to this fact of daily observation in such expressions as 'to give vent to one's feelings' to be 'relieved by weeping' etc. If the reaction is suppressed, the affect remains united with the memory. [The latter means the child carries the burden of traumatic memories which derail his emotional and social development.]
> (Freud and Breuer, 1909)

In other words, explain to the child how, when there was no space for their feelings (because Dad and Mum were expressing theirs so violently), feelings don't just go away. Tell the child how important it is for them to express their feelings about what they saw and heard with you, when they are ready. The feelings they need to express in particular are the protest (eg, 'How dare you do that to my Mum' and the grief, 'It broke my heart to see her hurt like that'). If the child cries about the domestic violence, shower them with praise for their courage in letting go in this way. It is brave and healing to cry. It is far easier to bottle it all up inside.

What to do if the child has moved into being aggressive with others

Children need to know that they are not bad or mad but that their own aggressive behaviour makes perfect sense in terms of what they have experienced. This is not excusing their aggressive behaviour, which needs to have consequences, but it is offering the child affirming empathy.

If they are between five and ten years old, read them the book *How Hattie Hated Kindness* (Sunderland, 2003a) and discuss it afterwards. If they are between ten and eighteen years old, read them the book *Smasher* (Sunderland, 2008a). Through the structure of a story, these books offer affirmative empathy in terms of why children who have suffered abuse, neglect or trauma, or who have watched parental violence, can end up being aggressive.

Talk about emotional ambivalence (if appropriate)

If you think the child is very confused, with major ambivalent feelings towards the violent parent, talk about how indeed it is utterly possible to love the very person you see hurting another person you love and perhaps from whom you also need protection.

Psycho-education about relationships, to help with the feelings of fear and confusion

Think about these things with the child:
- People don't have to hurt people with words or fists. It's often that people who do hurt in this way don't know other ways to get angry or what say when they want things to be different.
- Usually this is because in their childhood no adults showed them how.
- Some behaviour in parent-to-parent relationships is acceptable but hurting behaviour is not.
- Daddy/Mummy does some things that are not right. This can be confusing, painful, even heartbreaking.
- It isn't even a bit your fault and you are too little and young to be able to stop them. It is the job of other adults to stop your parents hurting each other in this way.
- Reiterate that violence is never OK, no matter how angry you feel.

If the domestic violence is still going on

Make a plan for if it happens again, so they feel more in control of the situation this time.

Always consider if you need to make a referral to social services. This is if you feel the child is at risk and/or the parent needs help from a social worker.

Educate children about who they can go to when they need help

As part of this, it is important to be familiar with organisations set up to support young carers, and to research those in your area. For example:
www.family-action.org.uk
www.youngcarers.net
ChildLine: www.ChildLine.org.uk Tel: 0800 1111

HOW TO HELP THE PARENTS TO HELP THE CHILDREN

First and foremost, the abused parent needs protecting. As Kelly (1994) stated, the one simple and key principle from which we can begin is that the protection of the woman is frequently the most effective form of child protection.

Second, research shows that domestic abuse causes mental health problems in the parent, which, as we have seen, will markedly affect the parent's ability to parent. So the parent must be encouraged to get help for the mental health impact of the domestic abuse. If she is reticent, asking her to do it for the sake of her child, and the impact that her depression or anxiety will have on him, can often be the motivational and galvanising factor.

Research shows that very few mothers talk to their children about violence

Research has found that less then one fifth of mothers talk to their children about the violence they experience (NCH Action for Children, 1994). This leaves the child struggling with their feelings on their own. As a result, the child has no choice but to defend against the feelings (and, as a result of that, develop some neurotic symptom and/or become emotionally numb) or discharge his feelings in aggressive behaviour. In short, the child discharges feelings in challenging behaviour or defends (physical or neurotic symptoms). There is no third choice! In addition, not talking about the awful event just exacerbates the child's fear and isolation.

'I felt sort of pushed out until she really sat down and told me and then I sort of understand' (NCH Action for Children, 1994).

Suppport the parent to talk about it with the child

So one of the best things to do is to support the parent to have a therapeutic conversation about what has happened. If the parent doesn't know how to do this, offer ways to engage the child and actual things to say.

Or suggest parent–child therapy, where the parent can give the child a clear understanding of what happened and why. It often helps to give the child some context – for example, 'Your Dad and I were both hit when we were children, so we had bad modelling in terms of how to make things better between us. We are going to get help to find better ways of arguing – ones that don't hurt us or frighten you.'

Example

Kara, a young mother, took in a lover who hit her. As a result, she threw him out. However, Stephan, aged six, saw what had gone on. He didn't talk about it to anyone but developed obsessive-compulsive disorder (OCD). He said to his Mum, 'Put the things on the mantelpiece in rows, Mum, or I will cut myself or attack you with a knife.' She realised that he was in a state of terror, rather than being angry or naughty. She came to us at The Centre for Child Mental Health and we suggested that he needed help to talk about what he had seen. We helped her find the words. So the next time he asked her to be part of his OCD ritual, at our suggestion, she took him on her lap and said, 'I am so sorry I did not protect you and you saw me and [the ex-boyfriend] fighting. I am so sorry I did not keep your world safe for you, so now you sometimes feel so frightened. Next time you feel like that, will you come and tell me? Will you come and say, "Hey Mum, I need some help because it's gone all unsafe again." Stephan cried and said, "You should have chosen another one [boyfriend], you should have chosen another." The conversation led to Stephan being able to do the two most important things in terms of healing: protest and grieving. He no longer has OCD rituals.

Empower the parent to apologise to the child

When a parent is aware, or helped to be aware, of how their child has been affected by domestic violence, apology to the child can be enormously therapeutic. For example, 'I am so sorry I did not protect you from seeing us fight', 'I am so sorry I did not leave your Dad earlier so you had to hear and see all that for so long.'

Support the parents to go into couple therapy

If the parents are both self-aware on some level and deeply regretting any violence between them, suggest couple therapy. Support them in actually accessing it. Inform them about Relate: www.relate.org.uk. Tel: 0300 100 1234.

CHILDREN WITH PARENTS WHO ARE SEPARATING, SEPARATED OR DIVORCED

SECTION ONE: WHAT LIFE CAN BE LIKE FOR THE CHILD WITH PARENTS WHO ARE SEPARATING, SEPARATED OR DIVORCED: THE RESEARCH, THE PSYCHOLOGY AND THE BRAIN SCIENCE

Children talking ...

Toby, aged seven: 'I want a proper family like everyone else in my class.'

Gabriel, aged three: 'Grown-ups live together, then they fight, then they can't live together any more' (Lieberman, 1995).

Wendy, aged ten: 'I had to choose who to live with, it was awful. I chose Mum just 'cos she knows more about what I need to get ready for school and stuff. Daddy cried when I chose and said that proves you don't love me. That made me want to be dead.'

Nathan, aged four: 'Dad moved out. I'm scared I won't see him anymore. Mum said I'll see him in a fortnight. I don't know what that means. To me it's like he's died.'

Sophie, aged fourteen: 'I just wanted the rows to stop, not for Mum and Dad to leave each other.'

Girl, aged eleven: 'I hate my parents arguing. Mum talks to me about her problems. Mum doesn't trust Dad and makes me spy on him and tell her what he's been doing. The stress of it is making me ill and made me lose friends' (NSPCC, 2008).

HOW COMMON ARE SEPARATION, DIVORCE AND FAMILY BREAKDOWN? THE STATISTICS

- Half of all couples who live together (unmarried) split up before the child's fifth birthday (Centre for Social Justice, 2007).
- Half of all children will see their parents split by the time they are 16 (Benson, 2010; Centre for Social Justice, 2011).
- For every three weddings there are now two divorces, and a quarter of children will experience stress due to family breakdown (Centre for Social Justice, 2011).
- One in five children live in a lone parent family.
- 1 million children live in step-families.
- 25 per cent of children watch parents screaming and shouting at each other (Joseph Rowntree Foundation, 1998).
- The taxpayer is spending at least £20 billion a year trying to repair the damage caused by family breakdown (Centre for Social Justice, 2011).
- Divorce is the fastest route into poverty when the mother is left on her own to bring up the children (Ely *et al*, 1999).
- Severe depression is three times higher among women and nine times higher among men who have been separated or divorced, compared to stably married and single men and women (Bruce and Kim, 1992).

About parents who separate or divorce

Let's face it, developing and deepening an intimate relationship over time requires immense skill. Considering the statistics above, it is crazy that the psychology of human relationship is not a compulsory subject on every school curriculum.

The key relational skills that don't come naturally to most of us are:
- empathy (especially with someone who you are angry with)
- attunement
- the ability to say sorry and find ways forward, rather than punish and blame
- the capacity to see how your partner's childhood past is contributing to their infuriating behaviour, and so have compassion for your partner's painful life experiences.

We all know the 'honeymoon period' ends, but then, without these key relational skills, most relationships will really struggle. We also know that the birth of a child is often not the joyous happy-ever-after event so many parents wish for. Research shows that married couples are 30 per cent more likely to split up after the birth of their first child than childless couples or couples with more than one child (Lunn *et al*, 2006).

The breakups after the new baby are also often because of having to readjust to a completely new life. It is so difficult to keep the romance going with all the tears, tantrums, excrement, endless mess and housework involved in bringing up a child. The sleeplessness makes people irritable and depressed and can drive a wedge between parents, one of whom may have to go to work in the morning and be resentful of their stay-at-home partner. The man can also be jealous of their partner's attention to the new baby, exacerbated by the fact that she just doesn't have the time or emotional space to look after him in the way she used to before the baby came along. In addition, rows often develop from disagreements over how to parent.

When parents are living in a troubled relationship with their partner, they can get depressed too. So some children can suffer all the troubles we have explored of being a child living with a parent troubled with depression. Some children see their parents falling into depression or moving into panicked, desperate behaviour, all of which can be very frightening. It can leave the child feeling unsafe, anxious and emotionally dysregulated.

HOW CHILDREN ARE AFFECTED

Even babies are affected

Fivaz-Depeursinge and colleagues (1999) developed a technique for looking at three-way interactions between baby, Mum and Dad. They found that even by 12 weeks, some infants are responding not just to emotional and physical cues from mother or from father but from what's going on between mother and father. So the behaviour of parents who are 'in sync' with each other is reflected in the infant's behaviour. For those who are not 'in sync', it appears that the infant is taking a go-between role and trying to regulate the parents' behaviours, even at that young age.

With separation and divorce, the problem is that the child needs the best possible parenting in terms of soothing, reassurance and empathy for their feelings of loss, fear and anger, just at a time when parents may be least able to give it to them. This is because the parents are often understandably struggling to manage their own emotional states let alone those of their child. But when children and teenagers are left with their own emotional turmoil, the fallout in terms of mental and physical health problems can be very marked as we see in the research below:

After parental separation or divorce, children and teenagers will be:
- 75 per cent more likely to fail at school (far more so than having lost a parent through bereavement)
- 70 per cent more likely to become a drug addict
- 50 per cent more likely to have alcohol problems
- 50 per cent more likely to have low self-esteem
- 50 per cent more likely to experience poor peer relationships.

They will be significantly more likely to have:
- health problems
- increased risk of behavioural problems (eg bedwetting, withdrawn behaviour, aggression, antisocial behaviour)
- increased likelihood of anxiety or depression, poor peer relationships, being admitted to hospital following accidents, leaving school and home when young, becoming sexually active and becoming pregnant.

They will be more likely to:
- end up without qualifications and claiming benefits
- experience breakups of their own partnerships.

Despite far more acceptance that people divorce today, the effects on children have not got better. When outcomes for children of divorced parents in the 1970s were compared with children now both groups were equally likely to lack qualifications, be on benefits and suffer from depression.

(Sources: Centre for Social Justice, 2007; Centre for Social Justice, 2011; Murray, 2007; Kiernan, 1997)

In addition:
- 75 per cent of children and young people who have experienced parental separation or divorce shift from secure to insecure attachments (Murray, 2008).
- 20 children a year are killed on access visits during separation (*Dispatches*, Channel 4, 13 July 2009).

Parental death can be less damaging than parental separation and divorce

Research suggests that parental death is less damaging for many children than parental separation and divorce. It shows that parental death does not carry the same risks of poorer educational attainment, lower socio-economic status, poor mental health and long-term risk of substance abuse as we see in children who experience parental separation or divorce (Joseph Rowntree Foundation, 1998).

It's the conflict that causes the mental health problems in the child not the separation or divorce per se

Research shows that it's not the separation or divorce per se that causes distress to the child, it's the atmosphere of conflict in the family home or between the parents after the separation, which can cause such fallout for the child in terms of emotional and behavioural problems (Hall, 2008).

Waiting for it all to happen again with the next marriage or partnership

Research shows that second marriages are twice as likely to break down than first marriages, so some children in step-families are just waiting to experience another family breakdown with another set of losses (Centre for Social Justice, 2011).

SECTION TWO: HOW TO HELP THE CHILD WITH PARENTS WHO ARE SEPARATING, SEPARATED OR DIVORCED: WHAT TO DO, HOW TO BE AND WHAT TO SAY

HOW TO HAVE A THERAPEUTIC CONVERSATION WITH THE CHILD

Many children are not helped by anyone to talk about the whole host of feelings they are left with when their parents split up, and as a result, are catapulted out of their childhood into a troubled adult world. This so often results in them being overburdened with too much knowledge of conflicts in adult relationships: financial strain, the courts, arguing, knowledge about affairs.

It is vital that children are helped to talk about their feelings with someone who can really hear them, empathise and attune, so that they don't have to go on to fail at school or suffer from mental health problems, low self-esteem or drug or alcohol problems, as detailed in the awful statistics above.

The practitioner needs to be aware of and empathise with the following range of feelings:

Grief

Kate, aged nine: 'Daddy broke my heart by leaving me.'

When their parents separate, like their world has fallen apart. So many losses: friends, familiarity, lovely family rituals, the family home or the family home as they knew it.

At watching a parent leave, children often also witness the other parent becoming depressed. So they lose their previously enlivened parent to depression.

Abandonment and feeling unloved

Kyle, aged seven: 'Dad said it was not me he was leaving, just Mum. But by moving out he was leaving me too. If they can stop loving each other they can stop loving me too.'

Rejected or excluded

Girl, aged twelve: 'My step-Dad moved in over the summer. I feel like Mum and him want me out of the family and that he has taken my Mum away … I want my Mum back' (ChildLine, 2008).

Girl, aged fourteen: 'My step-Dad is not my real Dad. I don't feel loved or included in anything but my younger brother is … I hate the atmosphere in the house' (ChildLine, 2008).

Feeling let down by the parent who has gone

Dayle, aged eight (Daddy moved out, said he would visit but didn't):
'It would have been easier if he had died rather than saying he would come back and see me, but he doesn't, he just doesn't.'

Anger, resentment and arguments

Gemma, aged eight: 'When Mum keeps crying I hate it. I thought parents were supposed to be the big, strong ones – now I am having to be that for her.'

Boy, aged eighteen: 'I've just had a massive argument with my Mum. It happens a lot. Today she threw all my stuff out on the street. It's been bad since Dad left' (NSPCC, 2008).

Hate

Tom, aged twelve: 'I knew Mum was miserable with Dad but aren't Mums supposed to put their children first, because we weren't miserable with Dad? I hate her for putting herself before us.'

Fear

When parents keep shouting and crying, have out-of-control feelings and/or are seemingly unable to cope with life, it can be truly frightening for a child.

Fear of losing everything familiar and known, all that makes them feel safe in the world – their home, their toys, their school, their friends, their routines and rituals.

Fear of the people they love.

Fear of the world, as they have known it, ending.

Guilt
When choosing which parent to live with, feeling that they let down the parent they did not choose. The unchosen parent may 'guilt trip' the child, consciously or unconsciously.

Feeling guilty when going out to have a good time instead of staying in to look after the parent who is now single.

Gerry, aged fourteen: 'I would feel too guilty leaving home now because Mum needs me to help her with her unhappiness.'

Shock and powerlessness
The majority of children have had no idea parents want a divorce, until it is voiced. They wanted the fighting to stop, not for Mum and Dad to separate.

Feeling stuck in the middle
Many children and young people feel stuck in the middle of their parents, used either as a messenger between them, or to report back to one about what the other is doing or feeling.

Resorting to secrecy
Sophie, aged nine: 'My Mum hates my Dad more because I used to tell her about all the lovely things I did at his house. She cried. I don't tell her anymore. If she asked what I did I say really boring things.'

Feeling that they don't matter
Kerry, aged twelve: 'My opinion doesn't matter. I told her what I felt about them splitting up, but I know I don't come into it.'

Confusion
Bailey, aged six: 'If he loves us, why has he gone?'

Also, confusion of being pushed into taking sides.

Caron, aged nine: 'Mum says Dad was selfish and useless, but I love my Dad, he is so kind and fun. It doesn't make sense.'

Peter, aged six: 'Mum says we will see Dad on Saturday. Is that a long time or a little time?'

Jealousy

Claire, aged seven: 'I hate it that my friends' parents are still together. I could scream when I see them kissing each other or holding hands.'

Jealous of new step-siblings, feeling their parent or step-parent finds them more interesting and lovely to be with than them.

Denial in terms of reunion fantasies

Pablo, aged seven: 'It's OK. If I work hard at it, I will be able to get them together again.'

Helping the child to grieve

For many children, parental separation and divorce means major adjustment to a very different life and extremely painful losses. Sometimes, the remaining parent is struggling with half their previous income, so the child has to make lots of sacrifices: far fewer new toys or clothes, not going to usual dance clubs or karate, no more lovely holidays abroad. Some children also feel they have lost their loving, warm, playful parent as that parent is now repeatedly angry or depressed. For others, their home no longer feels like their home, as half of the furniture and important homely items are gone, such as family photos. So children need help to talk about all these losses, not just some of them, and to grieve and protest. The best way is to cry and get angry. The child who has few civilised feelings about such a huge event is being defended or is in denial.

Helping the child to adjust

Many children then have to contend not only with all this loss but to living in a new family with new family members. This is because of step-families and second marriages. Children can be thrown into another family where maybe they don't like some members. They would never choose them as their friends. Yet they may be sharing a bedroom with one of these children. When this is the case, children need help to express anger and resentment but at the same time to learn social skills such as negotiation, de-escalating so that unhealthy fights and rows can be avoided, and finding 'me time' and 'me space' somewhere in the family home. They may need help with how to speak to their parent to ensure they get this.

HOW TO HELP THE PARENTS HELP THEIR CHILDREN

First and foremost parents need help in how to talk to their children about what is going on and what is going to happen

Often when parents are splitting up, they don't know how to talk to their children about it, or they don't even realise that they need to talk to them about it because they are so caught up in their own grief. A lot of children ring ChildLine because they can see that their parents are having a lot of problems and they're worried about what's going to happen, but neither parent has said anything to them.

What parents need to know

- The research shows that it's the conflict which often causes the child psychological damage, so staying together in conflict is as damaging as separating.
- Their children are at risk of developing physical, mental or behavioural problems, problems academically and with employment, if they are not helped to talk about their experience of the separation, divorce or parents' frequent arguing. In particular, they need someone who can acknowledge their hurt, anger and loss and their often very 'here-and-now' sense of abandonment. So if parents feel unable or unwilling to talk about things with their child, they need to ensure that their child has easy and readily available access to a very empathic relative (eg be able to talk to on the phone or get their calls returned that day). If this is not possible, the child needs to see a professional counsellor or therapist.
- Their ability as parent to manage and process their own distress directly impacts on their child. So it's vital that they get other adults to help them do this or, better still, seek professional help from a therapist or counsellor.
- The ability of parents to recover from their own psychological distress associated with the separation directly impacts on a child's ability to adjust.

- One of the most damaging things for the child is when a parent criticises the other parent to the child, gets the child to take sides, or uses them as a confidante, counsellor or go-between.
- It is essential to treat with grace the fact that the child is missing the other parent and that she or he needs to feel free to talk about this and get empathy from the other parent, not criticism.

Informing parents how to prevent making the child's suffering worse

- Don't allow the child to listen to parents' phone calls or arguments.
- Don't cross-examine the child for what happened when they stayed with the non-resident parent.
- Don't take down or throw away the photos of the non-resident parent.
- Don't use the child as a messenger or go-between.
- Don't get upset in front of the children during the transition from you to the other parent.
- Do let the child ask as many questions as they like.
- Do ensure the child knows you are always there if they want to speak about how they are feeling. Welcome the child's desire to talk about it.
- Don't assume that talking about it once is enough. Most children need to talk about it again and again and it's a really good sign if this is happening.
- Don't say to the child, 'It's far better now because Mum and Dad are happier now apart.' It is often not 'better' for the child, so it's not helpful saying this.
- Don't assume that older children will handle it better. Their grief can be just as great as that of younger children.
- Don't lie to the child about where the absent parent has gone. Be clear if they have left. Lies about anything at this time can lead to a deep sense of betrayal when they find out the truth. When children aren't given the information about why their parents are splitting up or are in conflict, they will make up their own version of the truth. The human mind needs closure, so a child needs a story of why this has happened. Here are some crazy stories children have made up because no one sat down with them and told them what was happening and why it was happening:
  - Boy, aged six: 'Daddy left because Mum kept losing the car keys.'
  - Girl, aged ten: 'Daddy went off Mum when she had a "semi-permanent". I never really understood what that was, I just knew I hate that hairdresser.'

Things to say to open up the subject with the child again

'You remember what I said the other day? I wondered if you had been worrying about it? What do you remember? I wondered if I had told you properly…?' (Segal, 1993).

'I don't know if you want to talk about it, but it's great if you do, when you are ready. And I promise I will really listen and not talk at you or lecture.'

What happens after the separation or divorce?

It's very important that warm, relational contact is maintained with both parents. Ironically, the non-resident parent often gives more time to the child than they did when they where living in the family house.

Carly, aged nine: 'Daddy was never around much before the divorce. He always came back from work when we were in bed and then had to dash off in the morning. We actually see far more of him now Mum and him have separated. That's the good thing out of all this.'

What can schools do?

Personal, social and health education (PSHE) in its current form, with its common emphasis on 'managing emotions' will for many children and teenagers not be sufficient in alleviating the negative effects of family breakdown. This is because the feelings involved are just too intense, too deep and too painful to be simply 'managed'. A general exploration of anger or grief will not offer these children the level of therapeutic conversation they need to be able to heal.

Anda *et al* (2006) and Van der Kolk (2006), both child trauma specialists, have found that a cognitive approach, typically an agenda of 'managing feelings' in healing children of family breakdown, simply doesn't work. This is because the child's or teenager's pain is subcortical (Damasio, 2000). This means that the parts of the brain highly activated are the genetically ingrained systems of rage, fear and grief and the flight or fight systems deep in the reptilian and old mammalian parts of the brain (Panksepp, 1998). These systems mean that the child or teenager has intense embodied emotional experiences, which, if not talked about, are often discharged in violent behaviour or defended against (eg neurotic defences such as phobias, obsessions, eating disorders, self-harm). As Van der Kolk (2007) says, 'the body keeps the score'. Thus a very different sort of intervention is required; namely, children need help to feel those intense feelings and to release the shock, grief and rage from their body – to cry, to howl, to let go into shaking, to sob in someone's arms. It is only after this that they will be able to take a more solely cognitive approach. Prior to this, stress hormones will simply flood the child's frontal lobes, making it impossible for them to think well, to attend and concentrate on what the teacher, counsellor or other adult is saying.

In light of this, schools would be well advised to invest in some form of skilled-facilitator small-group-work support for these children and teenagers. Given that by the age of fifteen, almost half of all children are no longer living with their parents (Centre for Social Justice), and given that the fallout is so awful, every secondary school should invest in such a group. In these groups, entitled something like 'Family issues', pupils could discuss their feelings about family and family breakdown more freely with attuned, empathic response from a trained adult leader who is very aware of the issues and feelings common to children and teenagers experiencing family breakdown. Exercises such as those offered in Part Two would be a good starting place. As an example, Standish Community High School in Wigan has a Pupil Services Unit. The teachers are vigilant as to which particular emotional issues in their student groups are interfering with learning. As a result, theme-based mentor-led learning groups are formed.

CHILDREN WITH PARENTS ADDICTED TO DRUGS, ALCOHOL OR SOLVENTS

SECTION ONE: WHAT LIFE CAN BE LIKE FOR CHILDREN WITH A PARENT ADDICTED TO DRUGS, ALCOHOL OR SOLVENTS: THE RESEARCH, THE PSYCHOLOGY AND THE BRAIN SCIENCE

Children talking ...

Ana, aged eleven: 'Dad has been drinking. He always drinks and then hits us and says it's our fault and that he wishes we hadn't been born' (NSPCC, 2008).

Jade, aged eight: 'My picture shows a family that are drug-takers and drink too much. Their child is left alone in her room because her family doesn't look after her properly. I think this is the most important thing to change because it's not nice to always be alone' (Centre for Social Justice, 2008).

Ben, aged seven: 'I think my Mum prefers her drink to me.'

Kyla, aged fifteen: 'My Dad drinks and shouts all the time. I feel upset, like crying and killing myself. I look after the little one – feeding him, getting him ready for bed, getting things ready for the morning and telling him stories. It's like I've got kids of my own' (ChildLine case notes 2008, family relationship problems).

Tyler, aged nine: 'I used to stay off tae make sure my Ma did nae get drugs and all that ...'cause I hate it ... I'd follow her and not let her doe it ... like I would make sure she stayed in the house with me' (Centre for Social Justice, 2008).

Terry, aged thirteen: 'Mummy takes pills because she says it makes her better. But then it makes her worse. It gets so bad sometimes that she can't be a Mummy to me anymore.'

HOW COMMON IS PARENTAL ADDICTION? THE STATISTICS

✫ Over a quarter of all adults in the UK drink alcohol to the point where it brings risk of physical or psychosocial harm (Singleton *et al*, 2001).

✫ On average, 200,000 people go into drug treatment each year in the UK – more than ever before. Only 3 per cent leave treatment drug-free (*Dispatches*, Channel 4, 'Mummy Loves Drugs, Not Me', 3 November 2008).

✫ A drug user dies of a drug overdose every 10 hours in the UK. Most of these people are parents.

✫ 30 per cent of men who assault their partners do so under the influence of alcohol (Cabinet Office, 2004).

✫ Over 1 million children in the UK live with a parent who drinks too much (Cabinet Office, 2004).

✫ 350,000 children have parents who have a serious drug problem. Nine out of 10 children live with their drug-addicted parents (Advisory Council on the Misuse of Drugs, 2003).

✫ 3,500 babies are born to heroin-addicted mothers a year; that's nearly 10 babies a day.

✫ If one of your parents is an addict, you have a 50 per cent chance of becoming an addict. If both of your parents are addicts, your odds could be as high as 75 per cent. If your father was addicted at a very young age, was violent when drinking, and you are a male, your odds are as high as 90 per cent (Clayton, 1997).

✫ Billions of pounds are spent on helping drug addicts, but there are almost no services for supporting children and grandparents.

About parents who are addicted to drugs or alcohol

When drunk or drugged, parents who are addicts often lose their loving, warm parental feelings. Many become a very different parent indeed. They lose their ability to be emotionally attuned to the needs of their child. They lose their capacity for emotionally regulating their child, soothing their distress, helping calm and reassure them when they are frightened. It is as if the child is abandoned and sometimes bereaved during these times. One little girl so aptly said to her mother, 'You were deaf when you were drunk', in the sense that her mother, when drunk, could not connect with her or respond to her on any meaningful level. At these times, it is as if the child has indeed fallen out of their mother's mind.

Picture of a Child Who Fell Out of His Mummy's Mind

Today he fell out of her mind,
Her arms became too limp and long.
He fell right down the front of her,
Got all-torn-up and paper-binned.

Now searching for his littered self,
He walks among his dreadful grief
And finds a lethal world of just-himself,
There is no lovely here.

He longs
That she might read the calling of his eyes
remember me, remember me,
That she might see
just once,
And feel his falling from her mind.
Yet has no words to speak of how he'd tried to cling
But helpless, lost his grip
And blown away like little dust.

He only wanted life,
He could not find it without her.

(The author)

This devastating failure to connect with the child due to being drunk or drugged is because higher brain functioning (capacity to reason and reflect, self-awareness, awareness of the other and empathy) is shut down. It is the higher brain that enables a parent to be attuned to the needs of their child, to hold them in mind, to respond to what the child needs, to connect with them. As one child on telephoning ChildLine (2008) said, 'Dad's an alcoholic, and constantly shouts at me and Mum. In all my life, I don't think he's ever said something nice to me.'

Due to the shutdown of higher brain functioning (pre-frontal cortex) the drunk or drugged parent can end up being deeply hurtful, angry, violent, insensitive, neglectful and/or abusive to their child. In effect, they are parenting at these times with the lower mammalian and reptilian parts of their brain in the driving seat. As a result, primitive aggressive impulses can have a field day, often terrifying the child. As Serena, aged thirteen, said, 'It's like having two different Mummys. The lovely kind one when she's sober and the angry monster when she's drunk.'

Furthermore, the brain chemicals released from desperately needing the drug or drink, taking one or both, and then the withdrawal period, can block maternal brain chemicals. One parent I worked with said that, when needing a drink, she knew that alcohol mattered far more to her than her child.

The commonality of neglect or abuse for the children involved

Your mother has left you alone with your siblings and locked the door. You are starving. Mum smokes crack so there is no money left for food. The neighbours know about your hunger and sometimes throw you cupcakes through the letterbox. They are too frightened to tell social services because mother's boyfriend might attack them. The cupcakes are a good day. On a bad day you draw pictures of food on paper and swallow them instead.
(Kids Company, 2011)

Many children of parents who are addicted to drugs or alcohol are on the cusp of being taken into care. It's that precarious. This is because, with parents addicted to drugs or alcohol, abuse or neglect of their children is very common. Some children are very aware of the fact that they might be taken into care, and hence often keep everything secret and don't call out for help. If they are taken into care, the pain of the rupture and yearning for the parent can be excruciating, even if that parent has been frequently neglectful and/or abusive. This fact is often underestimated by social workers and other child professionals, some of whom are cut off from their own grief and so cannot appreciate the child's pain. In one case, I was supervising a teenager who was allowed an access visit to her drug-addicted mother once a month. The teenager couldn't bear the pain of missing and yearning for her mother. So she found a way to visit her mother secretly once a day. 'I would die for my mother' said the teenager. One only has to think of the film *Rabbit Proof Fence* to appreciate that trying to sever a parent–child close bond is a terrible thing and the drive for reconnection can be immense.

Chaotic and bleak home environment

When their parent is a drug addict, some children live in a chaos of people coming and going, taking drugs, selling drugs and then rent money spent on drugs. Some children are told to shoplift to get money. The chaos to them is normal, as they don't know what normal is.

Example: Billy, aged seven

Billy's mother had a drug problem. Billy's siblings were glue-sniffers and stole to bring food back for Mum. Billy's father kept leaving and coming back. Billy was on the Child Protection Register for neglect. In a counselling session, Billy wrote the following story: 'There are octopuses coming in the house, dustbins are flying through the windows and knocking everything over. A baby is hiding in the wardrobe. It is crying. Someone rings the police for help. But the police fall in a pond and are drowned on the way there. The next day the lollipop lady falls asleep on the job, so the children get run over. I guess it's easier for the mother that way.' In another of Billy's stories, little cars fell off the toy garage 'into hell under the pavement'. Billy found it terribly difficult and anxiety-provoking to move from the classroom to the counselling room or from the counselling room to the classroom. It was as if he was frightened of falling off the edge of both of them.

Parents as addicts are often cut off from their feelings of hurt, guilt, grief and hopelessness about their own lives and how their addiction might be affecting their children. This is because to feel those feelings would often be unbearable. In fact, often people take drugs or alcohol as an emotion blocker, because they can't face feeling their feelings. As a result, vulnerable, sad or hurt feelings in the home tend not to be talked about openly by anyone. In contrast, there can be lots of interactions of blaming, anger, defensive exchanges and irrationality. The parents suddenly say things to their child that they didn't mean to say or would never dream of saying when sober or clean – 'You're a little slut dressed like that', 'You are the reason I keep needing a drink'. As a result, children often learn not to show feelings as it's not safe to do so (they might get shouted at or shamed in some way) or they learn actively to hide them. In addition, the atmosphere in the family home is often one devoid of any humour, fun or joy and a desolate sense of bleakness often hangs in the air.

HOW CHILDREN ARE AFFECTED

What happens when a pregnant woman takes drugs – how the foetus is affected

Cocaine, heroin, amphetamines and other drugs cross the placenta and enter the baby's body. The elimination of the drug is slower in a foetus than in an adult. This means that the drug remains in the baby's body much longer than it does in the mother's body.

The critical period of when the major organ systems develop is in the first trimester – it starts at about 17 days post-conception. So drugs being transferred from the mother's body can be particularly lethal at this time. But the baby's organ systems and central nervous system can still be adversely affected in the second and third trimesters. We also know that drugs and alcohol can affect the brain development process known as migration. This means that cells might not move to the right place in the brain. As a result, there can be one or more of the following:
- growth retardation
- foetal death
- miscarriage
- bleeding within the brain (intracranial haemorrhage)
- placental abruption (separating of the placenta from the uterus) resulting in severe bleeding
- damage to the developing brain and other organs.

Smoking marijuana means the baby is breathing in lethal levels of carbon monoxide and carbon dioxide, which also reduce oxygen supply to the brain vital for healthy brain and body growth. This can lead to all the factors outlined above and in the section on newborns, below, as well as developmental delays and behavioural and learning problems.

How the newborn can be affected by the parent taking drugs

Babies can be born dependent on the drug (eg cocaine or heroin) and suffer from withdrawal symptoms – for example, tremors, sleeplessness, muscle spasms, irritability, convulsions, diarrhoea, fever, sleep abnormalities, joint stiffness and feeding difficulties.

In addition these are common symptoms:
* premature birth
* low birth weight
* still birth
* infant death
* small size
* small head
* growth and development may be slow
* brain damage
* heart problems
* organ defects
* breathing difficulties.

With ecstasy, infants are much more likely to have limb and heart defects.

The risk of cot death (http://www.babycenter.com.au/a419/cot-death-sids) for babies exposed to heroin in the uterus is also much higher than average. (Sanberg, 1961; Bada *et al*, 2012; Gouin *et al*, 2011; Richardson *et al*, 2013)

Additional effects showing up in the teenage years
First trimester cocaine exposure significantly predicted earlier adolescent marijuana and alcohol initiation (Richardson *et al*, 2013).

What happens when a pregnant woman drinks too much – how the foetus is affected

The more alcohol drunk by the parent, the greater the risk of brain damage to the child. Some researchers say there is no safe limit and so advocate that no alcohol is drunk in pregnancy (Mukherjee *et al*, 2005). The alcohol travels freely between parent and foetus and the latter's liver can't detoxify it.

Foetal alcohol syndrome (FAS)

Children differ in the severity of damage to brain and body. Children with lesser severity are referred to as having foetal alcohol effects. It is rated to be the most common cause of mental and behavioural problems in children but that about three to four live births per thousand suffer from FAS and one to two per thousand suffer from foetal alcohol effects (Abel and Sokol, 1986).

The brain development process known as migration can be adversely affected, so cells do not go to the right place. Along with other badly affected developmental processes, this can lead to gross brain abnormalities and underdeveloped structures – in particular, damage to the corpus callosum, cerebellum, frontal lobes and hippocampus. This can lead to the child suffering from:

- low birth weight
- small head circumference
- developmental delay
- organ dysfunction
- facial abnormalities
- muscular deformities
- cleft palette
- learning difficulties
- behaviour problems (often misdiagnosed as ADHD)
- learning disabilities
- poor impulse control
- poor personal boundaries
- intrusive behaviour
- poor attention or concentration (ADHD)
- poor cognitive skills
- poor judgement
- slower cognitive processing
- poor language skills
- lack of understanding of metaphor, humour and irony
- sensory integration (SI) disorders
- inability to read nonverbal or social cues
- 'chattiness' but without substance
- severe hyperactivity (in 75 per cent of cases) seen in head banging, body rocking, head rolling as self-stimulating activities.

The average IQ of a child with foetal alcohol syndrome (FAS) is 65; the population average is 100. (www.patient.co.uk/doctor/Fetal-Alcohol-Syndrome.htm)

People with FAS often develop secondary disabilities as they mature. In research studies, these included:
- In 90 per cent of the cases the people suffered from mental health problems – clinical depression or other mental illness.
- In 60 per cent of the cases, there was disrupted school experience – suspended or expelled from school or dropped out of school (aged twelve or over).
- 60 per cent experienced trouble with the law – charged or convicted with a crime.
- 50 per cent needed inpatient psychiatric care, inpatient chemical dependency care, or were incarcerated for a crime (aged twelve or over).
- Inappropriate sexual behaviour – sexual advances, sexual touching, or promiscuity, experienced by about 50 per cent of the subjects (aged twelve and older).
- 35 per cent experienced alcohol and drug problems (aged twelve and older).

Two additional secondary disabilities exist for adult patients:
- 80 per cent needed some form of dependent living or some sort of assisted living (age twenty one or older).
- Problems with employment – required ongoing job training or coaching, could not keep a job, unemployed.
- Major problems with social and emotional intelligence for the rest of their lives.

(Bookstein *et al*, 2005; Floyd *et al*, 2005; Autti-Rämö *et al*, 2002; Bada *et al*, 2012)

Newborns of parents who drink in pregnancy
Newborns of parents who drink in pregnancy are often born jittery and have sleep problems.

How the parent's bond with the baby can be affected
Research shows that substance-dependent mothers have poor interactions in feeding and play with their six-month-olds – flat, empty, constricted affective tone of interaction (Savonlahti *et al*, 2005). It also shows that infants of substance-dependent mothers are more withdrawn, depressed, with avoiding behaviour, and less alert with poorer attention (Savonlahti *et al*, 2005).

The pain and loss of childhood for many children at having to be a young carer and the addicted parent's comforter

Kids with addicted parents often have to grow up very fast and have to be too mature. That's because they often have to do what their parents don't do. They can end up bringing up younger siblings. 'My sister is like my child not my mum's child' says one fourteen-year-old who had an alcoholic mother. All family members can come to view one child as the primary carer for all of them. She or he becomes everyone's rock. This one child can be keeping the family functioning on some level, despite the devastating effects of the parent's addiction.

The agony of on-off parenting love – awakening too much longing and yearning in the child

Since the child is acutely aware of the times his mother is loving, it makes the times of her non-response, when drunk or drugged, and the 'slap' of her disinterest, misattunement and emotional neglect at these times, even more painful and bleak in contrast. Research has shown that the physically present/emotionally absent parent can activate higher levels of stress chemicals in the brain than if that parent is not there at all (Field, 1994).

The addictive nature of the on-off parent and the psychology of intermittent reinforcement

On-off parental love means a rollercoaster ride for the child, from strong activation of opioids in their brain (the emotion chemicals that make us feel all is well in the world and give us a sense of calm, warmth and psychological safety) to an extremely painful opioid withdrawal. The latter leaves us feeling anxious, depressed and irritated or angry. This cycle often awakens an intensity of yearning for that 'exciting/rejecting' parent (Armstrong-Perlman, 1991).

Research shows that if rats are given peanuts down a chute, but the chute supplies peanuts very irregularly or less and less frequently, then the rat will become more and more unable to move away from the chute and get on with exploring and moving around. This is called 'intermittent reinforcement'. It is totally different for the rat who receives a steady flow of nuts (equivalent to consistent parental love), and for the rat who receives no peanuts from the chute (equivalent to some children whose parent is not good at loving at all, rather than on-off love). These rats are able to move away from the chute (equivalent to being able to move away from the parent and get on with exploring the world). Intermittent reinforcement is what is happening when parents offer on-off love.

There have also been recent brain scans showing that feelings of rejection (the emotionally unavailable parent when drunk or drugged) really do hurt, in that the brain areas activated in rejection are also those activated during physical pain (Panksepp, 1998). So, in short, the language of rejection and loss is the language of pain. Particular parts of the brain light up when scanned, with both physical pain and emotional pain, such as rejection. One structure involved in this is called the anterior cingulate cortex (Eisenberger *et al*, 2003).

Sometimes children have a parent who is on-off at predictable times during a day. We all have a rise in cortisol (a stress hormone) in the morning as a wake-up call. As a result of the rise in cortisol, some parents are highly irritable or outright hostile in the morning. They then move into a far better mood once dopamine and serotonin (some of which is triggered from having had food) are activated in their brain, and the early morning cortisol level drops. This will be especially relevant to parents who wake up with a hangover or drug 'come-down' in the morning.

The legacy for the child in terms of their ability to sustain and enjoy loving relationships in later life

For a young child, the experience ... of losing [his mother's] love is in very truth a bereavement.
(Bowlby, 1978)

On-off parental loving means that the panic/grief system in the child's lower mammalian brain (the limbic system) can be repeatedly triggered (Panksepp and Biven, 2012). An overactive panic/grief system in childhood can lead to loving in torment in later life. The child can grow up with no trust in the constancy of love because they have never known it in their early relationships. Instead, they can grow up linking love with fear. This can involve persistently thinking your loved one is going off you, so every look away, every little absence, every yawn or moment of lack of interest can trigger feelings of panic, distress or paranoia.

SECTION TWO: HOW TO HELP CHILDREN WITH PARENTS ADDICTED TO DRUGS ALCOHOL OR SOLVENTS: WHAT TO DO, HOW TO BE AND WHAT TO SAY

HOW TO HAVE A THERAPEUTIC CONVERSATION WITH THE CHILD

The practitioner needs to be aware of and emphasise with the following range of feelings:

Grief and heartbreak

For many children their heart gets broken time and time again, every time they see their beloved mother out of her mind, or sleeping in her own vomit, or beaten up by her drug dealer, or being cruel to one of their siblings.

Research shows that witnessing cruelty to a sibling is far, far worse for the majority of children than watching domestic violence. There is a greater resulting depression, somatisation, anxiety and anger (Teicher and Vitaliano, 2011).

The pain of loss every time Mummy moves from sober to drunk, from normal to drugged.

Loss of how life used to be (if ever it was better than this).

The grief of watching your Mum go down hill physically and mentally as the addiction sets in.

The loss of a previously warm and funny mother, with shared laughter, to a mother who is snappy, moody and critical most of the time.

One teenager can remember vividly the time before her mother was an alcoholic. She remembers warm towels on the radiator. Now there are just cold, wet, vomit-soiled towels on the floor.

Anger

Amy, aged nine: 'Mummy should try harder to give up the drug/drink. If she really loved me she would try a lot harder.'

Constant worry

Worry or dread about coming back from school and finding Mum drunk again, the police there, no Mum at all, Mum dead, Mum overdosed.

The child often lives with the worry that their parent might die through drug abuse, and indeed they might. As Clayton (1997) states, 'There is only one difference between a drug and a poison, and that is the quantity. Any drug that will alter your mood will also kill you if used in a large enough quantity.'

Every time you use cocaine the effects are so strong that you can have a heart attack, a stroke or go into a coma. Furthermore, many children of parents troubled in this way know that if drugs (prescription or otherwise) are mixed with drink it can kill you. In reality, many children will suffer the death of their parent from overdose, or sometimes from suicide.

Worry about being taken into care: 'I might be taken into care if they realise that my Mummy can't look after me properly anymore.'

Fear or terror of the parent when drugged or drunk

Mattie, aged nine: 'When Mummy goes from sober to drunk I often get frightened of her – it's like I lose this lovely Mummy and an angry monster who shouts at us all the time enters the room. Sometimes I just want to die.'

Billie, aged nine: 'My dad scares me when he's drunk – I am worried he will kill me or my Mum.'

Tom, aged ten (the son of an alcoholic father) wrote the following story: 'Sometimes, if you walk across the grass, the grass giant will make the earth scream so loudly that it will pierce your eardrums. But sometimes, if you walk across the grass, there is no grass giant and it's fine. But this means that you can never know anything for sure.'

Let down, disappointed, dashed hopes

The parent saying to the child that they will give up drugs, drink, and so on. 'When I get well we will do xxxx together.' It never happens. Often the parent may manage resisting the drugs or drink for a short period of time and then they go back to their addiction, often worse this time.

Despair or hopelessness

A sense of 'this is my lot' or 'this is my misery'. Just waiting to be an orphan, just waiting to be taken into care. Often too few or no role models in their life for using life well.

Cut off from what they feel

Due to the walking on eggshells and how painful it is to witness endless bouts of emotional volatility in the parent, many children of addicts learn not to have feelings. It's safer that way. If they have feelings, it might trigger yet another parental explosion or falling apart. This cutting off from feelings is important to know, as sometimes when asked what they feel they can't say, because they don't know. They know what Mum or Dad feels but not what they feel. As a result, many children whose parents are addicts need help not just to talk about their feelings but to have their feelings in the first place. When this is the case, they need our help to find words for feelings, to give them a vocabulary to help them move from an 'unthought known' (I know it, but I have never had help to know it) to a 'thought known'.

In addition, children of addicts often don't have a sense of identity either, as they are so involved with their parent. They haven't the space in their mind to think about what they want, their beliefs, their opinions, their boundaries, what they want to say no to and what they want to say yes to.

Feeling unloved

Talia, aged seven: 'Mummy prefers her booze to me – her booze is more important than me.'

Deep hurt

The child can so often be hurt by the cruel things Mum or Dad can say or do when drunk or drugged. Many parents are verbally abusive when drunk. Martin Teicher, at Harvard University, has found that verbal abuse can be as toxic in terms of damage to the child's developing brain as physical and sexual abuse (Teicher *et al*, 2006).

Feeling powerless

The painful feeling that they cannot make Mummy better, cannot stop her taking drugs or getting drunk.

Shock, horror or alarm

Children often feel alarmed by their parent, rather than experiencing them as 'home', a place of safety and solace.

Horror at the awful things that Mummy can say or do when drunk or drugged.

Shock at Mummy or Daddy's vomit, lack of personal hygiene, unkempt appearance and at a damaged Mummy, if beaten up by her partner or drug dealer.

Shame
The child often doesn't want people to visit the house – in case Mum is drinking or drugged again.

Confusion
'She loves me yet she says she can't stop drinking/taking her pills, even when she knows how much it hurts me.'

Over-serious
Over-seriousness comes from having to grow up too quickly and not having a carefree childhood.

Alone or lonely
Like in a little boat on a hostile sea – no one supporting them.

Sunil, aged eight: 'When Mummy is with her bottle she has her bottle. Me? – I'm on my own then.'

Feeling blamed or being blamed in actuality
Cindy opened the bathroom door to find her father mainlining heroin, holding a needle, a cord tied around his arm. He screamed at her, 'What do you expect? You and that mother of yours! I wouldn't need to do this if it weren't for you!' (Clayton, 1997).

Self-hate or low self-esteem
The child can so easily take in all the verbal abuse so common from parents who are addicts, and believe it. One little girl wrote Santa a note saying, 'You don't have to bring me anything this year. Give it to someone who's nice' (Clayton, 1997).

Mistrust
So much chaos, uncertainty, broken promises, shifts from sober Mum to drunk Mum and back, results in many children finding it difficult to trust that any adult who says they care will ever really mean it in a consistent, reliable way.

KEY THINGS TO SAY OR CONVEY IN THERAPEUTIC CONVERSATION WITH A CHILD WHOSE PARENT IS ADDICTED TO DRUGS OR ALCOHOL

Empathy

The following statements and psychological messages are suitable for the child who is open to listening, and is not stuck in a denying reality and an idealising of their parent. Where this is the case, such statements will not be useful. The child is likely to feel that you are attacking their parent and so get very defensive.

Examples of empathic statements

'I guess sometimes you must be hurting so much inside about your parent and you and your life together.'

'It is often so very painful to love someone who is addicted to drink/drugs and to have to see what it does to them.'

'It can be a huge burden for any child or teenager to live with a Mum or Dad who drinks too much or is addicted to drugs.'

'It is so understandable that you want to make your Mummy better and save her from her illness.'

Help them find their protest

For example, Danny found a way to talk to his Mum via puppets. He said, 'I feel so angry with you Mum that you don't get help to get of the drugs/drink and try to get better.'

Help them to grieve

You might open up the possibility of this by saying something like, 'However much you try to help your Mum to stop being addicted, in the end, it must be her who wants it so much that she succeeds. Sometimes it's better to find the courage to grieve (let go into sadness) the fact that your parent may continue to be addicted, perhaps for a long time, perhaps for the rest of their life.'

How to talk to the despairing child or teenager

As one teenager said, when asked what he wanted to be when he left school, 'I am going to end up under a bridge somewhere begging for money for drugs – alone.'

Sometimes it is that bleak, but at other times, the teenager has just lost sight of the hope and there is a significant, warm, loving adult in their life. In the case of Tim, a 17-year-old with two parents addicted to crack, there was a loving Grandpa. In such cases, you could say something like, 'Imagine Grandpa comes and sits with you under the bridge and says I am so sorry your life has been so hard, I am so sorry your heart got broken, I am so sorry your Mum and Dad got hooked on drugs.'

Empathy is all about the most healing form of human connection. It is without such connection that people often turn to drugs.

Key psychological messages the children may need

'You don't have to suffer like this. There are people who really understand what it's like for a child to live with a parent who is drinking too much or taking drugs. Many children have felt a huge relief talking to these people.'

'You need a safe place in your life and that means safe grownups, people you can trust. Let's think about who that might be for you. It might be your friend's Mum or a teacher or an adult who runs a club at school. It's really smart to find someone who you can trust and who you can turn to when things get too much.' (Support the child to think how they might 'call' on these safe adults more, go to these adults more, ask for help from them more, and then bring them to mind more often when they are feeling unhappy. They need someone who can really listen and help them process what is happening to them, grieve, protest and express other painful feelings.)

'Of course, you want to try to "fix" your parent. But often trying to fix an addicted parent doesn't work. That's because it isn't your job' (Clayton, 1997).

'Think what you want for your life – rather than just what you want for your parents' life.'

'You don't have to be the person looking after your Mum. We need someone who will help to look after her and to look after you.'

'You have rights – a right for help, a right to have a childhood, a right not to parent your parent, a right to feel carefree, a right to do things other children do in their free time without being worried about your parent.'

'You need time away from your parent in your house. Grownups call it respite care – school trips/school times away. Otherwise it is so easy to lose perspective on life.'

'How can I help you find the courage to talk about what is happening at home?'

Let the child ask as many questions as they like

Here are some common questions:

'Why do people need to keep drinking alcohol/taking drugs?'
You might say something like:
'Sometimes it's because when they drink or take drugs they forget their problems and with some drugs they feel good about themselves and without the drugs they feel bad about themselves.'

'Sometimes very painful things happen in a parent's own childhood. So they start to drink to make the hurt go away because no one helped them to talk about the hurt when they were little. They had no one in their life who was warm and kind and listened to them.'

'Why does Mummy/Daddy become so sad/angry after the drug/drink has worn off?'
Explain about the down after the up, that taking drugs and drink mean you crash into the natural drug store in your brain (feel-good brain chemicals) and use them all up. Then the feel-good chemicals take a while to replenish.

Explain that parents coming down from taking drugs called uppers – like speed or cocaine – can be depressed, angry, abusive or violent. When they are high they can be playful for a while. Some children enjoy this – it's like getting their lovely Mum back. Other children don't enjoy it as the child is always waiting for the down time just around the corner.

'Why does Mummy/Daddy become a monster when she/he is drunk?'
'While your parent is drugged or drunk the part of her brain that makes her

warm and friendly and responsive to you and your needs and your feelings is turned off. It gets turned on again when she is sober.'

Explain how the part of the brain that is all about reasonable behaviour and ability to think and feel about other people's feelings is not working properly when you drink or take certain drugs.

'Why does Mummy need her drink? Why aren't I enough for her?'
'Her body and brain are now addicted to the drink/drug. This means that, without it, her body and brain crave it more and more. It's not about love as she loves you; it's about a body need. Wanting drugs or drink so much is a kind of illness. You can't just tell yourself not to want them.'

The information the child needs about what drugs/drink do to their parent's brain and body

'Drugs can make good people act bad' (Heegaard, 1993).

'Drugs/drink can turn off the part of your Mummy's brain that feels love. It doesn't ever mean that she has stopped loving you. The loving part of her brain gets turned on again when the drug or drink wears off.'

'Drugs change people's feelings and thinking; sometimes it makes them act in strange, odd or violent ways that might frighten you.'

'Your parent can get help but the help has to come from doctors who have the right medicine and adults who know about drugs/drink and what they do to your Mum's mind, brain and body.'

Help the child navigate their parents when they act in hurtful ways when drugged or drunk

For example: 'Don't get angry with them – they often get more defensive – it's a smart thing instead to stay calm and say afterwards (when they can hear you), 'I feel so hurt and in pain when you drink/take drugs". Toby, aged seven, for example, said to his father when sober, 'When you drink, I feel like you are not my parent anymore.' It was enough for his father to go and get help from Alcoholics Anonymous.

If you fear the child is tempted to start taking drugs themselves

This is something you could say, so well put here by Clayton (1997): 'It could take up to twenty years for a forty-year-old who starts to develop a full-blown addiction. A twelve-year-old can do it in less than six months. A ten-year-old can do it in two months. The younger you start, the easier it is to get hooked, and the more severe the addiction. This doesn't mean that you will ever get old enough for drugs to be safe.'

HOW TO HELP THE PARENTS HELP THEIR CHILDREN

Empower the parent to talk to their child about their addiction

Often in families with parents addicted to drugs or alcohol, there is a culture of not talking about feelings. Indeed, parents often have taken drugs or drink to avoid painful feelings in the first place. So, parents may need help to find the right words to convey empathy to the child about the painful times involved in living with them. Empower the parents to talk to the child when they are sober or not on the drugs, so that they can be as warm and empathic as possible. Apology can go such a long way, for example, 'I know this is hurting you and I am so sorry I am having such difficulty giving up.' The child needs to know about addiction and why it's not easy for Mummy to 'just stop it'.

Example
'Amy, Mummy has got into a bit of a mess. Because I took drugs for quite a while, now my body needs it, so it's very difficult for me to stop. I would like to be able to stop because I know you are hurting so much when you see me take the drug/getting drunk.'

'When I drink/have my pills, it makes my brain think and feel differently, and so sometimes I might say things to you or do things that I really don't mean – but that's not me talking, it's the drug/drink. So take no notice of any hurtful things I do or say when I take the drug/get drunk. I will get help because I love you so much I don't ever want to hurt you in this way.'

Such conversations are often vital to maintain loving feelings in the child for the parent. Some parents think their children will love them forever, whatever they do or say when drunk or taking drugs. Some are wrong about that, as sometimes the pain of the hurtful things can go to so deep that one day something snaps and the child just stops loving their parent.

'We should never hold an addict responsible for his addiction. But we can and should hold an addict responsible for his recovery!' (Clayton, 1997)

And there is help out there; parents who are addicts need to be informed how vital it is for the sake of their foetus, newborn, infant or child to get help. That said, how this is conveyed to parents is very important so they don't feel blamed and shamed.

They can be given the research findings and statistics on the possible effects of their addiction on the foetus, newborn, infant and child and possible long-term consequences for their child's mental and physical health (see above).

Alcoholics Anonymous or Narcotics Anonymous can offer so much support. In addition, users of the NSPCC's Family Alcohol Service (FAS) report that parents value its therapeutic approach. They also appreciate its flexibility, including the provision of taxis for clients, the willingness of staff to work out of hours, and the provision of home visits. 'Such therapeutic services should be more widely available, and should adopt the FAS model of working with children' (NSPCC, 2009).

If the parent is taking illegal drugs and thinking of having a baby, it is really important that they talk to their midwife or doctor. They need to know that the parent is taking drugs, so that they can give them the right care and support during their pregnancy. The parent also needs to know that the midwife or doctor won't judge them for taking drugs. Telling them about the drugs shows how much the parent cares about their baby. The more the doctor knows, the more they can help the parent and unborn child to get the right treatment. The parent in this position should also be given the good news story that substance abusers who stop their drug use early in pregnancy tend to have perfectly healthy children (Hjerkinn et al, 2009).

CHILDREN WITH A PARENT WHO IS ILL OR DYING AND THE PLIGHT OF THE YOUNG CARER

All children, at some point in their childhood, think about the possibility of their parents leaving them, or becoming ill or helpless, or even dying.   (Segal, 1991)

SECTION ONE: WHAT LIFE CAN BE LIKE FOR THE CHILD WITH A PARENT WHO IS ILL OR DYING AND FOR YOUNG CARERS: THE RESEARCH, THE PSYCHOLOGY AND THE BRAIN SCIENCE

Children talking ...

A thirty-three-year-old (a health-care executive in New York who lost both his parents to cancer before he was 13): 'I'd give up a year of my life for just half a day with my parents' (Zaslow, 2010).

Rebecca, aged seventeen (she has been a young carer for six years): 'I would come home from school, do my homework and then have to help Mum take Dad upstairs, which was always quite difficult as there were numerous tasks involved. So by the time all that was done, the night was over and it was time for bed.' (www.barnardos.org.uk)

Stacey, aged nine: 'You can have some good days and some bad days but the good days aren't really good.' (www.barnardos.org.uk)

Jody, aged two: When her mother got upset or angry for any reason Jody would say to her mother, 'Don't worry, Mummy, you go lie down, I'll look after you' (Segal, 1991).

HOW COMMON IS SERIOUS PARENTAL ILLNESS OR DEATH? THE STATISTICS

- Every 22 minutes a child in Britain is bereaved of a parent; this equates to 24,000 new children each year (Winston's Wish, 2012).

- Children who lost parents young are more likely to be hospitalised for depression or to commit violent crimes (Zaslow, 2010).

- Children whose parents commit suicide are three times as likely to commit suicide later in their lives (Wilcox et al, 2010).

How common is it for a child to be a young carer?

The 2001 census found 175,000 young carers in the UK of which 5,000 were aged between five and seven. Many of these will have significant unmet need. Out of these, 72 per cent cook and clean; over 50 per cent provide general care; 20 per cent help with intimate care such as showering and toileting (www.barnardos.org.uk). Research shows that most young carers are aged between eleven and fifteen; most are girls and over half live in one-parent families. Only about one in 10 had been assessed by social services (The Children's Society and The Princess Royal Trust for Carers, 2002).

About parents who are ill or dying

We are talking here about parents with physical and/or mental health problems. Children look after parents with physical disabilities, broken limbs, multiple sclerosis, cancer, brain damage, strokes, depression, anxiety disorders such as agoraphobia, social phobias, drug and alcohol problems and many more.

Many parents are aware of the burden that their illness is to their children. Some feel very guilty about not being able to parent in the way they want to. Some become too indulgent as a result and don't lay down necessary boundaries. Some feel they give their child nothing because they are so physically needy that they can only take. Many such parents need to be reminded of the ways they are still giving, the ways they are still being a parent. For other parents, their 'little carer' becomes so accomplished that the parent starts to take the help from the child for granted and become complacent about finding other forms of support so that they can release their child from the task. In such circumstances the cost to the child in terms of quality of life is high.

For many parents, the feeling that you are going to die or might die while you still have children who live at home is unbearable. It can be experienced as a catastrophic abandonment of their children, flying in the face of all their instincts to protect their child from physical or emotional harm at all times. The pain is knowing that they cannot spare their children the dreadful grief of losing a parent so early in life. Furthermore, the worry is who is going to look after them and how can they possibly look after them as well as me?

HOW CHILDREN ARE AFFECTED

When a parent dies or is dying

The suffering of missing a parent too much can run very deep. Its intensity may feel unbearable to a child. In effect, such a child can be dragging around too heavy a burden of grief, a desperate and yet often mute cry of 'Come back! Come back!', 'Don't leave me! Don't leave me!' For some children, their longing and yearning for Mummy or Daddy makes the world seem not just bleak, but at times actually hostile. A motherless place in a child's mind can all too easily evoke a sense of a cold, rejecting, unfriendly world outside.

Research shows that, if children are not helped to grieve, they are vulnerable to experience depression, now and/or in later life, their academic work goes downhill, and they can fail to thrive emotionally, socially and academically. Sudden death, such as losing a parent in a car accident – where there is no goodbye, no preparation through collecting memorabilia, taping and videoing messages for the child to be played after the parent's death, and so on, no crying in the parent's arms while they are alive – can, of course, be far worse than, say, a parent dying of cancer over several months or years.

Children can suffer from one or more of the following:
• regression to any earlier age
• anxieties – (eg that the other parent will die)
• depression
• anger

- separation anxiety (eg not wanting to go on school trips)
- guilt at not being more helpful and better behaved when the parent was alive
- remorse for what could have been and for hurtful things that were said (particularly teenagers).

(Christ et al, 2002)

What happens to the brain of the grieving child?

The attachment system is deep in the mammalian part of our brain. It is known by many neuroscientists as the care system (Panksepp, 1998). The key emotion chemicals of this system are opioids, oxytocin and prolactin. When a loving relationship with someone has strongly activated these chemicals in our brain, we can feel a deep sense of peace and calm. We feel safe enough in the world to want to be creative, to explore, learn, play and relate to others. A milder version of this chemical activation comes from feelings of belonging and acceptance. But when we lose the person who makes us feel like this, the pain is awful. This is caused by an 'opioid withdrawal' and an activation of various pain centres in the brain. All too often this means a rollercoaster of intense feelings of rage, betrayal, grief and depression. Opioid withdrawal can also make animals behave very nastily to each other and/or fall into a terrible depression. Because of this biochemically evidenced pain, some children, after experiencing loss, try to cut off from their attachment needs and put a wall around their hearts. As a result, they do not dare to love any more in any long-term, committed way, and yet the price of this is usually a feeling of emptiness, hopelessness and/or a flat depression. To avoid this, many people try to compensate by having an often insatiable desire for material possessions: the latest clothes, gadgets, and so on. What follows are some more scientific examples as to why the pain of loss hurts so much.

When we lose someone we love, then the distress system in the lower mammalian brain is activated. The distress system is a system of grief, desolation and loneliness. (Scientists can artificially stimulate with electrodes the distress system of young mammals, causing them to howl for their mothers.) The distress system is also referred to as the panic system. The panic aspect of this system is particularly in evidence in children, who scream and scream if they can't find their Mummy or they have to let her go. When the distress system in the brain is strongly activated, for example, when we are missing someone or fear we have lost them or lost their love, it will flood our minds with thoughts of the lost person and impel us to try to find them again, to reconnect with them (hence the awesome power of the mobile phone!).

As stated, the activation of the distress system means opioid withdrawal in a key part of the brain known as the anterior cingulate. When opioids are optimally activated in the brain they can naturally diminish fear and anxiety. So with opioid withdrawal, fear and anxiety can flood in with a vengeance. Also opioid systems are involved in the regulation of emotional states, so with opioid withdrawal we can feel extremely stressed without being able to regulate our feelings properly. Here is an adapted list from a world-leading researcher in neuroscience, Professor Jaak Panksepp (1998), who has compared coming off heroin (which taps into the brain's opioid system artificially) to coming off a person. They both hurt like hell.

Coming off a drug	Coming off a person
Emotional pain	Emotional pain
Crying or the wish to cry	Crying or the wish to cry
Despondency	Depression
Loss of appetite	Loss of appetite
Sleeping problems	Sleeping problems
Irritability or aggressiveness	Irritability or aggressiveness

All too frequently in the news we hear about 'love made angry'. Many children who are bereaved move into very difficult and angry behaviour. Some are even expelled from school for it. When we look at the brain chemistry of broken hearts, this is not at all surprising.

Losing someone we deeply love results in the following:
• Strong activation of the brain chemical corticotropin releasing factor (CRF) for a sustained period. This in turn activates the pumping out of high levels of stress hormones (one of which is cortisol) into the brain and body. These can block the release of positive arousal chemicals (including dopamine, opioids and oxytocin). It also activates stress response systems in the brain leading to depression, anxiety disorders and/or problems with aggression.
• Strong activation of glutamate. Key to the brain's distress system is a chemical called glutamate. Strong activation of glutamate can dramatically increase crying, whereas blocking glutamate in the brain can dramatically

decrease crying. If high levels of glutamate are artificially activated in the brain, the comforting effects of such things as music and lovely company are lost.

- A drop in serotonin. Low serotonin can increase aggressive impulses, hence some of the angry outbursts of people with broken hearts, jealous feelings or threat of loss. Also, due to the depletion of serotonin, which optimally acts as a mood stabiliser, you are wide open to impulsive outbursts of irritation, anger, rage or attacks on the self, as in self-harm.
- Strong activation of acetylcholine. When there is a withdrawal of opioids in the brain, then what is known as 'opponent forces' are released. These opponent forces involve the release of high levels of a chemical called acetylcholine. At optimal levels, acetylcholine can help us concentrate and feel alert. These high levels of acetylcholine can once again make people angry, hostile and attacking.

In terms of the above, it is vital that any child who has suffered the pain of loss gets comfort over a sustainable period. If a child has someone in their life who will comfort their grief (eg the other parent or grandparent or school counsellor), help them reflect on it and work it through, this awful brain chemistry, which can set a child on the road to emotional numbing, depression and/or hostility, does not need to happen. The physical comforting of grief will release opioids and oxytocin in the brain. These will then stop the release of the toxic brain chemistry we've described above. This is why it is vital for children who are suffering from the pain of loss (even if on the surface they look just fine) to receive comfort. Schools in particular need to be aware of children who have lost a parent. So many children suffering the pain of loss or rejection behave in very angry or aggressive ways because of their changed brain chemistry. Tragically, it's then all too easy for other people to start to hate them, punish them and want to exclude them rather than help them. Hopefully, increasing public knowledge about these dramatic changes in brain chemistry will help to improve levels of compassion in society.

Many children need help to feel sad

One of the most important life skills is knowing how to suffer well and grieve well. If we don't have this skill, or if it doesn't come naturally, then, if we are not helped, the cost to self and others can be very high indeed. Research shows that sometimes people and animals do actually die of a broken heart (Goodall, 1990; Martikainen and Valkonen, 1996). Parents who have not been helped to work through the painful losses and separations that they have experienced in their lives may find that their parenting is adversely affected as a result of their grief. Their children may start to develop emotional or behavioural problems. When they go into counselling or therapy, their child's problems often completely stop.

How children are affected by being young carers

'The term young carer should be taken to include children and young people under 18 who provide regular or ongoing care and emotional support to a family member who is physically or mentally ill, disabled or misuses substances … a young carer becomes vulnerable when the level of care-giving and responsibility to the person in need of care becomes excessive or inappropriate for that child, risking impacting on his or her emotional or physical well being or educational achievement and life chances' (ADASS and ADCS, 2009).

Quality of life for the young carer

What young carers often have to do:
- Two-thirds of young carers provide domestic help in the home.
- 48 per cent of young carers provide general and nursing type care.
- 82 per cent of young carers provide emotional support and supervision.
- 18 per cent of young carers provide intimate personal care.
- 11 per cent of young carers also provide child care for their siblings.

Other tasks for young carers include household administration (eg bills) and accompanied hospital visits. Many adults who do all this get paid.
(Dearden and Becker, 2004)

Girl, aged fourteen: 'After school and on weekends and holidays I have to look after everyone. I sometimes go to bed after midnight, having cleaned, cooked, washed and ironed' (ChildLine, 2008).

No time for themselves or to be themselves or to be a child
They had very little time for themselves or to see friends, or to play with other children. Relational play is key for the developing brain (Panksepp and Biven, 2012). They are not free to enjoy what other children enjoy and do what other children do.

One ten-year-old girl said: 'I've got too much to think about, I don't have any time to play or see my friend. I've only got one friend' (ChildLine, 2009).

So often these children don't know how to behave like children, only little adults.

Relationship problems

Isolation is a major problem for the young carers. Many just can't spare the time to go out with friends from school and are too ashamed to bring people back to the house. Their evenings are not free to do what they want. Instead they may be dressing their parent, feeding her, helping her go to the toilet, cleaning her, bathing her, opening bills and thinking what to do with them, babysitting, helping all the siblings get fed, clothed or go to bed. They often feel there is no one there for them. There often isn't (Becker *et al*, 2000).

Mental health

The Children's Society and The Princess Royal Trust for Carers (2002) found that 70 per cent of former young carers suffered long-term psychological effects, and 40 per cent had mental health problems.

The psychological effects include:
- problems relating to people
- difficulty making friends
- depression
- stress
- low self-esteem.

What adults said when looking back at their life as a young carer

- The people interviewed were between the ages of twenty-five and seventy but talked about very similar experiences overall.
- 28 per cent had suffered physical health problems, such as bad backs due to lifting relatives.
- 70 per cent said their education had been affected: missed lessons, missed days, no time to do homework due to all the caring needs, so poor exam results, or exams not taken in the first place, resulting problems in terms of finding work. Several went into caring professions.
(Dearden and Becker, 2000)

When they get to leaving home age

Some young people will leave and go a long, long way away, such as to another country. 'They feel they need to be that far away in order to breathe again' (Segal, 1991). Others don't leave home and carry on looking after their parent, so once again missing out on living their own life.

SECTION TWO: HOW TO HELP THE CHILD OF A DYING PARENT AND HOW TO HELP YOUNG CARERS: WHAT TO DO, HOW TO BE AND WHAT TO SAY

It is still the case that many young carers are not getting the support that they require.
(Barnardo's, 2006)

HOW TO HAVE A THERAPEUTIC CONVERSATION WITH THE CHILD WHOSE PARENT IS DYING

The practitioner needs to be aware of and able to convey empathy for the following range of feelings:

Terrible sadness (with a dying or dead parent)

Some children are too young to understand death, and so when their parent does die, they feel abandoned by her or him. Some have fantasies that Mum left because she didn't love them. Some keep believing that Mum will come back. But whatever the circumstances, when you lose a beloved mother the pain can feel unbearable. These children are desperately in need of someone who is not afraid of talking about their awful pain and can stay with it rather than trying to take the child out of it prematurely to 'happier feelings'.

Wanting to die

'I want to die first so I don't get left if Mummy dies.'

Worries and fears

Fear about becoming an orphan. For example, the counsellor said to Matthew, 'Sometimes children worry about what will happen to them if both their parents die. Do you Matthew?' Matthew suddenly turned on her and said scornfully, 'Of course I do' (Segal and Simkins, 1993).

Worry that the parent will die when the child is absent.

Worry they could harm their parent and so bring on an even earlier death, for example, through their naughtiness, neediness, strong feelings or crying.

'She was terrified of crying or getting angry (with her mother) … this would be dangerous for her mother's health. She did sometimes cry on her own.' (Segal and Simkins, 1993).

When a parent has to go into hospital – fear of medical complications are common and that the parent will die (even when it is clear that the parent is not fatally ill) (Romer *et al*, 2006).

Fear that they may die prematurely. In such cases a medical check-up for assurance against genetic transmission can be a good idea.

Feelings of failure or inadequacy: 'I can't make Mummy well again.'

Panic distress

Some children with very ill or dying parents come to school full of utter panic and are in desperate need of someone to sit down with them and help them with their feelings and, in particular, help them to grieve, giving a really positive message of, 'It's fine to cry and if you feel like crying with someone please ask to see Miss X' (hopefully an available counsellor).

Here is an example of panic distress in a boy that resulted from him knowing that his father was dying:

Terry, aged eight, was desperately trying to manage the pain of his father dying of throat cancer from smoking. His father had been told that he had only months to live. Terry's mother smokes. He was told off for cutting up her cigarettes.

Before counselling, he was discharging his panic through aggressive behaviour. Now at least he can panic in front of the counsellor whose job it is to empathise, validate and emotionally regulate him. Prior to this he has been alone with his panic – a state known as catastrophic aloneness.

Terry picks up a tiger hand puppet and tries to wrap playdough around its neck.

Terry: 'You will live. You will make it. I will put tiger's flesh around your neck.
(Trying to mend the dinosaur): 'I don't like him but I have to mend him.'
'I don't know why I bother mending him, he will just get into another fight and die.'
(He repaired the puppets that were attacked in his play): 'I can't leave them like that.'
He was furious that a pencil got broken 'because I can't mend it.'

He said to the counsellor, 'You have killed my mother and my father.'
She was able to empathise with his rage and agony displaced onto her. She said, 'So it's like I have taken from you so brutally the people you so deeply love.'

Because she has responded instead of just staying silent or putting him right about who he was really cross with, he felt so profoundly safe with her. He cried in her arms for 20 minutes.

Anger

Anger with the ill parent for dying or not getting well. They may know this is irrational or unfair.

Denial that their parent is dying/blocked grief

This is so understandable regarding what can feel like unbearable pain. We know that the brain is capable of cutting off from feelings and so living in a world of thinking and acting instead. Some children cut off from pain and move into an 'I don't care' attitude.

> The counsellor gently said that it seemed very difficult for William to see that his father wasn't going to get better enough to drive again. William looked stricken and frightened. The counsellor said she wondered if William was afraid that if it was said it would become true, and that as long as nobody said it, it would not. William was silent.
> (Segal, 1991)

When you block grief, however, often that means blocking love, caring and compassion as well. So some children with 'blocked grief' and also who are full of angry feelings about their awful situation can become bullies. As they don't feel their own pain they don't feel the pain of the child they hurt, apart from enjoying the effect they are having. Some children with 'blocked grief' in the teenage years get into gangs, get drunk to dull the pain, cut off emotionally, because it's all far too serious and dreadful.

Talking to the child whose parent is dying: tasks for the practitioner

- Help the child to face their absolute fear.
- Help the child to accept that, whatever they do, they can't change the direction of their parent's illness.
- Help the child to accept they have no control of the situation and none of it is their fault.
- Help the child to grieve for the losses in their own life and for their pain at seeing their parent in pain.
- Help the child to know that they aren't responsible or to blame in any way for their parent's imminent death.

What a conversation needs to cover in preparing a child for the possible death of their parent

Go into the feelings of what life might be like if their Mum were to die. Who would they go to for cuddles and to cry?
- Try to change fear and anxiety to grief, but reminisce about the times when she was well, the happy memories.
- Giving an image can be helpful, that it can feel like the world has ended, but actually it is not the whole world but a part of the world. Some parents like to say something like this, 'Wherever you see light, like a star in the sky, that's me looking down and sending all my love to you.'
- It can feel like the child is left with nothing but in fact they are left with lots – all the memories of the lovely times they had with Mum (so the importance of a memory box full of photos of Mum, taped messages from her, talking photo books, etc).
- Life will go on with the family and so definitely is worth having, so in losing this parent you have not lost everything.
- Feelings can take time to be felt:
  - People don't cry for ever, even when someone they deeply love dies. Your grieving process will end, and life will feel good again.
  - You will probably carry on loving you parent for ever. You will probably never forget them. What they have given you and the lovely times you shared together will continue to warm you and live in you as a source of strength and emotional nourishment for the rest of your life.

Help the parent have that painful conversation with the child about death

Support the parent to tell the child the bad news in good time rather than at the last minute

The child will need to spend time with the person who is dying, assimilate the news and grieve while they are still alive, reminisce and share good times together. If the news is last minute they are deprived of all of this and are far more likely to feel that their world has fallen apart, and so to suffer post-traumatic stress disorder.

But if the parent feels unable to have this conversation, have a third person, for example a doctor, social worker or counsellor, to be there in the room to tell the news.

Help the parent to keep talking about it after the first conversation about their going to die

This is vital to check what the child is feeling and thinking about it, and to check that things have not been misunderstood or that the child is having self-blaming fantasies (eg, if I hadn't been so naughty/demanding Mummy would have been OK).

Also to give space for any questions the child may have.

How to help an ill or dying parent talk to the child when the child doesn't want to listen

If we don't talk about it, I can pretend it's not true

For dying parents, the most terrible thing can be to feel that you are leaving your children. Dying parents will feel guilt and/or fear that their child will not be looked after well enough, so it's not surprising that parents put off talking to their child about what is going to happen. Death and illness can then become an 'elephant in the room' or, if it is talked about, it can be talked about in an unrealistic way – 'Don't worry we are doing everything we can to make Mummy better' – rather than talking about the fact that she might die.

Some children will avoid these painful conversations, say something like 'blah blah blah' so they don't have to listen, or run away or switch on a distraction when parents try to talk. If this is the case, encourage the parent to talk in a different way with their child, using miniature people or drawings.

Conversations that need to happen if it is uncertain whether the parent will die or not

Conversation about whether Mummy or Daddy can be 'mended' or not, and whose fault it was that he or she was damaged (Segal and Simkins, 1993).

If the parents have just received news about the ill-health of one of the parents, tell the children after the parents have had time to feel and think and emotionally regulate it, so they are not told in a frightening or overwhelming way.

When the dying parent is still alive

- Make a memory box together – a treasure trove of photos of parent and child together, or memorabilia of things done together, a permanent object which remains after she is gone.
- Get the parent to make a video to play after her death, 'What I have loved about knowing you/ what I loved that we did together...'
- Get the parent to make an audio recording of loving messages that the child can play when they want.
- A video message and card for every birthday up to and including the eighteenth.

Adult whose father died when he was four: 'I haven't heard my father's voice since I was four years old … It doesn't exist [on tape]. It hurts not to hear him … I feel envious of children who lose parents today, because they have so many more digital images to hold on to' (Zaslow, 2010).

If the parent has to go away to hospital

Skype is great if a parent has to go away or to hospital. It stops the worry that Mummy has gone, died or is never coming back.

Get the other parent to take over while the parent is still alive

As the parent gets more ill, they often withdraw, and do not have physical or emotional strength to truly engage with the child in a deeply contactful way. So it's a good time for the other parent or family members to start to take over while the parent is still alive.

Is it OK for the non-ill parent to cry in front of the child?'

In some situations it may be a relief for the parent and child to cry together. This can be reassuring for a child. However, parents' loud distress can frighten children, and some parents prefer to allow their children to know they are upset and to know that they cry in private, but not actually to cry with them (Segal, 1998).

HOW TO HAVE A THERAPEUTIC CONVERSATION WITH THE YOUNG CARER

The practitioner needs to be aware of and able to convey empathy for the following range of feelings:

Feelings of loss
- loss of freedom
- loss of a carefree childhood
- loss of leisure time
- loss of time to develop friendships with peers outside school
- loss of a parent who was once able to parent them well but who has become one who can't
- loss of a parent who could once parent them but who has become someone that the child has to parent instead.

Worries and fears
Fears of the parent getting worse or dying.

Fear of asking for help in case someone takes them into care, or their parent into care, if they say anything.

'Some children we met actively tried to prevent themselves being "a burden" to their parents, and so deprived both themselves and their parents of a close relationship' (Segal and Simkins, 1993).

Anger

Angry fantasy (and sometimes a reality) that the parent doesn't want to get better.

Anger about living as a young carer, working so hard and/or living with fears and worries about the carer. But anger is usually felt to be too dangerous an emotion to express with the parent (in case it makes them worse). So the child can then express anger to other people in other settings, for example school.

Example: Nico, aged seven

Nico's mother was very ill and depressed. She was bed-bound and taking heavy doses of valium each day. She only wanted Nico and didn't want to relate to or see anyone else. Nico looked after her so well. When he came home from school he would sit holding her hand for hours in a dark room because she hated light and noise. This meant they could never watch TV together. At school Nico flooded the washbasins on a regular basis, defecated on the floors and denied it. He just couldn't concentrate on anything the teacher said. In counselling, he talked about his fear that his head might one day fall off because it was so full of worries and heaviness.

Anger with the other parent if well: 'You should be able to fix her Daddy, you are not helping enough.'

Resentment

'I am looking after her needs. Who is looking after mine? Mum should be looking after me but I am looking after her.'

Being far too good

To avoid upsetting the ill, depressed or addicted parent, avoiding arguments with them for fear of making them worse.

Overwhelmed, can't go on any more with the present situation

One fifteen-year-old girl, who cared for her disabled relative, called ChildLine asking for the number to: '… put myself in a care home. I can't do it any more without any outside help' (ChildLine, 2009).

Feeling undervalued

People who matter, for example teachers, relatives, other significant adults (for example the well parent), not giving sufficient acknowledgement, praise or respect for all the young carer is doing.

Acting big on the outside, feeling lousy on the inside

Trying to be the big person in the house but screaming and crying endlessly on the inside.

Identity issues

Who am I, other than Mummy's helper?

Envy of children whose parents are well and alive

It is very painful seeing other parents relate to their children or do things with their children that the young carer can't do with their own parents.

Guilty

If they are having a nice time (ie when Mum is so miserable or ill).

Huge loyalty

To the ill or dying parent.

No relief

The young carer can feel like they are living out an indefinite prison sentence. There they are living in the world of adult work (but unpaid) with very long hours and very little free time, 'me time' or leisure time, and missing out so badly on so many things that other children enjoy.

Tasks for the practitioner

Help the child to be able to feel, and voice and have heard, the resentment and anger of being the carer for their parent, their fear and all the feelings outlined above.

Help the young carer to appreciate that what they are doing in terms of reversal of parent/child roles is not normal but something that they are doing nevertheless.

Help the young carer to be able to let themselves be looked after by others (tuck them up in bed in the counselling room – read a book to them).

Help the child to know that they themselves don't have to be ill, depressed or sad to deserve care.

Help the child to understand that they are in no way responsible for their parent's moods, feelings, mental or physical health.

Help the child to grieve for the losses in their own life and for their pain at seeing their parent in pain.

Need to help communication between parent and child to sort out the fantasies

Young people who have come to the usual age for leaving home often have fantasies that the parent wants them to stay and care for them. This can be inaccurate. Parents need to be supported to discuss things with their teenager at this most important life stage.

What schools can do

Schools need to be able to bring the phenomenon of 'young carers' to children's awareness – so that they know that sometimes children have to start looking after parents. Then to give the message to the whole school that if that happens to any of them they can go and get help by talking to the school counsellor.

Useful information references and support services

Does that child need to be offered an assessment under the Framework for the Assessment of Children in Need or the Carers Act?

Young carers are entitled to an assessment of their needs under the Carers (Recognition and Services) Act 1995 and Children Act 1989 (see paragraph 3.61–3.63 Framework for the Assessment of Children in Need). Carers aged over sixteen are also entitled to a Carer's Assessment from Children's Services under the Carers and Disabled Children Act 2000. Any assessment of the young carer under this Framework results in the review of what they need and parenting support for the parent. Crisis provision is also considered.

The idea is also for adult and children's social services, schools and health care workers to communicate with each other regarding a proper assessment of needs of the adult and the child and what needs to change to ensure

against levels or care that adversely affect the child's quality of life and mental state.
(See Framework for the Assessment of Children in Need and their Families (Department of Health, 2000) and Common Assessment Framework (www.cwdcouncil.org.uk/caf))

The above can be enormously helpful for the child and can result in a practitioner making regular family visits, or an adult coming in to help in the home, counselling for one or both parties, or family therapy, extra help at school if necessary and a phone number for the child when things get just too much. (Supporting young carers and their families: Include Programme, The Children's Society, 2011)

See also:
The Whole Family Pathway – free online resource for practitioners supporting young carers' and their families (www.youngcarer.com/resources/whole-family-pathway).

Frank J (2002) *Making it Work: Good practice with young carers and their families.* The Children's Society with The Princess Royal Trust for Carers, London.

Frank J & McLarnon J (2008) *Young Carers, Parents and their Families: key principles of practice. Supportive practice guidance for those who work directly with, or commission services for, young carers and their families.* The Children's Society, London.

Helping Children of Troubled Parents

PART TWO

OBJECTIVE/INSTRUCTIONS/DEVELOPMENT

About the exercises

These exercises are designed to open up a rich and meaningful dialogue with child or teenager. They offer an opportunity for them to start to reflect on their feelings about their troubled parents, and so begin to make sense of their life and their world.

There are many scientific studies, known as 'affect labelling studies', which show that helping a child to put words to feelings, as in all of these exercises, can be profoundly emotionally regulating – for brain, mind and body. The child or teenager is then supported to think and reflect, resulting in marked emotional, cognitive and social development, instead of moving into emotional hyperarousal, neurotic symptoms or difficult behaviour (Lieberman, 2011; Lieberman *et al*, 2007; Tabibnia *et al*, 2008; Pennebaker and Chung, 2011).

Good to talk

Research shows that many children and teenagers with troubled parents do not talk to friends about what is happening at home. This is because they may feel ashamed of not having normal parents or ashamed that their parent has a problem, say, with depression, drink or drugs. Some think it's a private matter and feel they are betraying their parent by talking. So it is vital that they have an adult to whom they can speak. For many children and teenagers this is a trusted teacher, social worker or youth worker, as we see in these examples:

'I used to talk to my teachers about that [Mum's drug use] 'cause they used to look after me as well while I'm at school. I used to cry at school a lot and everyone used to take the mickey out of me and they thought I was a whining baby and I actually wasn't...' (Houmoller *et al*, 2011)

'First thing (when they split up), I went straight to my teacher, said, "Miss, could I talk to you?" And then she said, "What's up, Ben?" And I says, "My Mum and Dad have split up."' (Houmoller *et al*, 2011)

The problem is that, when approached by a child or teenager to talk in this way, many adults feel de-skilled or do not know what to say or how to respond. So the exercises in this section of the book are designed as a support to enhance the therapeutic value of any conversation when a child or teenager is hurting in some way about what is going on at home.

How to use the exercises

Decide which of the exercises might be of value for the child or teenager with whom you are working. (In widening your choice, you may like to use this book in conjunction with worksheets in *Draw on Your Emotions* (Sunderland, 1997), *Draw on Your Relationships* (Sunderland, 2008b) and books in the Helping Children with Feelings series (Sunderland, 2001a, 2003b, 2003c, 2003d).) Once you have chosen your worksheet, familiarise yourself with it before seeing the child or teenager.

■ The Objective section

The Objective section is for you, and not to be read out to the child. You may, however, speak about some of the ideas and concepts in this section as you work with the child or teenager, if appropriate.

■ The Instruction section

Familiarise yourself with the Instruction section. The instruction should not be read out to the child or teenager. Instead, put it in your own words. If you do read it out, you will lose some of the vital energy you are bringing to the task and also your eye contact with the participant.

■ The Development section

The Development section offers another angle on the issue explored in the worksheet. It is obviously only relevant to use the tasks offered in this section if the child or teenager with whom you are working has been fully engaged in the exercise itself and clearly has more emotional energy around the theme. You may also find that you have all manner of other creative ideas on how to develop a theme, rather than using the developments offered here. Allow your creative juices to flow! Only you know the particular needs of the child or teenager with whom you are working. So don't be afraid to offer developments that follow the participant along their own rich vein of ideas and feelings.

Safety issues

Two things in particular make a conversation about feelings with a child or teenager unsafe.

These are:

1 Lots of questions and no empathy.

2 Telling the child or teenager what they are feeling.

1 Lots of questions and no empathy

What children value more than anything is someone who will listen. Children's anger towards their social workers (in some cases, not all, of course) became clear from the excellent study called Juggling Harms (Houmoller *et al*, 2011). The children and teenagers reported that what was so awful was the barrage of questions from the adults involved:

'They would just ask me all the questions all the time and I used to just didn't like it… 'cause they was so direct. They wasn't nice, it wasn't as if they'd come and say, "How are you?" It was coming in "Okay, so you're living with your Mum and your Mum's blah, blah, blah and you…" and they were so direct… and aggressive and straight to the point. It was horrible.' (Deena)

Practitioner: 'So did it help in any way, that social services got involved?' Child: 'Just thought they was a bunch of um… nosy gits.' (Paul)

The report also makes the following statement: 'Our data suggests that young people tend to interpret direct questioning, in the absence of trust, as interrogatory and confrontational.' As we see, the girl in the example above said it would have been so different if the social workers had shown such human compassion and concern and asked 'How are you?'

Within a therapeutic conversation, we often need to ask questions in order to ascertain the meaning of an event or experience for a child or teenager. But the questions are there to inform our empathy. Questions without empathy can never result in a therapeutic conversation.

2 Telling a child or teenager what they are feeling

This is dangerous. Telling a child what they feel and being wrong is a gross misattunement and flies in the face of empathy. It also feels awful to be on the receiving end. Here are some examples:

'You must be angry that your Dad is in prison.' (The child in question was actually not angry but heartbroken.)

'Must make you angry that Mum is using [drugs] again.' (The child in question was not angry but terrified.)

Some children will just agree with what you're saying to get you off their back. So always enquire, so as to get the child's meaning of an event, and then empathise. For example:

Practitioner: 'What is it like for your Dad to be in prison?'
Child: 'My heart is in bits.'
Practitioner: 'Wow, so it hurts you SO much...'

Other key safety rules

1 Never assume that you know what something means to the child or teenager. It may mean something seemingly obvious to you, while actually meaning something entirely different to them.

2 Before you empathise, if you are at all unsure about the meaning of an image or drawing, ask for more information. Never assume.

3 Watch out for hidden, incorrect, assumptions in the choice of words you use in response to an image or drawing.

4 Make sure you ask open questions. These are questions such as 'What is that like?', 'What do you feel about that?'
   A closed question is a question that requires a yes or no from the child, such as 'Do you feel angry about that?'

5 Avoid 'Why?' questions. They take the child or teenager away from their feelings.

6 Process your own emotional pain, trauma and loss. Go to see a counsellor to work through your own emotional baggage. You will be a far more effective practitioner if you do.

7 Always allow time for reflection at the end of a session and summarise in an empathic manner what has happened in the therapeutic conversation, particularly referring to the child's feelings.

8 Know your limits of competence and, if a child protection issue arises out of your conversation, refer on.

9 Have a supervisor or someone to whom you can talk about, and get feedback for, your work.

Safeguarding: Your concerns and worries about the welfare of the child or teenager

If you are talking to a child or teenager and what they say is concerning in terms of their welfare or safety being put at risk, ask other agencies to intervene.

If, as a result of talking to a child or teenager, you are concerned that there is an inappropriate level of caring, you will need to communicate with other agencies (eg social workers, school, staff, GP). Some schools have a staff member designated to respond to young carers. If not there is always a member of staff at the child's or teenager's school who is responsible for child protection issues. When schools respond in a way you are not happy with, you can also ring the Education Welfare Officer in your area or social services.

When the issue you are concerned about involves a young carer, the agencies should then action the following:
- an effective assessment of the needs of the young carer
- an assessment of inappropriate caring
- an assessment of the needs of the adult
- consideration of whether there is a safeguarding issue
- consideration of what support can be offered to the whole family
- a working together between adult's and children's social care (working in partnership with health and third sector partners)
- an end to inappropriate caring.

(Adapted from ADASS & ADCS, 2009)

If you are working with young carers, it is important to be familiar with organisations set up to support them. For example:
www.family-action.org.uk
www.youngcarers.net
Family Action, for example, go out and speak to the young carer and they can also communicate to the school so they can support the young carer more. They can give the child a break from their caring roles (when parents can't take them to places) helping them to have a life of their own.

Confidentiality

If you are having a therapeutic conversation with a child or teenager, the best thing to say is, 'What you tell me will remain with me. That said, if I think some people could help you to feel happier, I will want to tell them, but I will tell you that I will want to tell them. Otherwise, I would only tell someone something you said if I felt you or someone else was being harmed or hurt or were in danger of being so.'

The child's fear that 'telling' will result in them being taken away

So many children are worried that if they speak about their parent's drug or alcohol problem or their parent's inability to parent well due to another trouble, they will be taken into care. Where this is an issue, children and teenagers need to be given the correct information that, in most cases, if a referral to social services needs to be made, they will usually want to support and encourage the parents to parent in more effective ways. A child is only taken into care as a last resort and sometimes this is just for a short time, while the parent gets help. (See Families First social work model in supporting families affected by parental substance misuse (Woolfall, 2008).) In addition, all the Young Carers' organisations have the same agenda, to support both the parent/s and the child. See www.family-action.org.uk and www.youngcarers.net.

But what if the child or teenager I am working with is making it quite clear that talking about their troubled parent is strictly 'off-limits'?

Some children find it far too threatening, shaming or disturbing to talk about their troubled parents. Some want to maintain the delusion that their troubled parent is perfect. It is not OK to directly challenge this. If you take away the child's defences you leave them with nothing. So, with such children and teenagers you can still convey empathy but through what's known as 'indirect expression'. This means that you talk indirectly about the emotional themes in the child's life without ever making direct reference to their troubled parent. A great vehicle for indirect expression is therapeutic story. (The storybook vitally relevant for children with troubled parents is *Monica Plum's Horrid Problem*, the book that accompanies this workbook.)

In therapeutic stories, no actual parent, mother or father is ever referred to, but the stories convey empathy and understanding, psycho-education and ways forward. Even Sigmund Freud, so long ago, knew that the unconscious of one person can communicate to the unconscious of another person without going through the conscious mind! So by reading the story to the child, they will feel connected with and understood in terms of the pain, worry and difficulties they experience. You can also make up your own therapeutic story, being careful to sufficiently disguise aspects of the child's own life. See *Using Story Telling as a Therapeutic Tool with Children* (Sunderland, 2001b), to provide you with a key set of tools for this.

Sandplay

Sandplay therapy is ideal for children and teenagers. They can use the sandbox as a quasi-film set or little theatre. Where they get very stuck with words, children and teenagers often make breathtakingly powerful images about their life in the sandbox.

Ideally, what you need is a sandbox about 23 × 29 × 3 inches (57 × 72 × 7cm). It should be painted blue on the bottom to represent water. The box becomes the frame or forum for the child's or teenager's symbolic statement about some important aspect of their life, life event or overview of their life. Because of the sand, they can bury things or bomb things, and everything stands up easily. When the sand is wetted, they can mould it into a fort, an island, a cave, and so on.

Then you need a big choice of miniature objects. These are usually toys or ornaments. Your aim is to represent as many things in the world as you can. This is one reason why sandplay therapy is known as 'the world technique' (see Lowenfeld, 1991, for more on sandplay therapy). Having said that, I started off with about 30 miniatures with teenagers and they still made some amazing sandplay 'filmscapes'. The important thing is to have some miniatures from each of the following categories:

- transport (must include emergency service vehicles) as well as train, aeroplane, helicopter, car, bus, and so on
- people (to include figures of aggression or cruelty and figures of love or warmth, and so on, mythical figures such as trolls, witches and fairies, and family members)
- people in professions (for example, policeman, nurse, lollipop lady, teacher)
- monsters
- farmyard animals

- jungle animals
- buildings (for example, houses, prison, fort, and so on)
- furniture (for example, bath, bed, armchair, toilet) and food
- outside man-made world (for example, gate, road, fence)
- outside natural world (trees, flowers, hedge, stones, shells, cliffs).

How to explain sandplay to a child or teenager

Show the child or teenager the miniatures and the sandbox. Show them how you can then put miniatures in the sand by doing so yourself. Also use your hands in the sandbox to show the blue on the bottom for water, and how you can wet then mould the sand into a building, a wall or a dam, and so on, so you have a setting. Then ask them to choose objects from the selection and place them in the sandbox. If you are working in a directive way, you might say something like 'show your feelings towards event x in the sandplay.' If you are working in a non-directive way, just ask the child/teenager to make a picture in the sand or a film set or story (as appropriate).

Some teenagers may look at the images and say indignantly, 'I'm not playing with toys.' If this happens, simply explain that they are not to be used as toys. Rather, each miniature can stand for something. 'For example, someone might use this monster figure to represent their anger, or this very little duck to stand for their weak small feelings.' I have never had a teenager refuse to engage in the activity after this explanation. After the child or teenager has finished their sandplay image, you can converse about it. The conversation often changes perspectives on things, so it is always useful to ask the child or teenager at the end of your conversation, 'Is there anything you want to change in your film set/picture/story now that we have talked about it.'

MY FEELINGS ABOUT MUM OR DAD

■ Objective

This exercise is for any child or teenager who lives with a troubled parent and who acknowledges the fact and wants to talk about their experiences.

One maths teacher I knew was worried about being sacked because many of the fifteen-year-old boys in his class would come up to him and say things like 'Sir, can I tell you about my Mum, she's drinking again' or 'Sir, my Mum's got all sad again. What do you think I should do?' Such young people as this would gain hugely from a reflective space such as that offered in this exercise. With an empathic adult, it can be a real relief for a child or teenager to talk about and think about what it's like for them to live with a troubled parent. As a result, the child is able to think clearly about their emotional experiences rather than feeling flooded by them. The idea, developed by Christopher Bollas (1987), is to help the child to find words for feelings and move from a disturbing unthought known (troubling sensations, images, feelings that have never been symbolised in words and coherent thought – 'I know it but I have not had a thought about it') to a thought known.

■ Instruction for the child or teenager

It can be stressful and painful for a child or teenager to live with a parent who is unwell or unhappy. It can really get you down at times, and that's normal. Some people's parents gets very sad, or frightened or angry. Others get drunk or take drugs or have some other big problem.

Do you ever feel one or more of these feelings towards your parent when they are troubled or unhappy?
If so, look at the picture on the next page and tick or colour in any of the things that you feel. If it's none of these, write or draw the feelings you do feel in the empty box.

■ Development

Discussion

Talk about how it is so easy for children or teenagers to be too affected by what's happening to their parents.
Ask them to draw a picture or do a sandplay (for an explanation of sandplay see the introduction to Part Two) of the parts of their life they do enjoy so

that they can reflect on these too. Then you can lay the 'enjoyment' picture and their completed worksheet (as above) side by side. An important message then to the child or teenager is to say that it is important not to let the troubles at home affect the lovely parts of their life, for example, their joy at football, their love of scooting, their love of taking photos, their friendships at school, their real affection for certain teachers.

If the child or teenager has been unable to draw anything on the enjoyment page, and says it's because there is no time to do anything just for them, there is a real concern and it's time to communicate with other professionals and agencies (see section above entitled 'Safeguarding: Your concerns and worries about the welfare of the child or teenager').

MY FEELINGS ABOUT MUM/DAD

Worried-he/she might never get better.

Trying so hard to keep her/him happy.

Lonely-lost my parent to her/his problem.

Shock-at how bad it can get.

Guilt I am to blame for all their unhappiness

Desperate to make her/him well again

Hopeless- nothing I do seems
to make her/him better

Angry-she can't parent me like I need

Crying on the inside
With all the pain in our house

Worried- that I could damage
my Mum with my feelings

THE WORRY MOUNTAIN (WHAT IF SOMETHING VERY BAD HAPPENS – AND I DON'T KNOW WHAT TO DO?)

■ Objective

This exercise is about addressing a child's anxious thoughts and fearful or catastrophic fantasies. Some people say it's opening up a can of worms for a child to talk about such painful feelings. But that usually means that you simply leave the child alone with their painful feelings, which most times will include some catastrophic fantasies about what will happen to them and/or their loved ones. It is unfair and totally lacking in compassion to leave a child to manage their anxieties or catastrophic fantasies on their own, and children and teenagers with troubled parents often have lots. It would be like walking away from a child who has a huge gash in their leg. Many children stay awake at night plaguing themselves with their fears and anxieties, which go round and round in their heads.

Example: Molly, aged eight, who lived with her Gran, because her Mum was in prison for three years, lay awake each night with her catastrophic thinking. She was worried about what she would do if her Gran died in her sleep. She never came up with a solution. She would call out throughout the night 'Goodnight Granny', just to check that her grandmother was not dead. Her quality of life was vastly improved by doing this exercise with a listening adult.

The adult asked her if she knew where Gran's phone was. The little girl said she did. The adult asked her if she had any other relatives who cared about her. She said she had an Uncle. The practitioner wrote down on the paper the Uncle's number. 'But what if he doesn't answer?' asked Molly, so the practitioner wrote down 'dial 999'. The practitioner also asked how old Gran was. The answer was 54. The practitioner was able to tell the little girl that actually, although 54 might feel ancient to the little girl, it's actually middle, and not old, age. So the likelihood of Gran suddenly dying in her sleep was extremely small. Also, with her permission, the practitioner called in Gran to have a three-way session. Gran listened very well (she had been primed to do so with a phone call earlier) and reassured Molly but also said that the next door neighbour, Mrs Simpson, would be there for her too, in case of a problem, and she could always ring her doorbell at any time of day or night. Molly felt both heard and empowered. As a result, she started to sleep well for the first time in three years.

So this exercise is to support the child or teenager to speak about their anxieties, worries and fears, which for many will be the very first time they have done so. For some, it will never have occurred to them to speak about these and so they may have no 'felt experience' of the deep sense of relief and support they can get if they do.

So the exercise has a two-fold aim:
1 To enable the child to voice their fears that they may have kept to themselves for days, months or years, and to find that 'what is shareable is bearable'.
2 To give the child vital information or knowledge to empower them to manage better the feared event should it ever happen and to reassure as appropriate.

■ Instructions for the child or teenager

'One of his unrealistic beliefs was that if his mother fell over, it meant she was going to die.' (Segal and Simkins, 1993)

Sometimes worries can get so big and so troubling that they can spoil any good things that happen during the day and keep us awake at night. Some children and teenagers who have an ill or unhappy parent worry particularly about what they should do if a bad thing happens, whom should they tell, what would they say, and if anyone would help.

Look at the picture of the Worry Mountain. If you have any of these worries, tick the worry, or mark it in some way or colour it in.

THE WORRY MOUNTAIN

■ Development

The Fear Bag and the Phew! Bag

The exercise helps children and teenagers to have a novel and supportive vehicle for sharing their fears without actually needing to speak about them. It's great to provide them with two little bags. One should have 'Fear' written on it and the other 'Phew!' written on it. It makes the exercise more enticing! If, after the exercise, the child chooses to share one or more of his or her fears with you, it's good to praise them for their courage, offer empathy and then, if appropriate, offer advice, help or reassurance. If appropriate, tell them that you would like to tell a person in another service or agency (eg social worker, SENCo) to see if they can help.

Instruction to the child

Write your fears on separate little notes. Write H on the ones you would like help with. Put them in the Fear Bag.

How does it feel now they are in the Fear Bag rather than just in your head? If there are any of the H fears that you think you could share with me that would be great. When one of your fears has ended or got less fearful, cross it out and put it in the Phew! Bag.

THE 'IT'S ALL TOO MUCH' FEELING

■ Objective

This exercise is again designed to enable young carers to feel understood and valued in terms of what they are doing at home and the sacrifices they are making. Without this, they can feel so very lonely and isolated. As one nine-year-old girl said, 'I see my friends after school going to play in the park and I go home to do the cleaning, the cooking and the babysitting. Then to cap it all school often tells me off for not doing my homework! When am I supposed to do that? Mum needs me to help until late each night.'
The exercise also gives the child or teenager a vital opportunity to process their feelings rather than being overwhelmed by them. For many young carers they will never have had anyone really empathising with what life is like for them in this way: the too much, the too difficult, the too lonely. The exercise will be particularly useful for young carers of ill, disabled, depressed parents and those with a drug or alcohol problem.

■ Instruction for the child or teenager

Look at the picture of the 'It's all too much' feeling. When you feel the 'it's all too much feeling', do you ever feel like any of the things in the picture? Put a circle round any you do. If none of these are right for you, just draw or write your feelings.

■ Development

Objective

This exercise is to help the child or teenager to acknowledge that, as a young carer, they are having to act in a grown-up, responsible way, but not to lose sight of the child they are, who still needs looking after, comforting, time to be, feel and play as a child.

The responsible capable you

Make an image in play dough or clay of the responsible, capable you.
Show the feeling of this 'you' in a movement.
Play out in music what this 'you' feels like.
Draw a picture of you like this.

The child you

Now do the same for the child you.
Make an image in play dough or clay of the child you.

THE 'IT'S ALL TOO MUCH' FEELING

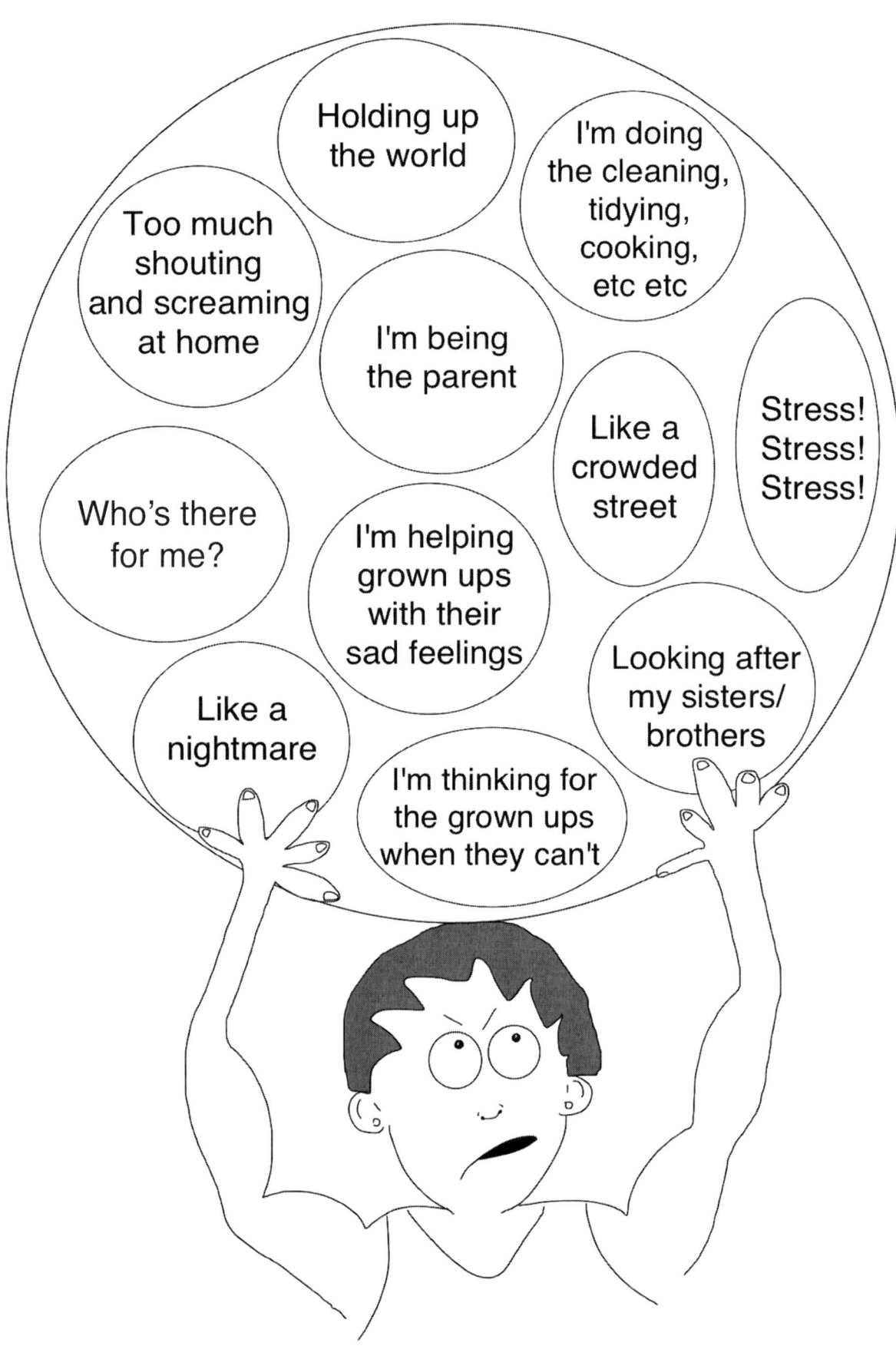

Show the feeling of this 'you' in a movement.
Play out in music what this 'you' feels like.
Draw a picture of you like this.

Put the images of the **responsible capable** you and the **child you** side by side. What do you feel when you look at both these aspects of you side by side?
What does the responsible part of you want to say to the child part of you and what does the child part of you want to say to the responsible part?

LOSS AND LONGINGS

■ Objective

This exercise is designed to support the child or teenager to grieve what they need to grieve in terms of having a troubled parent. So often so many losses are involved. It is also hoped that the child or teenager will be helped to understand the importance of grieving. As one child says, 'Crying lets the sad out.' If the sad is not 'let out', the unmourned grief can very commonly turn into depression in the teenage and adult years (see Panksepp and Watt, 2011) and all manner of mental and/or physical ill-health. As Henry Maudsley said, 'The sorrow that hath no vent in tears makes other organs weep.'

Before doing the exercise with a child or teenager it is recommended that the practitioner makes themselves aware of the territory, so to speak; the range of losses common to young carers. Here are some examples:

Longing for us to be a normal family
'When I went round to her house and her Mum and Dad are together, it was weird how they had dinner at the same time every day, and they had to have a bath, 'cause I stayed there, and they woke you up in the morning and it was just completely different and I really liked it … and it made me feel uncomfortable to go back to my Mum's … knowing what I was missing.' (Houmoller et al, 2011)

Longing to be related to, like other parents relate to their children. Longing to be cared for, like other parents care for their children
'I feel like I didn't have a Mum or Dad. Like a proper one … where you just spend time with them and they speak to you … and they ask you questions about what you're doing … and things.' (Houmoller et al, 2011)

So many children whose parents are addicted to drink or alcohol are all too aware of what parent–child love looks like and should feel like. They have seen it on TV or at the school gates or in the shopping centre. They are also often very aware of how their parent can't give that sort of love and attention.

Heartbroken from watching how my sister/brother is affected by my parent's problems

'My Mum, she forgot my birthday and then she forgot my brother's birthday. That one was far worse – I mean he's only six and she didn't even get him a card. I can still see the sadness in his eyes.' (Taylor, aged twelve).

'I watched my little brother's pain as he was yearning to go back and live with Mum. He really wanted to move back [with Mum]. Like he really misses his Mum. And I didn't want him to move back on his own because I know that like, um, he wouldn't have been looked after properly.' (Houmoller et al, 2011)

The pain of missing out on vital things that other children get

One five-year-old boy with a troubled Mum (addicted to drugs) was taken to see Santa Claus by his social worker. He said to Santa, 'But why do you never come to our house?'

Yearning to have their well Mum back

'I miss the Mum I had. Now I've just got this drunk one instead.' (Carly, aged nine)

Being let down by people who say they've come to help

'I don't see the point of having social workers. No? 'Cause they don't really help and they just leave you after a while.' (Houmoller et al, 2011)

■ Instruction for the child or teenager

It's painful to feel sad feelings, but only by feeling them can we eventually stop feeling so sad and move on. It's a very brave thing to feel and think about your longings and losses but far better to grieve them with someone else than on your own.

Look at the picture. Which things in the picture do you sometimes feel? Tick, circle or colour in the ones that you do. If it's none of these, draw your own in the empty boxes.

LOSS AND LONGINGS

Longing for my parent
to be well

Longing for us to be
a normal family

Longing to be cared for
like other parents do

Longing for my parent to play/
have fun with me

Trying to let go of hoping that
my parent will ever change

Too many grown ups that help
or say they'll help just leave

Watching my brother's/ sister's hurting
because of Mum's/ Dad's troubles

■ Development

How unmourned grief can derail personal development

Jennifer (aged six) would talk about 'when Daddy gets better we'll...' It took a long time before her mother could bring herself to say to Jennifer, 'Daddy isn't going to get better, you know.' Jennifer was quiet, and later she and her mother cried together. (Segal, 1995)

A child's or teenager's life can be derailed by unmourned grief, leaving the child struggling emotionally, relationally and at school with their work. The child can feel like they can't really get on with anything. They can feel like nothing really matters any more, as Sigmund Freud said in his famous paper 'Mourning and Melancholia' (1915), 'as if the world cannot recall him'. Explain to the child or teenager that this is a common reaction to loss and longing but that the best way to get the train on the track again, so to speak, is to find the courage to grieve with someone they trust. So this exercise will help the child or teenager to reflect on this and, with the practitioner's help, to think about what they need to mourn properly and so move on.

When sadness gets in the way of everything

■ Instructions to the child

Look at the five trains in the picture. Two are running fine but three have been derailed by big blobs of sadness.

Think of losses, longings, disappointments or times that you were let down in your life that were so painful that it was like they derailed your life for a time, for example, spoiling your friendships, your happiness, your schoolwork. Perhaps they are still doing so. Write on the big blobs of sadness what each loss, longing, disappointment or feeling of being let down was and what age you were when they happened to you. What do you need to help you with all this? Who would you like to help you, so that you can move on and the trains can run on the track again?

WHEN SADNESS GETS IN THE WAY OF EVERYTHING

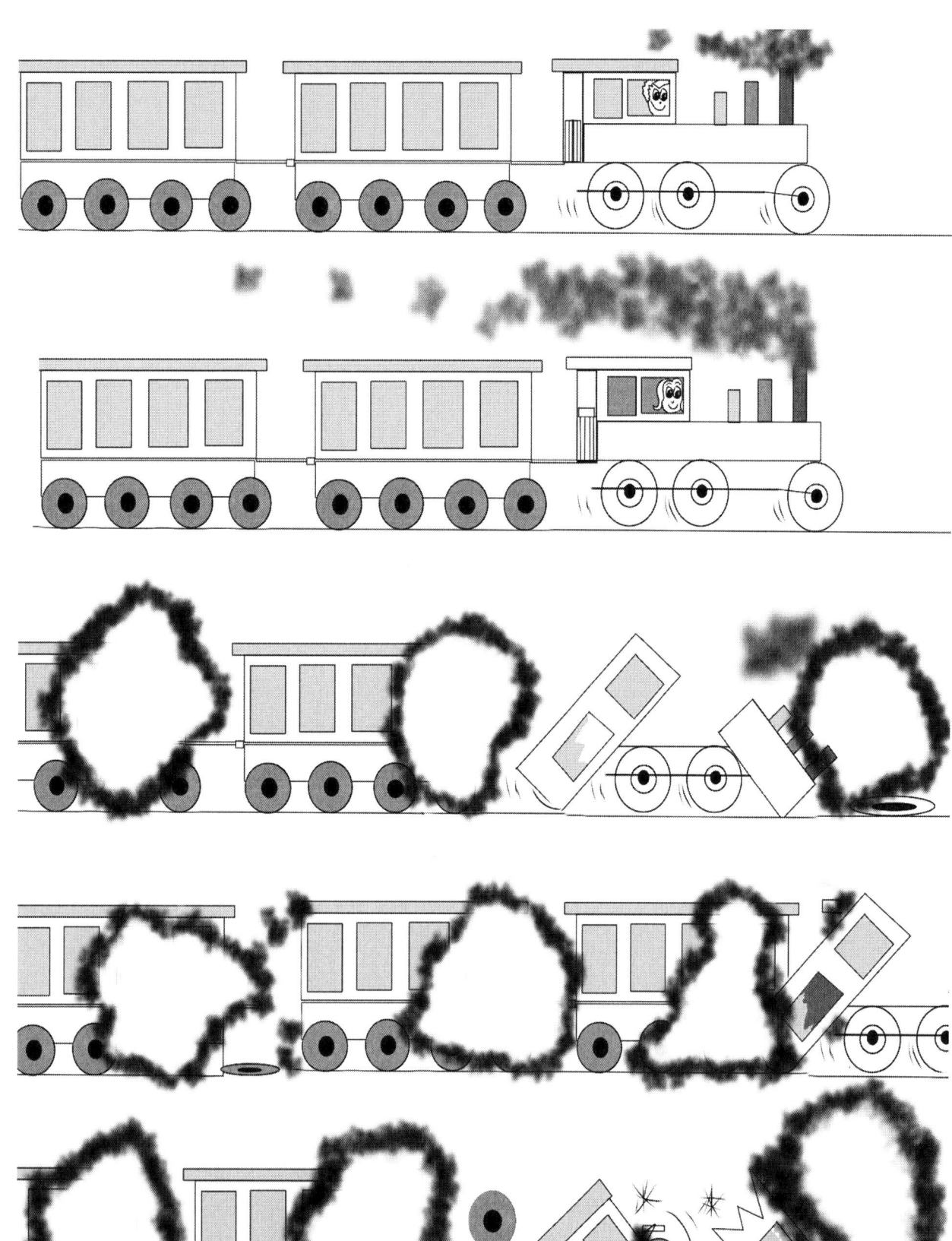

SHOCK

■ Objective

It is easy to begin to think that your life will carry on down roughly the same path. Then one day something happens that changes everything. For children of troubled parents often the change involves some form of loss; loss of their home, loss of a safe mother, loss of a healthy mother, loss of one of their parents who has moved out or gone to prison, loss of something safe and known in one's life; loss of a feeling of safety in being in the world. Whatever it is, things may never be the same again.

Terrible shocks are something the vast majority of us will have to manage at some time in our life. Yet, for many people, the parenting and education they receive provide them with few if any resources to know how to cope well with shocks. Without help to feel, think about and work through shock states, negative reverberations can cause long-term psychological problems. Also, when it is denied, shock can get locked in the body, resulting in all manner of illnesses and physical symptoms. As Bessel van der Kolk (1996), a famous researcher in traumatic stress, states: 'The body keeps the score.' Shock states can also badly affect the child's ability to concentrate at school. Again to quote van der Kolk: 'In traumatic stress we become frightened unthinking animals.'

This exercise is to help the child or teenager to reflect on the shocking experiences in their life. If, with the help of an empathic other, feelings are reflected on and shared through words and images, they no longer need to be discharged through neurotic symptoms or destructive actions. For some children and teenagers the exercise may be the first time they have acknowledged to themselves the power of the shocks they have experienced, so that they can be mourned and worked through. It may help to talk to children or teenagers, when appropriate, about the cost to emotional health of bottling up feelings about shock.

The practitioner needs to give lots of empathy. All too few children and teenagers who have suffered shocks have received empathy, but rather they have been given (voiced or not voiced) a 'get over it' or a 'put it behind you' message.

■ Instruction for the child or teenager

There is all the difference in the world between being able to prepare yourself for a bad thing that you know is going to take place (for example someone you love leaving) and a bad thing happening for which you had no warning and so it's an awful shock.

These are shocks that other children and teenagers have experienced:
- coming home and finding Mummy lying on the floor
- Father being taken into prison
- opening the door to find police on the doorstep
- something bad happening to a sibling
- parents telling them they are getting a divorce
- Mum has taken too many pills and is unconscious
- their parent dying
- their parent is rushed to hospital
- their parent has a bad accident.

Look at the picture and think of one or more shocks you have suffered in your life. Did any of them make you feel like any of the images in the picture? If so, tick those pictures. If it's not any of these, draw your own feelings about the shocks in the empty boxes and give each picture a title. What was the worst thing for you about the shock? What words describe what it felt like? How are the shocking things that happened to you still affecting your daily life? Looking back, did any good things come out of any of those events in the end?

■ Development: The shock energies

Ask the child or teenager to think of a shock they experienced. On a large piece of paper, ask them to show what the shock felt like. Alternatively, if you have percussion instruments, ask them to play out the energy of the shock. These visual and auditory images created by the child or teenager can be a vital first step to working through these forms of pain. Shock often leaves people feeling helpless, so encourage the child or teenager to take their power back by playing out, on percussion or through drawing, their protest or angry response to what had happened. Drums are ideal for this.

Be aware of children and teenagers who through the exercise might be describing states of post-traumatic stress disorder (PTSD). They need a referral to a doctor, psychiatrist or child psychotherapist if they are describing the following, resulting from the shocking experience:

- daily states of hyperarousal lasting a long time
- hypervigilance
- flashbacks
- startle reactions
- problems sleeping, eating, breathing (in PTSD the body is unable to regulate internal systems properly)
- social phobias
- generalised anxiety
- inappropriate flight/freeze responses (suddenly finding your thinking, feeling or doing is frozen, cut off or totally stuck).

SHOCK

A door slammed in your face

A terrible noise

Everything falling out of everything

Everything coming to a standstill

A punch in your gut

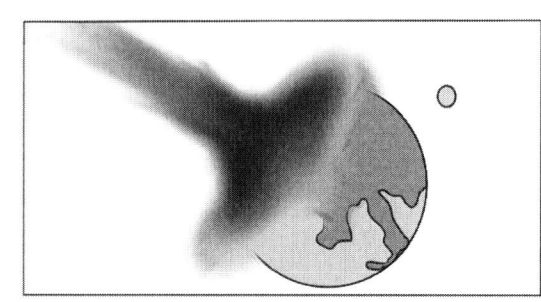

The world coming to an end

A great smash

MUSEUM OF RESENTMENTS

■ Objective

Talking about feelings can enable children and teenagers to take on board the emotional complexities of a situation, particularly where feelings of anger and resentment are involved. So, for example, instead of thinking 'I hate him', a child or teenager can be enabled to develop far more sophisticated thought processes such as, 'I hate him, because I feel so hurt by him,' and even, 'I guess he must have been really hurt by someone in his life, to call my mother names like that.'

When we help children and teenagers to talk about their feelings of anger and resentment, they can develop curiosity about how what has happened to them in the past colours their perception of the present. This is a sophisticated human capacity showing insight and self-awareness. Without help to speak about feelings, many children and teenagers will never develop that capacity. Instead, their anger and resentment moves all too quickly into blame and, perhaps, into fantasies of revenge. For example, before counselling, Toby, aged 13, said things like, 'I just hit him because he deserved it'. After counselling he could say, 'I think I hit him because he dissed me but I guess it was also because I was still feeling so let down by my Dad moving out.'

Some key research by Hauser *et al* (2008) found that teenagers who had committed violent crimes (eg shooting or stabbing), but who then developed capacity for insight and self-awareness in the ways described above, went on to do well in later life. The others, who lacked insight and awareness and who were stuck in years of anger, hate and resentment, did very badly. Furthermore, carrying around unspoken resentments for years costs. It takes up lots of energy that could be used for far more creative pursuits. Resentments take up too much thought time and the fact that they do is indication enough that they are unworked through. Rarely does a child or teenager get an arena where they can look at all the resentments in their life with a supportive, understanding adult, so that they can start the process of putting down that emotional baggage and moving on.

This exercise, in particular, will be of benefit for the young carer who is just 'too good' to find their own protest and is screaming inside about the situation at home.

Just to orientate you, here are some examples of resentments by young carers:

I resent that Mum cares more about her drink than me

'I always come second for my Mum and her drink comes first. I don't know, it really makes me angry because it's like if you love me you'd buy milk rather than that bottle of wine. Do you know what I mean?' (Houmoller *et al*, 2011)

I resent that my older sibling left home so I'm doing all the work at home now alone

Anna, resents that her older brother prioritised taking care of himself and left her alone with their mother: 'I remember thinking, "well there's not much good you being here now Mark [older brother] because you walked out and I was five years old and I had to look after this woman then who was like dribbling and not washing" and, yeah, it was really hard.' [Anna is 15 and her brother is 27]. (Houmoller *et al*, 2011)

I resent people who say they will help and then don't

'I phoned the social services to try to tell them that it was dreadful at home. But it didn't do any good because when they came round Mum just tidied everything up and made sure she was sober, so they said I was over-reacting.' (Emma, aged 15)

I resent it that Dad/Mum lies about their problem

'I couldn't do anything [with the knowledge I had], 'cause they can lie through their teeth. There's no point me going or saying to her, "Oh, are you on it?", because she'd lie … And then two months later I found her jacking up … I felt relieved because I thought am I going crazy and just imagining all this? When I found out I was like, no, I'm not going mad, she's the liar, and she is doing that again. Because no one really believed me.' (Houmoller *et al*, 2011)

■ Instructions for the child or teenager

Think of resentments you have. They may date back a long way or may be relatively new.

MUSEUM OF RESENTMENTS

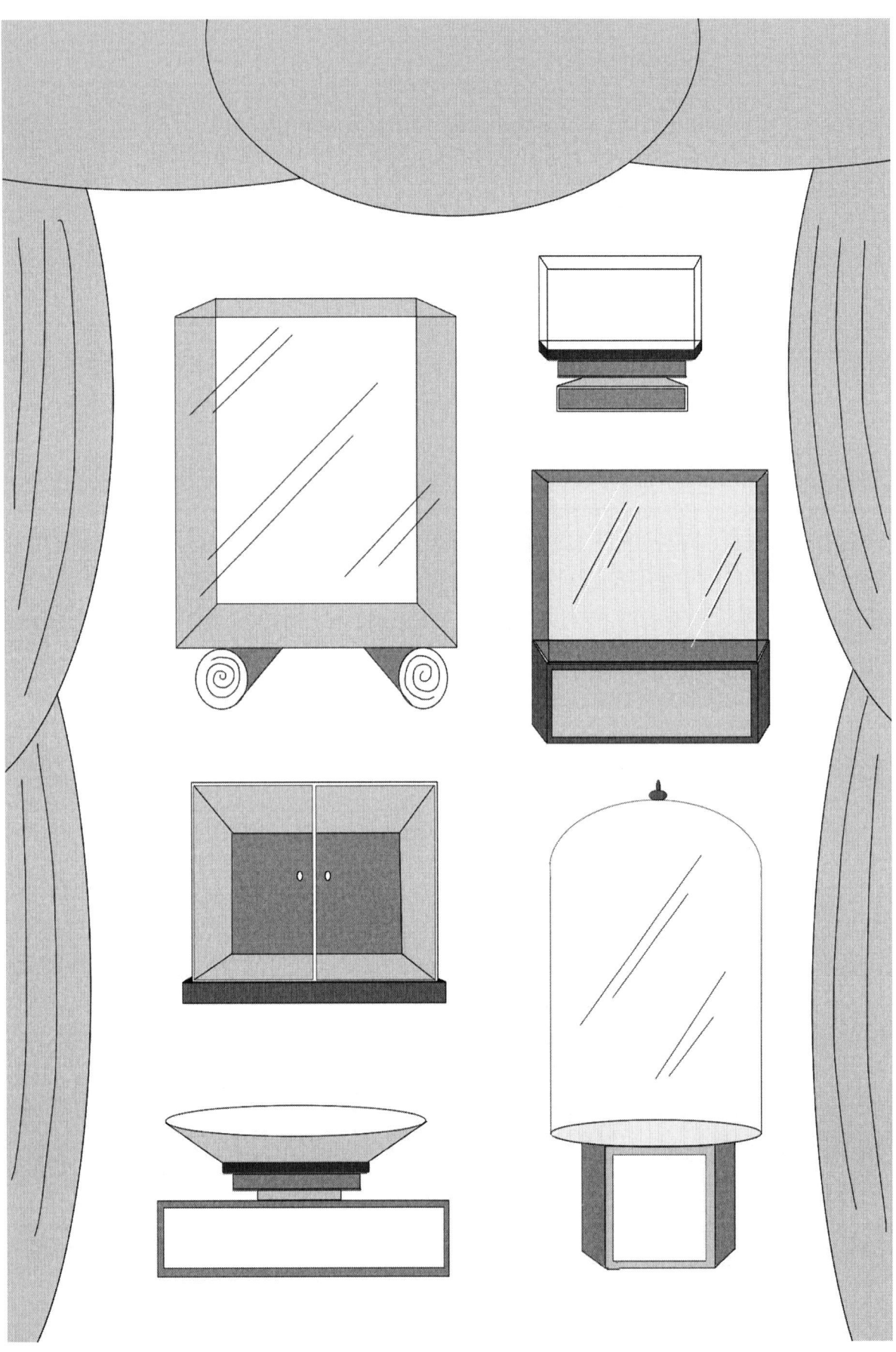

These are resentments that other children and teenagers with troubled parents have had:

I resent it that…
- my parent is ill
- my parent is so sad
- my parent lies about her/his problem
- my parent doesn't look after me like normal parents do
- my parent doesn't try harder to get better
- I can't fix this
- my parent doesn't go and get help
- people who could help don't
- there's nothing to look forward to for me and my parent
- my brother/sister left home so I'm dealing with this on my own now
- she has this problem but I love her.

Draw or label your biggest resentments on the exhibit stands in this Museum of Resentments. When you stand back and look at them all together, what do you feel? Which eats away at you the most? Is there any way you can resolve anything, make it better in any way. For example, you might think of writing someone you feel resentful towards a letter (that you may or not send). Talking about resentments with a grown-up who is good at listening can often resolve problems and empower you to confront the people in your life who you think need confronting.

■ Development: Museum of Hurt

■ Instructions

Look at this picture of the Museum of Hurt. Look at each exhibit in turn. Think of times or events in your life when you have felt very hurt. Choose the exhibit stands appropriate to your various hurtful experiences. For example, choose the 'ouch' stand for a little hurt and one of the others for a major hurt. Think of a title to describe the hurtful event and write this by the exhibit. What was the worst thing about it? What do you want the person who hurt you to know or understand? Try saying it to them now as if they were in the room.

MUSEUM OF HURT

What I want you to know is...

- 'I am so hurt that you…'
- 'I feel anger/hate because you…'

You can also develop this exercise by asking the child or teenager to pick their biggest hurt from the Museum and use clay to make a sculpture of the hurt, or ask them to do a sandplay (for an explanation of sandplay see the introduction to Part Two) about it, or to play it out in music. It may help to use all these languages of expression, as each offers a different perspective and different form of working through.

THE CLOUD WE LIVE UNDER

■ Objective

Some children and teenagers have lived for years with a parent who is emotionally and/or physically unwell. With the former, the parent may suffer from depression, anxiety or problems with anger. They may have an addiction problem or may have never properly grieved a traumatic loss. Others may be letting themselves be abused by a partner or spouse. Others suffered troubled childhoods themselves, so find it very difficult to parent now. Subsequently, there is often a bad family atmosphere with lots of negative emotion and energy, and very high stress levels.

Many children and teenagers in this position also feel impotent and helpless when they try and fail to mend their broken parent. They may be unable to focus on schoolwork as they are so worried about their parent. In some cases, school refusal is about wanting to stay at home because they are too anxious about what will happen to their Mum or Dad if they are not there to look after them:

'I used to stay off [school] tae make sure my Ma did nae get drugs and all that… 'cause I hate it… I'd follow her and not let her doe it… like I would make sure she stayed in the house with me.' (Advisory Council on the Misuse of Drugs, 2003).

So this exercise and these discussion points are designed to empower the child or teenager with a space to process feelings about their home life and relationships with parents and other family members, a vital knowledge base and some practical ways forward to cope with the cloud they live under at home.

■ Instructions for the child or teenager

When you feel that family stuff is getting you down you may find it useful to think about things in terms of what it is like for you, what has made you feel like this and what you can change. It might help to think about things with some pictures instead of just with words. Have a look at the pictures below. If you feel your life or concerns are like any of the pictures, please tick the box or colour them in. If it's not any of these things, draw or write in the empty boxes what you feel inside when you think about the difficult family stuff in your life.

THE CLOUD WE LIVE UNDER

I've got a Mum who got
broken and didn't get mended

I'm trying to mend mum/dad
but never managing

Our family can't seem to
save each other

I'm trying so hard to make
mum/dad happy/well

Full of silent screams
at having to watch stuff

In bits because of stuff
that happens at home

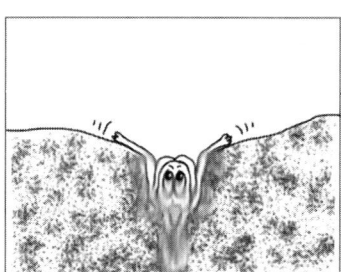

My parent's troubles: like sinking
sand, I get dragged down too

What hurts her hurts me

There is no one to make the
hurting stop

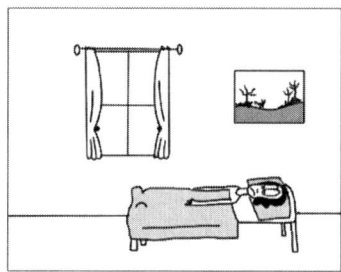

Just terribly terribly tired

When my parent isn't happy
no one is happy

When my parent wobbles
my world wobbles

■ Development

Discussion

Pick one or more of the topics below to discuss with the child or teenager as appropriate.

Talk about what it can feel like parenting your parent

If a child or teenager is parenting their parent, they need to have this named, empathised with and talked about. They will need help to consider the complexity of the situation with regard to the very different sets of needs – those of the child/teenager and those of the parent. They will need you to acknowledge that it can be very painful seeing a parent in physical or emotional pain and feeling that you can't do anything about it. They need to know that many children and teenagers never suffer in this way and are free to get on with their own lives and development, as they have parents who are clearly in the parenting role and don't have needs of the child. They will also need to be given information about how to get help for the troubled parent instead of parenting the parent themselves. They need to know that children and teenagers often feel a huge relief when a responsible adult takes over and looks after their parent.

Talk about how to confront the parent

Give them some ideas of what they might say and of what other children and teenagers have said (obviously, use age-appropriate language). Here are some examples:

'Mum I love you very much but feel at times as if you are using me as your counsellor. I feel inadequate to help because I am only a child. Would you ever consider professional counselling, as it is free if you go to the doctor?'

'I am aware how unhappy you are for much of the time.'

'I see how much pain you are in. I find your pain very painful.'

'We need to think of who we can ask to help you and the services that can help, so that I don't become your main carer all on my own.'

'Mum/Dad, I need you to know that I am finding it hard to concentrate at school because I keep worrying about you. So I am asking you to get professional help, by talking to the doctor or a social worker. If you do that it would be a great gift for me, as I would feel free then to get on with my own life rather than spending so much time worrying about you.'

If the child or teenager feels it is too hard or frightening to talk like this with their parent, they might like to write a letter instead. Also, check with them whether they would like you or someone else to support them to confront their parent.

Talk about drugs or alcohol

Talk about how, with a parent addicted to drugs or alcohol, it is common to feel less important to them than their drugs or alcohol. The child or teenager can feel literally cast aside and secondary in importance, as expressed so well in the following statement: 'While she was alone in the light of the kitchen, I saw her drink her white wine and I wanted to be the wine, to do her some good, to make her happy, to attract her attention' (Cardinal, 1993). The child or teenager needs to know that this feeling of being of secondary importance should never be taken personally because it isn't personal. Having the concept of emotional unavailability explained to them can help them recognise when their parent is physically present but emotionally absent.

Talk about any misplaced responsibility

Correct any confusion over unwell people in the family so that the child or teenager doesn't blame themselves. For example, 'Mum would be happy if it weren't for me.'

Talk about how important it is to get re-parenting from other adults

Discuss how, because their own parents are unable to parent them adequately, re-parenting from other adults as they go through life can make a huge difference. They can look to specific other adults in their lives to do some re-parenting for them, to offer them the comfort, soothing and listening that their parent can't give them right now. 'Other parents' might be a valued teacher, other members of the family, a friend's parent, a counsellor, or indeed any adult that can hold the child's best interests at heart, and who has the capacity to listen, empathise and imagine into what the child is going through. You can explain that re-parenting is a great thing, even if it doesn't first really happen until later in their life, even when they are an adult.

Quotations the child/teenager may find useful

'He imagined wiping away his mother's black moods and sullen withdrawals. Once and for all he would restore her world, which he was forever being told, with a thousand cues, raised eyebrows, and turned-down corners of a mouth, had collapsed because of something he had done or failed to do.' (Stolorow *et al*, 1987)

'There are actually families in which nobody is present. The fact of living under the same roof is the only link between its members.' (Odier, 1956)

'The [teenager's mind] may be infected by the fears which the mother refuses to recognise as her own.' (Wickes, 1988)

WHAT I WANT FOR ME AND MY LIFE

■ Objective

This exercise acknowledges the fact that young carers often de-prioritise their own needs and sometimes have not thought about what they want for themselves, their own life, their future. Some are so used to focusing on their parent's need that they mistakenly think it is selfish to think about what they need. Young carers need to know that they have the same rights as all children and young people, many of whom are actively pursuing hobbies and their own hopes and dreams for themselves!

As the 'Working together to support young carers' report (ADASS, 2009) states, 'Young carers should be able to learn, achieve, develop friendships and enjoy positive, healthy childhoods just like other children. This means taking account of their hopes, aspirations, strengths and achievements. Young carers are encouraged to have strong ambitions and good opportunities to realise their potential and to have the same access to education, career choices and broader opportunities as their peers.'

This exercise is designed to help the young carer focus on their life for a while, their needs and hopes and dreams, as opposed to their parent with all their wants and needs.

■ Instructions for the child or teenager

Sometimes, when children and teenagers are young carers, they put their own needs to the back of their mind. They stop having wants and needs for their own life now and hopes and dreams for their future. So this exercise is a time for us to look together at what you want, need and wish for and to think more about what you want to do with your life, instead of focusing on what your parent needs, feels, thinks and wants, and how they behave and suffer.

The needs and wants now picture

Look at the needs and wants in this picture. If you have one or more of these needs or wants put a circle round them. If there are other needs and wants that are not written here, write your own in the empty circles.

WHAT I WANT FOR ME AND MY LIFE

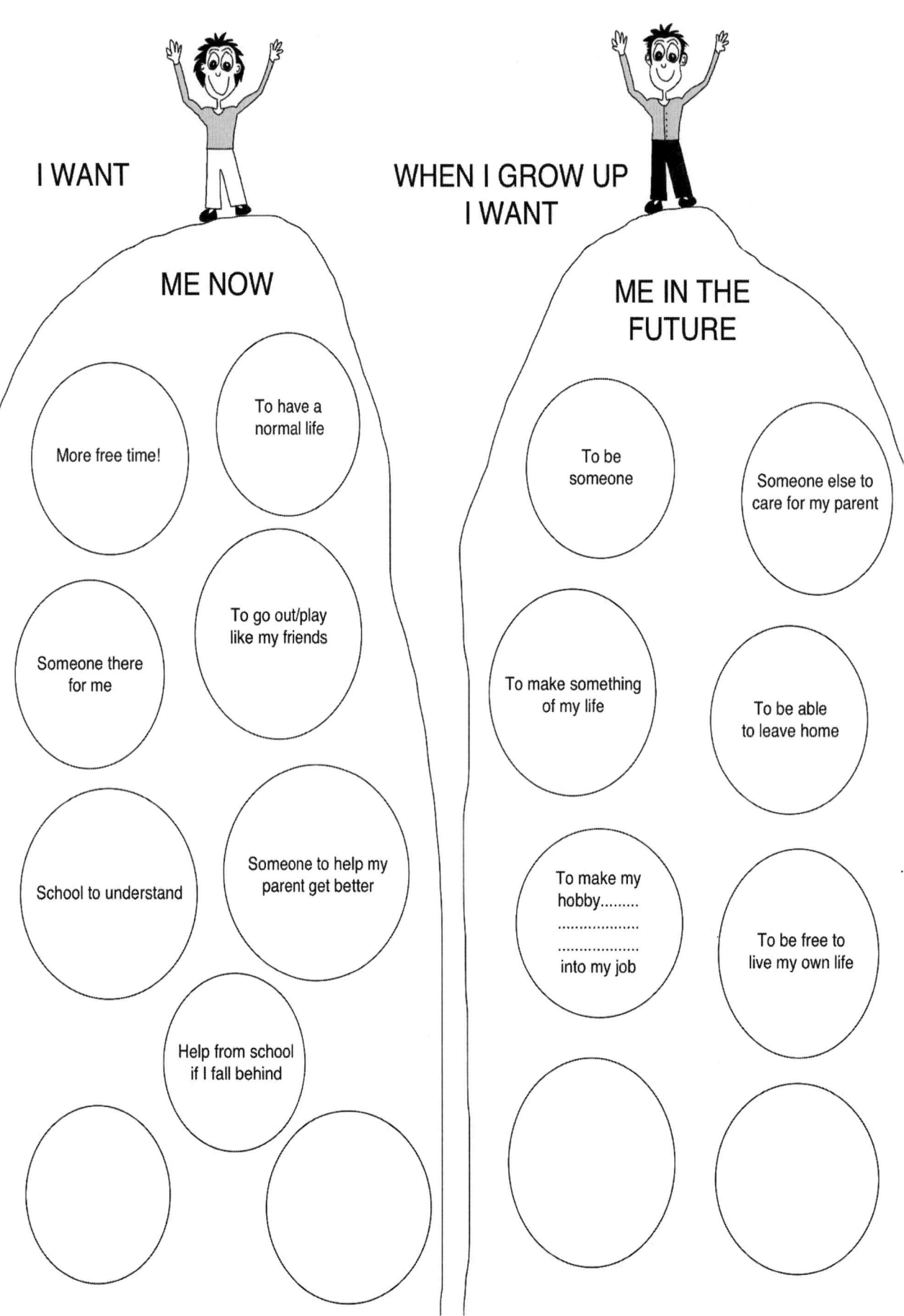

I WANT

ME NOW

More free time!

To have a normal life

Someone there for me

To go out/play like my friends

School to understand

Someone to help my parent get better

Help from school if I fall behind

WHEN I GROW UP I WANT

ME IN THE FUTURE

To be someone

Someone else to care for my parent

To make something of my life

To be able to leave home

To make my hobby.........
....
....
into my job

To be free to live my own life

The wishes and dreams for my future picture

Look at the wishes and dreams in this picture. If you have one or more of these wishes or dreams for your future, put a circle round them. If you have other wishes and dreams that are not written here, write your own in the empty circles.

■ Development: The Help Garden

'Defences are self-regulation [self-help] held too tightly. My job is to disrupt this self-regulation, so that the [child/teenager] finds healthier ways of managing their feelings.' (Grotstein, 2005)

It can be really difficult for a young carer to get their wants and needs answered, their wishes and dreams fulfilled, unless they have a crucial skill. This is the ability to ask for help from understanding, emotionally robust, compassionate adults. So this exercise brings that into focus, hopefully underpinned with psychological messages from the practitioner about how important it is for a child or teenager who is struggling at home to ask for help.

You can help a child or teenager who has opted for 'self-help' to consider what is perhaps so frightening or threatening for them in asking for help instead. For others, it is just that there has been no good modelling in their family of being able to ask for or use help well. For some children, this is a real eye-opener. They may not have realised up until this point that they have been doing the hard things in their life all on their own. It may never have occurred to them to ask for help.

■ Instructions for the child or teenager

When something in life gets too hard, you have a big choice to make. Do you stay in a horrid place in your mind like the horrid house in this picture with no help, or do you go into a place like the Help Garden, which means asking for help from a grown-up that you respect and like? No one needs to do something too hard on their own. There are always kind adults in the world that can help.

Look at the picture. If you have ever asked for help when something in your life has been too difficult or horrid, colour in one of the flowers in the Help Garden. If you have asked for help more than once, colour in more than one flower.

THE HELP GARDEN

WHAT I WANT FOR ME AND MY LIFE

If you have never asked for help, draw yourself in the horrid house which is a symbol of the pain of the aloneness of doing too hard things all on your own. If you haven't coloured in a flower in the Help Garden, what do you think stops you asking for help when things in your life get too hard? Is it perhaps that you don't trust grown-ups or you or think they won't be able to help? Or has it never really occurred to you to ask for help?

MUM/DAD: THE ROCK BOTTOM AND THE BEST BITS

■ Objective

Too few people take the time in their lives to sit down and look at the relational experiences that have changed them in some way, for better or worse. So this exercise is about offering the child or teenager a chance to stand back and review some of the most important, and therefore often life-changing, relational experiences in their life.

The exercise supports the need both to grieve the bad times and to celebrate the good times they have had with a parent. Doing both helps the child or teenager to process their past properly. For many children and teenagers, the rock bottom moments will have been traumatic and, as we know, trauma does not just go away. As Van der Kolk (1989) says 'The past will not go into the past until it is remembered in the present.' So this exercise is about doing just that.

■ Instructions for the child or teenager

Choose one of your parents to think about. Think of the most memorable good times with that parent and the most memorable bad times. These are times that you will never forget. The good times may have been funny, beautiful or exciting, or a time when you had a deep sense of connection with that parent. The bad times may have involved feeling terribly alone, angry, frightened, hopeless or desperate with or about that parent.

Write the rock bottom moments on the rock bottom picture. To get you thinking, you might be interested to see what some other children and teenagers who are young carers said were their rock bottom moments. If something they have said is true for you too, put a tick next to it.

Now turn to the magic carpet. Draw a little sign or use a word or two words for some of the best moments you can remember with your parent. Again, to get you thinking, you might be interested to see what some other children and teenagers who are young carers said were their best moments with their parent. If something they have said is true for you too, tick it.

After you have done this, talk about the bad and good moments you want to talk about: what they made you feel, how they are still affecting you today.

Mum/Dad The Best Bits

Other children's best moments

Me and my parent playing together
Me and my parent laughing together
Me and my parent on holiday
My parent looking after me
My parent being proud of me
The day someone came to help us
When we had warm towels on the
radiator not smelly wet ones on the floor

Mum/Dad The Rock Bottom Moments

Other children's rock bottom moments

That really bad row
When I couldn't stop the bad thing
happening
Mum crying (again)
Finding Mum/Dad on the floor
When my parent was really out of it
When s/he went to hospital
Opening the door to the police
When my pet died
When my sister/brother left home,
so only me now

■ Development: My different Mums/Dads

This exercise develops the child's exploration of their relationship with one or both parents and will be particularly useful for children and teenagers who feel that one of the main difficulties they live with is having a Mum or Dad who keeps changing, in terms of very contrasting mood states – like having a multiple-personality Mum or Dad! The child or teenager can never feel safe because, for example, when they are with their happy or playful Mum or Dad they always know the angry, cruel or depressed, silent one will be back soon.

■ Instructions to the child

Sometimes children and teenagers have a Mum or Dad who keeps changing in terms of the moods they are in. This can be very unsettling, particularly if you have a parent who can be very lovely with you one minute but then changes to being very angry, depressed or perhaps drunk or drugged the next. Perhaps, in this respect, you never know who you are going to meet when you come home each day from school. Look at all the different faces here. In terms of your parent, which are the ones you know the best? Which do you like the most and dislike the most?

MY DIFFERENT MUMS/DADS

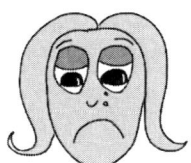 

Mum/Dad being sad

Mum/Dad being happy

Mum/Dad being kind

Mum/Dad being cruel

Mum/Dad being drunk

Mum/Dad on drugs

Mum/Dad being sober

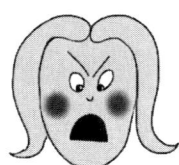 

Mum/Dad being angry

Mum/Dad being worried

Mum/Dad being fun

Mum/Dad not playful

Mum/Dad listening

Mum/Dad not listening

SEPARATION AND DIVORCE

■ Objective

So many children are affected by separation and divorce. Figures from the Office for National Statistics show that 42 per cent of marriages end in divorce (ONS, 2011). The above example is the ideal scenario for a child being able to talk to a trusted adult, in this case a teacher. But so many children of divorced or separated parents struggle with their feelings all on their own. This is borne out by the statistic from Professor Lynne Murray or the University of Reading, whose research showed that 75 per cent of children who are securely attached become insecure attached with parents separating or divorcing (Murray, 2007). Insecure attachment is highly associated with problems in relational, mental and physical health. So this exercise is designed to support the child to talk about the impact on them of parental separation and divorce and, in so doing, receive the comfort, emotional regulation and help to grieve that will prevent any shift into insecure attachment and help restore quality of life.

■ Instructions for the child or teenager

When parents separate it can be very painful for the children involved. Emotionally intelligent children and teenagers find an adult who they really trust to talk about what they feel. They know, intuitively or factually, that if they don't, their bottled-up feelings can turn into emotional baggage, which they can carry for years. Some children and teenagers find it hard to ask for help, particularly if in their past they have reached out to an adult but the adult hasn't helped. They might not remember this happening because such failed or misattuned responses may have occurred in babyhood.

Look at this list of feelings. These are painful feelings many children and teenagers who have experienced parental separation and divorce have said they feel. The statements in italics under the feelings are what children and teenagers have said. Have you ever felt any of these feelings too? (It doesn't matter if you have experienced these feelings but in a different way to the statements.) Tick the feelings you have had about your parents separating or divorcing. Then grade them from 1 to 10, with 1 a manageable feeling and 10 a very painful one. Now look back at the feelings you ticked. Which of them stand out for you? What do you think you need to make this feeling hurt less?

MY FEELINGS	TICK IF YOU FEEL THIS	THE PAIN LEVEL 1 = OK 10 = HORRID
Misunderstood 'No one understands what I'm going through.'		
Torn in two/stuck in the middle 'I feel torn in two between my two parents/split loyalties/'the go-between'/messenger from one parent to the other. I hate it.'		
Shocked 'I had no idea that they were going to split up. My world is falling apart.'		
In pain because they are in pain 'I hate watching Mum cry. It breaks my heart.'		
Guilt 'It's my fault they split up.' 'I feel so guilty choosing to live with Mum not Dad.'		
Feeling not good enough 'I am not good enough for Dad/Mum to want to stay living with us.'		
Not cared for 'My parents don't help me with my feelings because they're having too many of their own.' 'I'm looking after Mum/Dad, not them looking after me. It's not right.'		
Fear 'Nothing feels safe anymore.' 'What will happen to me now?'		
Let down 'I hate my Dad for all his failed promises.' 'Mum said she would keep in touch lots – that's a laugh. I don't think I can ever forgive her – birthdays, that's about it.'		
Betrayal 'The family photos in our album are a lie.'		
Desperate to get them back together 'I was trying to keep them together and now they've split up I'm trying to get them back together.'		

MY FEELINGS	TICK IF YOU FEEL THIS	THE PAIN LEVEL 1 = OK 10 = HORRID
Angry/resentful 'I'm just sick of all the fighting.' 'No one consulted me.' 'I get so angry at school. I think it's the divorce thing.'		
Powerless 'I can mend my bike and stuff but I can't seem to fix this in any way.'		
Relief 'At least there won't by all that arguing/all those bad moods in the house now.'		
Hate 'I hate it when Mum/Dad cries/gets cross.' 'I hate people in my step-family.' 'I hate my parent for kicking out my other parent.'		
Cut off 'I don't care about the divorce thing. It's their decision.'		
Worry 'I worry so much about them being on their own now.' 'I worry about Mum when I visit Dad and I worry about Dad when I visit Mum.'		
Mistrust 'Who can I trust now? It's like I am just waiting for another awful shock of some sort.'		
Not belonging 'Where do I belong now?" I don't feel I have anything in common with my step-brothers or step-mother.'		
Heartbroken 'I feel heartbroken by the parent who left me.' Hurting so much because of all the losses 'I have lost my friends, lots of lovely family rituals, lost the family home as I knew it, stuff we used to do together, its horrid.'		
Confused 'If Dad says he loves us why has he left us too?' 'Dad left. I love and hate him. It's confusing.'		

Development: Parents splitting up – 'Letting the sad out'

■ Objective

One of the key reasons why 75 per cent of securely attached children become insecurely attached after parents separate or divorce (Murray, 2007) is because of unmourned losses. There are so many losses involved when parents separate or divorce. It's a mistake to think it's just the main loss of the parent who has left. Due to the so many losses (see table below), there is often a sense for professionals helping these children of 'where do you start?' But we do need to start. As we know, the transition from unmourned loss to violence (self-abuse or abusing others) has a firm brain biochemical reality (see Panksepp, 1998 and Panksepp and Biven, 2012). In addition there is a mass of scientific evidence showing how unmourned loss is one of the main causes, if not the main underlying cause, of clinical depression and anxiety disorders (see meta-analysis, Panksepp and Watt, 2011).

■ Instructions for the child or teenager

Look at the table of losses below. The statements in italics under the feelings are what actual children and teenagers have said about these looses. Have you ever felt any of these feelings too? (It doesn't matter if you feel the feelings but in a different way to the statements.) Tick the losses you have experienced as a result of your parents separating or divorcing. Then put a number to indicate the hurt level by each of the ones you have ticked, 10 being a very painful loss and 1 a more manageable loss. In the three empty spaces draw or write any other losses that have not been mentioned here.

MY LOSSES BECAUSE MY PARENTS SPLIT UP	TICK IF YOU FEEL THIS	THE PAIN LEVEL 1 = OK 10 = HORRID
Heartbroken by the parent who's left 'I will never be happy again.'		
Lost my feelings of safety/security in the world 'I don't feel at home anymore now.'		
No more happy families 'I can't just smile and pretend.'		
Far less money now 'Since Dad left there's no money for my football coaching. It was what I loved.'		
Lost my sense of trust 'If they can stop loving each other surely they can stop loving me.'		
Lost my sense of identity 'I'm not sure who I am anymore.' 'Who am I in this family now?'		
Missing one parent when I'm with the other one 'When I'm with Dad I miss Mum. When I'm with Mum I miss Dad.'		
Lost everything good in my life 'What's the point in Christmas and holidays and stuff, when everything's ruined since they split?'		
Lost having that parent on hand 'Who's going to play football with me now Dad's gone?' 'I always used to talk to Mum about those things. It's not the same on the phone…'		
Lost my Mum/Dad to their new partner 'Whenever I go round there I feel like a gooseberry, it's all about her new boyfriend now.'		
Loss of my independence 'It should be me thinking of moving out in a few years, not Dad/Mum.'		

MY LOSSES BECAUSE MY PARENTS SPLIT UP	TICK IF YOU FEEL THIS	THE PAIN LEVEL 1 = OK 10 = HORRID
Lost my parent all over again when they got their new partner 'Just when things were getting back to normal Mum moves her boyfriend in and I'm out in the cold again.'		
Lost what we used to do as a family 'Since they spilt up everything's changed, we don't do weekends or birthdays or going camping together like we used to.'		
Lost the home as it was 'When Dad moved out he took the sofas and now we have to sit on fold-up chairs.'		
Write another of your losses here		
Write another of your losses here		
Write another of your losses here		

PARENTS FIGHTING

■ Objective

Watching bad fights between parents, particularly where someone gets hurt and when the child is too little to intervene, can feel to the child or teenager like being plunged into a nightmare. The research shows that the majority of children felt they have little choice but to endure the violence.

'Sometimes I just go and run and hide in the toilet it's so frightening.'
(Darren, aged six)

First and foremost, these children need to be empathised with as a way of re-establishing compassionate human connectedness and a sense that they are not alone in the world.

These are common feelings that need empathy:
*   The feeling of being stuck in the middle of two warring parents and desperate for it to stop.
*   The feeling that the very person who is supposed to protect you can't, because he or she can't protect himself/herself.
*   The feeling that the parent you love is not protecting you from seeing/hearing this nightmare.
*   The pain and confusion of loving someone who hurts someone else that you love so much.
*   The feeling that there was no one to stop the bad things from happening.
*   The pain of seeing your beloved parent damaged or broken in some way.
*   The feeling of not being able to get your parent's screams and cries out of your head.

■ Instructions for the child or teenager

If you have seen your parents argue or fight in bad ways, what did it feel like? In the picture you will see some of the feelings that it made other children and teenagers feel. If you have felt one or more of these things too, colour it in, tick it or put a circle round it. If you have felt something that is not in the picture, write or draw what it is in the empty boxes.

PARENTS FIGHTING

Like a nightmare got
stuck in my brain

It breaks my heart

Hating that I'm too
small to make it stop

My world ended
that day

I could cry forever

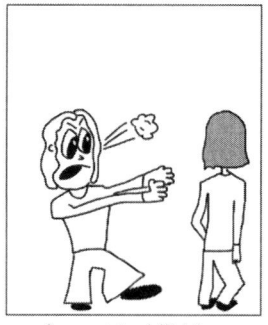

I want to kill him

I get terrified

I want to scream at them
to make them stop

Want to say-"can't you see
what this is doing to me"

Shock

Maybe it's my fault
they fight

Too scared to tell in
case I'm taken away

The muddle of loving
and hating him

Angry with Mum for
staying with him

■ Development: Carrying someone else's emotional baggage

Discuss and role-play through puppets, healthy ways of being angry. Show the child or teenager the power of negotiation, compromise, resolution and empathy for the other person's point of view.

■ Objective

This exercise is suitable for older children and teenagers due to its sophisticated concepts in dealing with intergenerational transfer. It is about helping the child or teenager to understand intergenerational transmission of misery. It is hoped that from this they will develop more compassion for and understanding of their emotionally troubled parent, thereby affording them the relief of having a coherent narrative for what is happening to them. In other words, it may help them see that their parent may not have been parented well when they were a child, in ways that would have helped them to thrive and be well. Older children and teenagers can be helped to know that when their parent is angry or cruel, it is not because of them, but something that lives on within the parent from their own childhood.

If a parent has suffered loss or trauma and doesn't go and get professional help such as therapy or counselling, their children can be deeply affected. Despite their very best efforts and intentions, the parent can pass on aspects of their own misery to their children. This can happen from generation to generation. Children and teenagers may be helped to understand that it only takes one person to break the cycle, by getting some form of counselling or therapy through which their pain can be addressed and successfully modified.

■ Instructions for the child or teenager

First, fill the suitcase entitled 'Your parents' emotional baggage'. Fill it by writing in the suitcase your parent's problems – for example, depression, worry, drinks too much – and also the painful life experiences that you know they have suffered – for example, 'Dad's father left when he was four', 'Mum lost her first baby', 'Dad was badly bullied as a child by his older brothers', 'Mum has a hang-up about germs'. It is fine to put both parents in the one suitcase!

Then look at what you have written. Consider which aspects of your parents' emotional baggage you've also ended up carrying in your own life in some way (meaning that you have been deeply affected by it). Write what these are on the suitcase entitled 'Your emotional baggage'. Look at what you have drawn. Now turn to the figure who has broken free from the suitcase and is flying high. Write on the kite the aspects of you that have not been blighted by your parents' emotional baggage – for example, your ability to take risks, your sense of calm, your courage, your generosity. Congratulate yourself on this. Finally, think how you could put down the emotional baggage you are carrying because of your parents' baggage.

■ Development

Discuss with the child or teenager the adults they know or have known in their life who seem pretty baggage-free. Ask the child or teenager how these adults have positively influenced their lives. If the child or teenager has a lot of interest in this, it's lovely to do a little celebration ceremony using candles, lighting a candle for each adult who has been important in their life.

CARRYING SOMEONE ELSE'S EMOTIONAL BAGGAGE

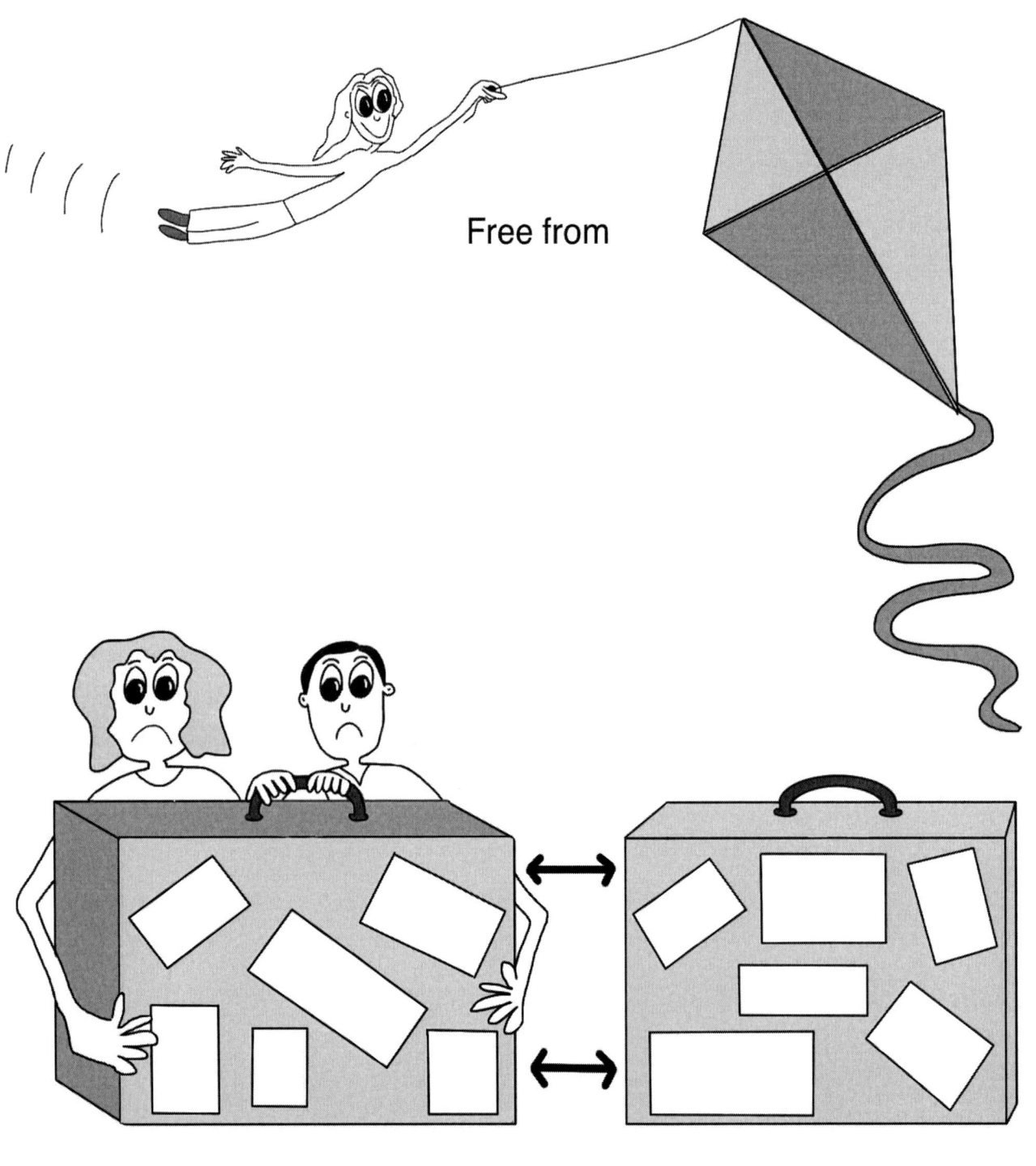

Free from

Your parents' emotional baggage

Your emotional baggage

LOVING SOMEONE WHO ISN'T GOOD AT LOVING BACK

Then come to me. I will give you a cold, cold kiss.
My roses are dead. My lips are grey. My eyes
Have neither iris nor pupil. They died, and now all is white;
White in a face of stone. Sister, cold lover, come.
(John Alexander Chapman, b. 1875, 'Gipsy Queen')

When they speak about their relationship, one wonders at their blindness. [Their parent] is incapable of reciprocating or loving, or [parenting them] in the way they desire. They had been pursuing an alluring but rejecting other, an exciting yet frustrating other. [The parent] has awakened an intensity of yearning, but is essentially the elusive object of desire, seemingly there but just out of reach. (Armstrong-Perlman, 1991)

■ Objective

This exercise is designed for older children and teenagers who are aware that their parent cannot love them or parent them well. Research carried out in 2011 by The London School of Hygiene & Tropical Medicine, entitled *Juggling Harms – Coping with Parental Substance Misuse*, found that while almost all of the young people expressed an enduring love for their parents, their accounts also revealed that over time many of them had actively withdrawn this love and care in an attempt to deal with, and protect themselves from, what felt like their parent's lack of care. However, withdrawing love was usually a short-term strategy and not one that could be maintained over time (Houmoller *et al*, 2011). Here is an example:

'The best thing in an ideal world would be to turn away from her and say, "You're causing me too much hassle, too much pressure, too much hurt. I don't want anything to do with you". But at the end of the day, I only have one Mum and even if I don't like her very much, I have to love her. I have to numb my feelings over it, 'cause I know she's drinking now ... I mean, I wouldn't be surprised if she's smoking now. But I just have to say, "Good morning" to her, "Have you eaten? Do you want me to make you a cup of tea?"' (Houmoller *et al*, 2011)

When children and teenagers love a parent who, because of their own childhood, isn't good at loving, they often try so hard to awaken the love in the parent by all manner of self-sacrifice, over-generous acts, compliance and over-tolerance. Sadly, this process often results in them putting their own development on hold. So, this exercise is designed to support children and teenagers to not take personally their parent's inability to love them in the way they want to be loved. It will help them to stand back and hopefully stop them yearning for what may never be and turn towards those who can respond to them in the way they need.

This exercise is not appropriate for children or teenagers who are not aware that their parent isn't good at loving and/or who cannot tolerate anything negative said about their Mum/Dad. Their defences must be respected. Rather this exercise is designed for children and teenagers who want to make sense of what they know is the sad reality that they are not being parented well.

■ Instructions

On the table laid out with a feast, colour in all the things that you wish your parent would give you in your relationship. Now turn to the table below it. On this table, draw or write what your parent is actually giving you. What does it feel like when you look at both drawings? How might you stop yourself from yearning for what may never be, because of how your parent was parented in their childhood. Think of the saying, 'When you are facing the gates of hell, you have got your back to the gates of heaven.' Perhaps there are adults in your life who are good at loving and/or who can give you some of the things you have drawn on the feast table. If you feel you don't know any grown-ups like this, keep looking for them. As with Monica in the story *Monica Plum's Horrid Problem*, if you keep looking for them, you will very likely find adults like this at some time in your life. It is such a clever and mature thing to know what you are not getting and what you need from parent figures.

■ Development

Life story work would be excellent here so that the child or teenager sees the parent within the overall context of what has happened in their family generationally and inter-generationally. This will help the child or teenager to think about their parent's own childhood and so stop any confusion between fears of their own unloveability and their parent's incapacity to love. The best book is Richard Rose's *Life Story Therapy with Traumatized Children: A Model for Practice*.

LOVING SOMEONE WHO ISN'T GOOD AT LOVING

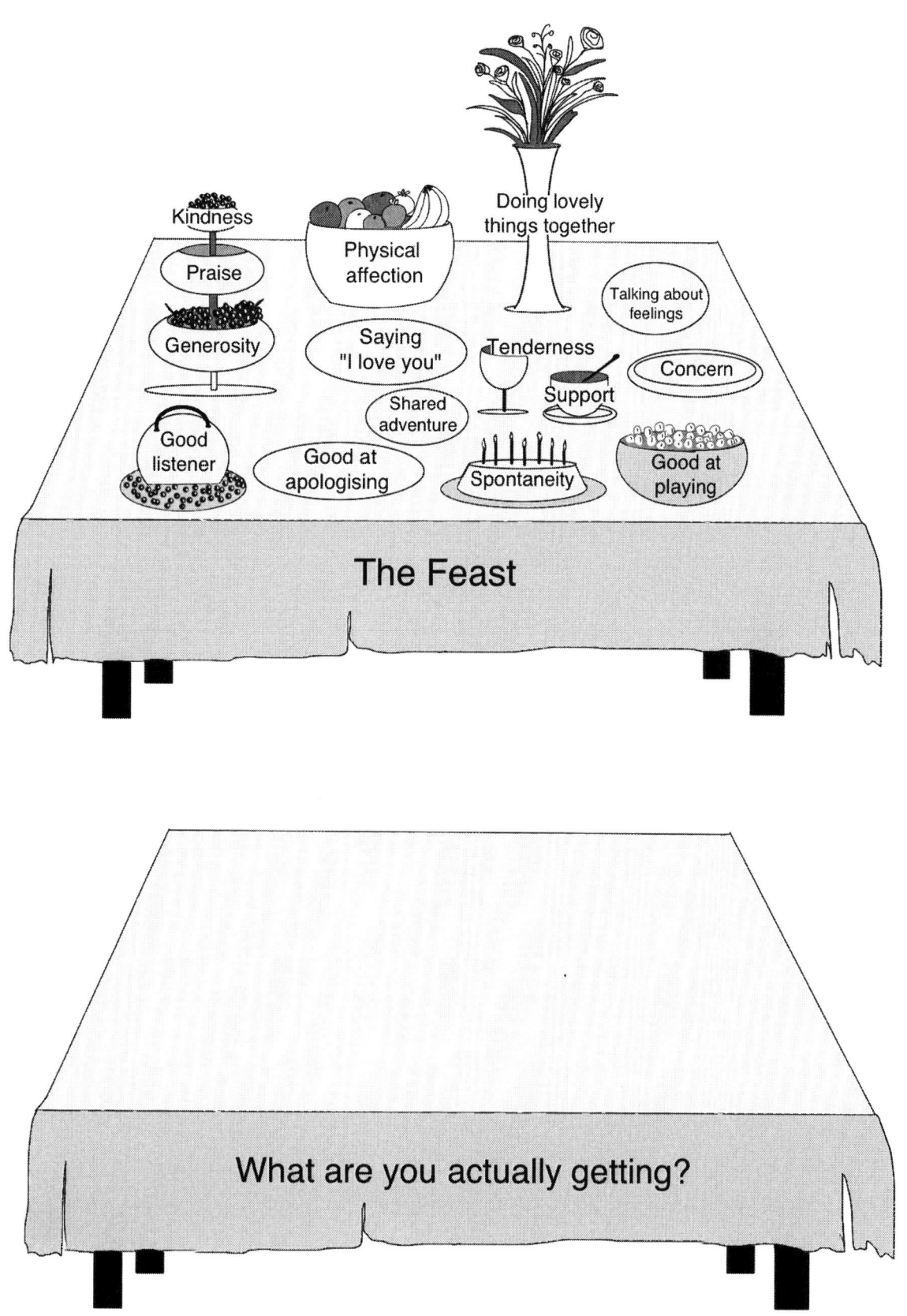

FACILITATING A HEALING CONVERSATION BETWEEN PARENT AND CHILD/TEENAGER

■ Objective

Parents and young people often struggle to communicate effectively with each other about what is happening at home and about the parent's troubles – for example, substance misuse, depression, unmourned grief, anxiety disorders. Research shows that many parents postpone disclosure about their addiction or alcohol problem even in the face of their children communicating to them that they know. Similarly, an NCH Action for Children report (1994) found that less than one fifth of mothers had talked to their children about the domestic violence they had suffered, even though the children had often heard what was happening. As one child said, 'I felt sort of pushed out until she really sat down and told me and then I sort of understood' (NCH Action for Children, 1994).

So this exercise acknowledges the need to support troubled parents and children and teenagers to talk to each other about what is going on at home. This is known as 'facilitated conversation'. It means that a practitioner is present with the two people to ensure that the conversation is therapeutic rather than destructive. Sometimes the practitioner will offer structured exercises with rules (as we shall see here) to keep things very safe, rather than just let the conversation between the child and parent take its own course.

Such facilitated conversation can:
• improve the quality of the parent–child relationship
• open channels of emotional communication between parent and child
• support the child to have a voice with the parent
• empower the parent and child with a wider range of relational options
• enable the child to feel heard by the parent
• enable there to be less stress in the family home due to all the secrets and bottled-up resentments.

The exercise can be particularly helpful if you are working with a child or teenager who is coping with a parent's raw feelings of depression, anxiety or anger and who has never really sat down with their parent to talk about the impact of all this on them.

Before you start the exercise

Not all troubled parents are able to offer their child or teenager a good experience in a facilitated conversation. So before offering this intervention to the parent and child always ask yourself the following questions:

(a) Will the parent be able to follow your instruction for rule-bound conversations? Will they be able to listen to the child when you ask and be able to reflect back what they have heard in a non-judgemental way?

(b) Does the parent have enough space in their mind to consider their children's needs as well as their own?

(c) Is the parent capable of saying sorry or might they blame the child for what is wrong or believe the child's behaviour is a major cause of their own problems?

(d) Is the parent able to reflect on how their own childhood may be impacting on their life now? Or does he or she think that it's just bad luck, or that other people are to blame for their own life's difficulties and so it's nothing to do with him or her?

If the answer is yes to all of the above, you need to speak to the parent before the session, to ensure they know what is expected of them in the therapeutic conversation time, and to establish the necessary boundaries.

There are a lot of unfinished sentences here. Before you see the parent and child for the facilitated conversation, select the ones you feel will be most helpful for the child or teenager. You will see that there are unfinished sentences to do with positive feelings interspersed with the more painful ones. This is deliberate to try to guard against the parent getting defensive and feeling attacked.

■ Instructions

What to say to the parent and child:

'I'm going to give you (the child/teenager) some unfinished sentences to finish. You can speak your answer, or do a quick drawing for your answer, or a combination of both. If you don't want to finish one of the sentences you can just say "pass". Mum/Dad, I will just ask you to listen to what [child/teenager] is saying. At the end of her/his time, I will give you some unfinished sentences to help you to respond to what your child has said.'

Sentences for the child or teenager to finish:

- When you get sad I feel…
- When you get angry I feel…

- When you get scared/anxious I feel…
- I like it when you…
- I love it when together we…
- I feel worried when you…
- I feel frightened when you…
- I am frightened of you when you…
- I am worried that what will happen is….
- I feel angry when you…
- I feel sad when you …
- My heart breaks when you….
- I don't like it when you…
- I feel so good about myself when you…
- I wish together we could…
- I want you to know that…
- It feels like you don't understand that…
- I hate it when you …
- I feel good when you…
- I feel like rubbish when you…
- I feel sad that we never seem to do … anymore.
- One of my best times with you was… [Good to finish on a positive note.]

(Don't reverse this by asking the parent to finish the sentences. This is because the child or teenager could feel further burdened by parental feelings.)

Parent's chance to respond

(Again select the unfinished sentences that you feel will be most helpful and leave out the other ones.) Only do the next part of this exercise if you know the parent will be appropriate in their answers, provide the child with a good experience over all, and not burden the child with their own worries, anxieties or a barrage of unspoken resentments, anger, lectures on behaviour, and so on.

'Mum/Dad, please finish these sentences in response to what you have heard your child say.'
- I was surprised when you said…
- I didn't know that you felt…
- I was sorry to hear that…
- I feel hurt that…
- Thank you for letting me know that…
- I am delighted to hear that you…

- I agree with you when you said that…
- I am really thinking about what you said about…

■ Mending relationships

In the session, you can also ask both parent and child to do a drawing or sandplay (for an explanation of sandplay see the introduction to Part Two) of their best times and worst times together. They should work separately and in silence. After completion, the parent will listen to the child first and the practitioner will reflect back to the parent what the child has said. This is then reversed, with the child listening to the parent.

The three wishes exercise can be really helpful too. This can be done in words or in painting or sandplay.
The child shares their wishes first. The parent then shares their wishes. With your help they can talk about it afterwards. If they need the response sentences, above, to make it safer, use them again.
- If I had three wishes for you they would be…
- If I had three wishes for me they would be…
- If I had three wishes for us they would be…
- The mess that we sometimes get into feels like this… [Do a sandplay or drawing.]

Example

Here is an example of nine-year-old Billy's best and worst times with his Mum. This was in a facilitated conversation with his parent:

Best times with you

Playing. Shopping. Just you and me, listening when I am sad.
Making a cake together. When we laugh about something. When we go to the coffee shop in the park and talk about stuff. When you tickle me.

Worst times with you

When you are so sad. When you are with my brother and not me.
When you just stare into space and don't play with me.
When you just to do the cleaning and don't play with me. [Mum had obsessive compulsive disorder around germs.]

As a result of this, the practitioner supported Billy in asking his Mum for an hour's quality time each evening. She was very moved and agreed that she needed to do more playing and give up some of her obsession with cleaning.

■ Development

A very powerful form of facilitated conversation can happen when the parent and child no longer live with each other. Perhaps the child has gone into care or the parent has gone to prison or moved out due to the parents separating. Before a meeting between the parent and the child, the child can be asked to write down questions they want to ask the parent. If the parent agrees, they can be sent the questions, prior to meeting with the child, to give themselves time to think what they might say. In an ideal world they can be helped, with a practitioner present, to formulate their answers.

Below are two examples of how healing these facilitated prepared conversations can be:

Examples

Here are the questions that Milly (aged eight) wrote before a meeting with her Mum who left the family to live with a new man abroad:

- Mum, why do you not visit much?
- Mum, why did you not want to keep me?
- Mum, why did you choose your new boyfriend over me?
- Mum, why did your love for me die?
- If you say you loved me, why didn't you stay?

Mum could hear Milly's hurt and reassured her that her love for her daughter had not died but rather she thought about her every day and missed her so much. She reiterated once more that she did not leave Milly but could not live with her father anymore. She said she would visit far more often from now on. She did.

Kyle (aged nine), whose parent had taken drugs and so left for rehab but then never came back, formulated these questions prior to seeing his Dad:

- Dad, why did you love the drugs more than me?
- Dad, you said you loved me but not enough to give up the drugs so you could be my Dad again. Why didn't you try harder?
- Dad, why did you not come back to live with us when you said you would?

How Dad responded:

'Kyle, I am so sorry I let you down so badly. I do not love the drugs, I hate them but they had taken hold over my body.

I fell in love with someone at rehab and your Mum and I split up. Kyle, I will love you forever and I got well in rehab because I was determined to be a better father. What motivated me to get better more than anything was a picture of you on my bedroom wall.'

The conversation was deeply healing for Kyle. His Dad arranged to come and have far more special one-to-one times with his son and he kept to his word.

References

Abel, EL & Sokol, RJ (1986) 'Fetal alcohol syndrome is now leading cause of mental retardation', *The Lancet*, 2, p1222.

Acquarone S (2004) *Infant-Parent Psychotherapy: A Handbook*, Karnac Books, London.

Adamec RE (1994) 'Modelling anxiety disorders following chemical exposures', *Toxicology and Industrial Health*, 10 (4–5), pp391–420.

Adamec RE & Shallow T (1993) 'Lasting effects on rodent anxiety of a single exposure to a cat', *Physiology & Behaviour*, 54 (1), pp101–9.

ADASS & ADCS (Association of Directors of Adult Social Services & Association of Directors of Children's Services) (2009) 'Working together to support young carers: A model memorandum of understanding between statutory directors for children's services and adult social services', ADASS/ADCS, London.

Advisory Council on the Misuse of Drugs (2003) *Hidden Harm: Responding to the Needs of Children of Problem Drug Users*, Home Office, London.

Alyahri A & Goodman R (2008) 'Harsh corporal punishment of Yemeni children: occurrence, type and associations', *Child Abuse Negl*, 32 (8), pp766–73.

Anda RF, Felitti VJ, Bremner JD, Walker JD, Whitfield C, Perry BD, Dube SR & Giles WH (2006) 'The enduring effects of abuse and related adverse experiences in childhood. A convergence of evidence from neurobiology and epidemiology', *European Archives of Psychiatry and Clinical Neuroscience*, 256 (3), pp174–86.

Andersen, SL & Teicher, MH (2004) 'Delayed effects of early stress on hippocampal development', *Neuropsychopharmacology*, 29 (11), pp1988–93.

Armstrong-Perlman EM (1991) 'The Allure of the Bad Object', *Free Associations*, 2 (3), pp343–56.

Armstrong-Perlman EM (1995) 'Psychosis: The sacrifice that fails?', Ellwood J (ed) *Psychosis: Understanding and Treatment*, London, Jessica Kingsley, pp93–102.

Ashman SB, Dawson G, Panagiotides H, Yamada E & Wilkinson CW (2002) 'Stress hormone levels of children of depressed mothers', *Development and Psychopathology,* 14 (2), pp333–49.

Ateah CA, Secco ML & Woodgate RL (2003) 'The risks and alternatives to physical punishment use with children', *Journal of Pediatric Health Care,* 17 (3), pp126–32.

Autti-Ramo I (2002) 'Fetal alcohol syndrome – a multifaceted condition'.,*Developmental Medicine and Child Neurology*, 44, pp141–4.

Bada H, Bann CM, Whitaker TM, Bauer CR, Shankaran S, Lagasse L, Lester BM, Hammond J & Higgins R (2012) 'Protective factors can mitigate behavior problems after prenatal cocaine and other drug exposures', *Pediatrics*, 130 (6), pp1479–88.

Bancroft A, Wilson S, Cunningham-Burley S, Backett-Milburn K & Masters H (2004) *Parental Drug and Alcohol Misuse: Resilience and Transition Among Young People*, Joseph Rowntree Foundation, York.

Barnard M (2007) *Drug Addiction and Families,* Jessica Kingsley Publishers, London.

Barnardo's (2006) 'Hidden lives, unidentified young carers in the UK', online, http://www.barnardos.org.uk/hidden_lives_young_carer_report.pdf (accessed February 2013).

Barter C, McCarry M, Berridge D & Evans K (2009) 'Partner exploitation and violence in teenage intimate relationships', online, https://www.nspcc.org.uk/inform/research/findings/partner_exploitation_and _violence_summary_wdf68093.pdf (accessed February 2013).

Baumrind D (1975) 'The contributions of the family to the development of competence in children', *Schizophrenia Bulletin,* 14, pp12–37.

Beatson J & Taryan S (2003) 'Predispositions to depression: The role of attachment', *Australian and New Zealand Journal of Psychiatry*, 37 (2), pp219–25.

Becker S (2000) *Young Carers: The Blackwell Encyclopedia of Social Work*, M. Davies (ed.) p378, Oxford, Blackwell.

Belsky J & Pensky E (1988) 'Marital change across the transition to parenthood', *Marriage and Family Review*, 12, pp133–56.

Belsky J, Spanier G & Rovine M (1983) 'Stability and change in marriage across the transition to parenthood', *Journal of Marriage and Family,* 45 (3), pp567–77.

Benson H (2010) 'Married and unmarried family breakdown: Key statistics explained', Bristol Community Family Trust, online, http://www.bcft.co.uk/2010%20Family%20policy,%20breakdown%20and%20structure.pdf (accessed February 2013).

Bergman K, Sarkar P, O'Connor TG, Modi N & Glover V (2007) 'Maternal stress during pregnancy predicts cognitive ability and fearfulness in infancy', *Journal of the American Academy of Child and Adolescent Psychiatry*, 46 (11), pp1454–63.

Berne E (1979) *What Do You Say After You Say Hello?*, Bantam, New York.

Bollas C (1987) *The Shadow of the Object: Psychoanalysis of the Unthought Known*, Free Association Books, London.

Bookstein FL, Connor PD, Covell KD, Barr HM, Gleason CA, Sze RW, McBroom JA & Streissguth AP (2005) 'Preliminary evidence that prenatal alcohol damage may be visible in averaged ultrasound images of the neonatal human corpus callosum', *Alcohol*, 36 (3) pp151–60.

Booth, P & Jerberg (2010) *Theraplay: Helping Parents and Children Build Better Relationships Through Attachment-Based Play*, John Wiley and Sons, New York.

Bowlby J (1978) *Attachment and Loss: Volume 3 – Loss, Sadness and Depression*, Penguin, Harmondsworth.

Brandon M & Lewis A (1996) 'Significant harm and children's experiences of domestic violence', *Child and Family Social Work,* 1 (1), pp33–42.

Brookman F & Maguire M (2003) *Reducing Homicide: A Review of the Possibilities*, Home Office, London.

Brown DW, Anda RF, Tiemeier H, Felitti VJ, Edwards VJ, Croft JB & Giles WH (2009) 'Adverse childhood experiences and the risk of premature mortality', *American Journal of Preventive Medicine*, 37 (5), pp389–96.

Bruce ML & Kim KM(1992) 'Differences in the effects of divorce on major depression in men and women', *American Journal of Psychiatry*, 149 (7), pp914–17.

Budinger CM, Drazdowski TK & Ginsburg GG (2013) 'Anxiety-promoting parenting behaviors: A comparison of anxious parents with and without social anxiety disorder', *Child Psychiatry & Human Development*, 44 (3), pp412–18.

Bugental D, Gabriela A, Martorella & Barrazaa, V (2003) 'The hormonal costs of subtle forms of infant maltreatment', *Hormones and Behavior*, pp237–44.

Butler I & Williamson H (1994) *Children Speak: Children, Trauma and Social Work*, Longman, Harlow.

Cabinet Office (2004) *Alcohol Harm Reduction Strategy for England*, Prime Minister's Strategy Unit, London, online, http://webarchive.nationalarchives.gov.uk/+/http://www.cabinetoffice.gov.uk/strategy/news/press_releases/2004/040315.aspxm (accessed February 2013).

Caldji C, Diorio J & Meaney MJ (2003) 'Variations in maternal care alter GABAA receptor subunit expression in brain regions associated with fear', *Neuropsychopharmacology*, 28, pp1950–9.

Cardinal M (1993) *The Words to Say It: An Autobiographical Novel*, Goodheart P (tr), Women's Press, London.

Carper J (2000) *Your Miracle Brain*, Harper Collins, New York.

Cawson P (2002) *Child Maltreatment in the Family: The Experience of a National Sample of Young People*, NSPCC, London, pp37–8.

Centre for Social Justice (2007) *Breakthrough Britain*, Centre for Social Justice, London.

Centre for Social Justice (2008) 'Couldn't care less: A policy report from the children in care working group', online, http://www.centreforsocialjustice.org.uk/UserStorage/pdf/Pdf%20reports/Couldn%27tCareLess.pdf (accessed February 2013).

Centre for Social Justice (2011) 'Mental health: poverty, ethnicity, and family breakdown: Interim Policy Briefing', Centre for Social Justice, London.

Centre for Social Justice (2013) 'Fractured families – Why Stability Matters', Centre for Social Justice, London.

Charney DS, Woods SW, Nagy LM, Southwick SM, Krystal JH & Heninger GR (1990) 'Noradrenergic function in panic disorder'. *Journal of Clinical Psychiatry,* 51 (Suppl A), 5–11.

ChildLine (2008) 'Children talking to ChildLine about family relationship problems', online, https://www.nspcc.org.uk/Inform/publications/casenotes/clcasenotesfamilyrelationships_wdf59010.pdf (accessed February 2013).

ChildLine casenotes, online, www.nspcc.org (accessed February 2013).

Christ G, Siegel K & Christ A (2002) 'Adolescent Grief "It never really hit me… until it actually happened"', *The Journal of the American Medical Association*, 288, Nov 10.

Clayton L (1997) *Coping with a Drug Abusing Parent*, Hazelden, Center City, Minnesota.

Cleaver H, Nicholson D, Tarr S & Cleaver D (2007*) Child Protection, Domestic Violence and Parental Substance Misuse: Family Experiences and Effective Practice*, Jessica Kingsley Publishers, London.

Cleaver H, Unell I & Aldgate J (2011) C*hildren's Needs – Parenting Capacity,* HMSO, London.

Cline F & Facy J (1990) *Parenting with Love and Logic*, Pinon Press, Colorado Springs.

Cline F & Fay J (2006) *Parenting Teens with Love and Logic,* NavPress, Colorado Springs.

Cole PM, Teti LO & Zahn-Waxler C (2003) 'Mutual emotion regulation and the stability of conduct problems between preschool and early school age', *Development and Psychopathology,* 15 (1), pp1–18.

Cooper P, Murray L, Wilson A & Romaniuk H (2003) 'Controlled trial of short- and long-term effect of psychological treatment of post-partum depression. 2. Impact on mother–child relationship and child outcome', *British Journal of Psychiatry*, 182, pp412–9.

Cowan PA & Cowan CP (1988) 'Changes in marriage during the transition to parenthood: Must we blame the baby?', Michaels GY & Goldberg WA, *The Transition to Parenthood: Current Theory and Research,* Cambridge University Press, New York.

Cowan PA & Cowan CP (1995) 'Interventions to ease the transition to parenthood: Why they are needed and what they can do', *Family Relations*, 44 (4), p412.

Cozolino LJ (2006) *The Neuroscience of Human Relationships, Attachment and the Developing Social Brain*, W.W. Norton & Company, London.

Damasio AR (2000) *The Feeling of What Happens*, Heinemann, London.

Davis RN, Davis MM, Freed GL & Clark SJ (2011) 'Fathers' depression related to positive and negative parenting behaviors with 1-year-old children', *Pediatrics*, 127 (4), pp612–18

Dawson G, Ashman SB & Carver LJ (2000) 'The role of early experience in shaping behavioural and brain development and its implications for social policy', *Development and Psychopathology,* 12 (4), 695–712.

Dawson G, Klinger LG, Panagiotides H, Hill D & Spieker S (1992) 'Frontal lobe activity and affective behavior of infants of mothers with depressive symptoms', *Child Development*, 63 (3), pp725–37.

Dearden C & Becker S (2000) *Growing Up Caring: Vulnerability and Transition to Adulthood – Young Carers' Experiences*, Youth Work Press for the Joseph Rowntree Foundation, Leicester.

Debiec J (2005) 'Peptides of love and fear: vasopressin and oxytocin modulate the integration of information in the amygdala', *Bioessays,* 27 (9), pp869–73.

Denham SA, Workman E, Cole PM, Weissbrod C, Kendziora KT & Zahn-Waxler C (2000) 'Prediction of externalizing behavior problems from early to middle childhood: The role of parental socialization and emotion expression', *Development and Psychopathology,* 12 (1), pp23–45.

Department for Education (2010) 'Children in Need' Census, online, www.data.gov.uk (accessed February 2013).

Department of Health (2005) 'Mental health of children and young people, 2004', NHS, London.

Dolan M, Deakin WJF, Roberts N & Anderson I (2002) 'Serotonergic and cognitive impairment in impulsive aggressive personality disordered offenders: are there implications for treatment?', *Psychological Medicine*, 32, pp105–17.

Dully H & Fleming C (2009) *Messing with My Head: The Shocking True Story of My Lobotomy*, Vermilion, London.

Ehlers A (1997) 'Anxiety disorders: Challenging negative thinking', Welcome Trust Review, London.

Eisenberger NI, Lieberma MD & Williams KD (2003) 'Does rejection hurt? An FMRI study of social exclusion', *Science,* 10, 302(5643), pp290–2.

Ely M, Richards M, Wadsworth J & Elliott J (1999) 'Secular Changes in the Association of Parental Divorce and Children's Educational Attainment – Evidence from three British Birth Cohorts', *Journal of Social Policy*, 28, 1999, pp437–45.

Faber A & Mazlish E (2013) *How to Talk so Kids will Listen and Listen so Kids will Talk*, Piccadilly Press Ltd, London.

Feder A, Coplan JD, Goetz RR, Mathew SJ, Pine DS, Dahl RE, Ryan ND, Greenwald S & Weissman MM (2004) 'Twenty-four-hour cortisol secretion patterns in prepubertal children with anxiety or depressive disorders', *Biological Psychiatry*, 56 (3), pp198–204.

Feijo L, Hernandez-Reif M, Field T, Burns W, Valley-Gray S & Simco E (2006) 'Mothers' depressed mood and anxiety levels are reduced after massaging their preterm infants', *Infant Behavior and Development,* 29 (3), pp476–80.

Felitti VJ, Anda R, Block R (2003) *Adverse Childhood Experiences Study.* Centers for Disease Control and Prevention, San Diego, online, http://www.cdc.gov/NCCDPHP/ACE/index.htm (accessed February 2012).

Field T (1994) 'The effects of mother's physical and emotional unavailability on emotion regulation, *Monographs of the Society for Research in Child Development*, 59 (2/3), pp208–27.

Field T & Hernandez-Reif M (2001) 'Sleep problems in infants decrease following massage therapy', *Early Child Development and Care*,168, pp95–104.

Field T, Diego M, Hernandez-Reif M, Deeds O & Figueiredo B (2009) 'Pregnancy massage reduces prematurity, low birthweight and postpartum depression', *Infant Behavior and Development,* 32 (4), pp454–60.

Field T, Diego M, Hernandez-Reif M, Salman F, Schanberg S, Kuhn C, Yando R & Bendell DJ (2002) 'Prenatal anger effects on the foetus and neonate', *Obstetrics and Gynaecology,* 22 (3), pp260–6.

Field T, Grizzle N, Scafidi F & Schanberg S (1996a) 'Massage and relaxation therapies' effects on depressed adolescent mothers', *Adolescence,* 31, pp903–11.

Field T, Hernandez-Reif M, Hart S, Theakston H, Schanberg S & Kuhn C (1999) 'Pregnant women benefit from massage therapy', *Journal of Psychosomatic Obstetrics and Gynecology*, 20 (1), pp31–8.

Field T, Henteleff T, Hernandez-Reif M, Martinez E, Mavunda K, Kuhn C & Schanberg S (1998) 'Children with asthma have improved pulmonary functions after massage therapy', Journal of Pediatrics,132, pp854-858.

Field T, Kilmer T, Hernandez-Reif M & Burman I (1996b) 'Preschool children's sleep and wake behavior: effects of massage therapy', *Early Child Development and Care*, 120, pp39–44.

Floyd RL, O'Connor MJ, Sokol RJ, Bertrand J & Cordero JF (2005) 'Recognition and Prevention of Fetal Alcohol Syndrome', *Obstetrics and Gynecology*, 106(5), pp1059–64.

Forehand R & Scarboro ME (1975) 'An analysis of children's oppositional behavior', *Journal of Abnormal Child Psychology*, 3(1), pp27–31.

Francis DD, Diorio J, Plotsky PM & Meaney MJ (2002) 'Environmental enrichment reverses the effects of maternal separation on stress reactivity', *Journal of Neuroscience*, 22 (18), 7480–3.

Frank J (2002) *Making it Work: Good practice with young carers and their families,* The Children's Society with The Princess Royal Trust for Carers, London.

Frank J & McLarnon J (2008) *Young Carers, Parents and their Families: Key Principles of Practice. Supportive practice guidance for those who work directly with, or commission services for, young carers and their families*, The Children's Society, London.

Freud S (1926) 'Inhibitions, symptoms and anxiety', Richards, A & Strachey J (eds), Strachey J (tr), *On Psychopathology, Inhibitions, Symptoms and Anxiety,* Vol. 10 of The Penguin Freud Library (1979), Penguin, Harmondsworth, pp237–333.

Freud S (1984) 'Mourning and Melancholia', *On Metapsychology: The Theory of Psychoanalysis*, Richards, A (ed), Strachey J (tr), Vol. 11 of The Pelican Freud Library, Penguin, London, pp245–69.

Freud S & Breuer J (1909) *Studies in Hysteria*, Penguin Modern Classics, New Edition (2004), Penguin, Harmondsworth.

George DT, Nutt DJ, Walker WV, Porges SW, Adinoff B & Linnoila M (1989) 'Lactate and hyperventilation substantially attenuate vagal tone in normal volunteers: A possible mechanism of panic provocation', *Archives of General Psychiatry,* 46 (2), pp153–6.

Ginsburg GS (2009) 'The child anxiety prevention study: Intervention model and primary outcomes', *Journal of Consulting and Clinical Psychology,* 77 (3), pp580–7.

Glover V, Bergman K, Sarkar P & O'Connor TG (2009) 'Association between maternal and amniotic fluid cortisol is moderated by maternal anxiety', *Psychoneuroendocrinology*, 34 (3), pp430–5.

Goodall J (1990) *Through a Window: Thirty Years with Chimpanzees of Gombe*, Weidenfeld and Nicolson, London.

Gordon NS, Burke S, Akil H, Watson SJ & Panksepp, J (2003) 'Socially-induced brain 'fertilisation': play promotes brain derived neurotrophic factor transcription in the amygdala and dorsolateral frontal cortex in juvenile rats', *Neursoscience Letters*, 341(1), pp17–20.

Gottman J & DeClaire J (1998) *Raising an Emotionally Intelligent* Child, Prentice Hall, New York.

Gottman J, Katz L & Hoover C (1996) 'Parental meta-emotion philosophy and the emotional life of families: Theoretical models and preliminary data', *Journal of Family Psychology,* 10 (3), pp243–68.

Graham-Bermann SA & Seng J (2005) 'Violence exposure and traumatic stress symptoms as additional predictors of health problems in high-risk children', *Journal of Pediatrics,* 146 (3), pp309–10.

Green L & Thachil A (2010) *Mental Health in Pregnancy*, The Royal College of Psychiatrists' Public Education Sub-committee, London.

Greenfield S (2000) *The Private Life of the Brain*, Wiley, London.

Grotstein J (2005) 'New views of patient-analyst mutual influence and their clinical implications', *How Psychodynamic Psychotherapies Change the Mind and Brain Conference,* Los Angeles, Lifespan Learning Institute.

Gunnar M, Nachmias M, Mangelsdorf S, Parritt RH & Buss K (1996) 'Behavioral inhibition and stress reactivity: the moderating role of attachment security', *Child Development*, 67(2), pp508–22.

Hagman RR (1932) 'A study of fears of children of preschool age', *Journal of Experimental Education*, 1, pp110–30.

Hall P (2008) *How to Have a Healthy Divorce: A Relate Guide*, Vermillion, London.

Halligan SL, Murray L, Martins C & Cooper PJ (2006) 'Maternal depression and psychiatric outcomes in adolescent offspring: A 13-year longitudinal study', *Journal of Affective Disorders*, 97 (1–3), pp145–54.

Ham J & Tronick E (2006) 'Infant resilience to the stress of the still-face: infant and maternal psychophysiology are related', *Annals of the New York Academy of Sciences*, 1094, pp297–302.

Hauser S, Allen J, Golden E (2008) *Out of the Woods*, Harvard University Press, Cambridge, MA.

Heckman J (2011) *The American Family in Black and White*, The American Academy of Arts and Sciences, Cambridge, MA.

Heegaard M (1993) *Children Can Cope With Grief From Drug and Alcohol Addiction*, Woodland Press, Chapmanville, WV (work book for using with children, from the 'When a family is in trouble' series of workbooks).

Hernandez-Reif M (2001) 'Sleep problems in infants decrease following massage therapy', *Early Child Development and Care*, 168, pp95–104.

Herrera E, Reissland N & Shepherd J (2004) 'Maternal touch and maternal child-directed speech: Effects of depressed mood in the postnatal period', *Journal of Affective Disorders,* 81 (1), pp29–39.

Hibbs ED, Zahn TP, Hamburger SD, Kruesi MM & Rapoport JL (1992) 'Parental expressed emotion and psycho physiological reactivity in disturbed and normal children', *British Journal of Psychiatry,* 160, pp504–10.

Hjerkinn B (2007) 'Substance Abuse in Pregnant Women, Experiences from a Special Child Welfare Clinic in Norway', *Biomedical Central: Public Health*, 322.

Hofmeyr GJ, Nikodem VC, Wolman W, Chalmers BE & Kramer T (1991) 'Companionship to modify the clinical birth environment: effects on progress and perceptions of labour and breastfeeding', *British Journal of Obstetrics and Gynaecology*, 98 (8), pp756–64 .

Holmes M (2000) *A Terrible Thing Happened*, American Psychological Association, Washington.

Home Office (1992) *British Crime Survey*, online, www.homeoffice.gov.uk (accessed February 2013).

Houmoller K, Bernhas S & Rhodes T (2011) *Juggling Harms – Coping with Parental Substance Misuse*, School of Hygiene & Tropical Medicine, London.

Howard LM, Trevillion K, Oram S & Feder G (2012) 'Experiences of domestic violence and mental disorders: a systematic review and meta-analysis' *PLoS One*, 7(12).

Howard S & Johnson B (2000) 'The resilient and non-resilient behaviour in adolescents', *Trends and Issues in Crime and Justice, Australian Institute of Criminology*, 183.

Howe D (2005) *Child Abuse and Neglect: Attachment, Development and Intervention*, Palgrave Macmillan, Basingstoke.

Hughes T (1985) From 'Sheep' (part III), *Collected Poems of Ted Hughes*, Faber and Faber, London (2005).

Humphreys C & Stanley N (eds) (2006) *Domestic Violence and Child Protection*, Jessica Kingsley Publishers, London.

Hunter M (2001) *Psychotherapy with Young People in Care – Lost and Found*, Brunner Routledge, Hove.

Jones N & Field T (1999) 'Right frontal EEG asymmetry is attenuated by massage and music therapy', *Adolescence*, 34 (135), pp529–34.

Joseph Rowntree Foundation (1998) *Divorce and Separation: The Outcomes for Children*, Joseph Rowntree Foundation, York.

Kelly L (1994) The interconnectedness of domestic violence and child abuse: challenges for research, policy and practice, *in Children Living with Domestic Violence* (eds A. Mullender and R Morley) Whiting and Birch Ltd, London, pp 43–56.

Kids Company (2011) online, www.kidsco.org.uk (accessed February 2013).

Kiernan K (1997) *The Legacy Of Parental Divorce: Social Economic And Family Experiences Of Childhood*, Joseph Rowntree Foundation, York.

Kitzinger S (2005) *Understanding Your Crying Baby*, Carroll and Brown Publishers, London.

Kohut H (1977) *The Restoration of the Self,* International Universities Press, New York.

Kohut H (1984) *How Does Analysis Cure?* University of Chicago Press, London/Chicago.

Kohut H & Wolf ES (1978) 'The disorders of the self and their treatment', *International Journal of Psycho-Analysis,* 59, pp413–24.

Koo JW, Park CH, Choi SH, Kim NJ, Kim HS, Choe JC & Suh YH (2003) 'The postnatal environment can counteract prenatal effects on cognitive ability, cell proliferation, and synaptic protein expression', *FASEB Journal,* 17 (11), pp1556–8.

Korhonen M, Luoma I, Salmelin R & Tamminen T (2012) 'A longitudinal study of maternal prenatal, postnatal and concurrent depressive symptoms and adolescent well-being', *Journal of Affective Disorders,* 136 (3), pp680–92.

Landry SH, McGrath SK & Kennel JH (1998) 'The effects of doula support during labor on mother-infant interaction at 2 months', *Pediatric Research*, 43, p13.

Levine P (2006) *Trauma Through a Child's Eyes*, North Atlantic Books, New York.

Li D, Liu L & Odouli R (2008) 'Presence of depressive symptoms during early pregnancy and the risk of preterm delivery: A prospective cohort study', *Human Reproduction*, 24 (1), pp146–53.

Lieberman A (1995) *The Emotional Life of a Toddler*, Simon and Schuster, New York.

Lieberman MD (2011) 'Why symbolic processing of affect can disrupt negative affect: Social cognitive and affective neuroscience investigations', Todorov A, Fiske ST & Prentice D (eds), *Social Neuroscience: Toward Understanding The Underpinnings Of The Social Mind*, Oxford University Press, Oxford, pp188–209.

Lieberman MD, Eisenberger NI, Crockett MJ, Tom SM, Pfeifer JH & Way BM (2007) 'Putting feelings into words. Affect labeling disrupts amygdala activity to affective stimuli', *Psychological Science*, 18, pp421–8.

London School of Economics and Centre for Economic Performances Mental Health Policy Group (2012) How Mental Health Loses out in the NHS, June, LSE and Centre for Economic Performance.

Lowenfeld M (1991) *Play in Childhood*, MacKeith Press, London.

Lunn P, Fahey T & Hannan C (2006) *Family Figures: Family Dynamics and Family Types in Ireland, 1986–2006*, Economic and Social Research Institute, Dublin.

Lyons-Ruth K (1996) 'Attachment relationships among children with aggressive behaviour problems: The role of disorganised early attachment patterns', *Journal of Consulting and Clinical Psychology,* 64 (1), pp64–73.

Mahler M (1968) *On Human Symbiosis and the Vicissitudes of Individuation*, International Universities Press, New York.

Malphurs J, Raag T, Field T, Pickens J & Pelaez-Nogueras M (1996) 'Touch by intrusive and withdrawn mothers with depressive symptoms', *Early Development and Parenting*, 5, pp111–15.

Martikainen P & Valkonen T (1996) 'Mortality after the death of a spouse:

Rates and causes of death in a large Finnish cohort', *American Journal of Public Health*, 86 (8), pp1087–93.

McHale JP & Fivaz-Depeursinge E (1999) 'Understanding triadic and family group interactions during infancy and toddlerhood', *Clinical Child and Family Psychology Review,* 2 (2), pp107–27.

McLearn KT, Minkovitz CS, Strobino DM, Marks E & Hou W (2006) 'The timing of maternal depressive symptoms and mothers' parenting practices with young children: Implications for pediatric practice', *Pediatrics*, 118 (1), 174–82.

Mental Health Foundation (2007) *The Fundamental Facts: The Latest Facts And Figures On Mental Health,* The Mental Health Foundation, London.

Mental Health Foundation (2009) *In The Face Of Fear: How Fear And Anxiety Affect Our Health And Society And What We Can Do About It,* The Mental Health Foundation, London.

Moffitt TE & Caspi A (1998) 'Implications of violence between intimate partners for child psychologists and psychiatrists', *Journal of Child Psychology and Psychiatry* 39 (2), pp137–44.

Mousavi S, Chatterji S, Verdes E, Tandon A, Vikram P & Bedirhan U (2007) Depression, chronic diseases, and decrements in health: results from the World Health Surveys, *The Lancet*, 370, pp851–8.

Mukherjee R (2005) 'Low level alcohol consumption and the fetus', *British Medical Journal*, 19, 330(7488) pp375–6

Murray L (2007) Presentation from Professor Lynne Murray University of Reading to the Early Years Commission, The Centre for Social Justice, London.

Murray, L (2008) Personal communication, Early Years Commission, Centre for Social Justice, Westminster.

Murray L, Arteche A, Fearon P, Halligan S, Goodyer I & Cooper P (2011) 'Maternal postnatal depression and the development of depression in offspring up to 16 years of age', *Journal of the American Academy of Child & Adolescent Psychiatry,* 50 (5), pp460–70.

NCH Action for Children (1994) *The Hidden Victims: Children and Domestic Violence*, NCH Action for Children, London.

NHS *Generalised Anxiety Disorder,* online, http://www.nhs.uk/conditions/anxiety/Pages/Introduction.aspx (accessed February 2013).

Noland VJ, Liller KD, McDermott RJ, Coulter ML & Seraphine AE (2004) 'Is adolescent sibling violence a precursor to college dating violence?', *American Journal of Health and Behavior,* 28, pp813–23.

NSPCC (2009) 'Children talking to ChildLine about family relationship problems', online, https://www.nspcc.org.uk/Inform/publications/casenotes/clcasenotesfamilyre lationships_wdf59010.pdf (accessed February 2013).

Odier C (1956) *Anxiety and Magical Thinking,* International Universities Press, New York.

Office for National Statistics (2011) 'Divorces in England and Wales', online, http://www.ons.gov.uk/ons/rel/vsob1/divorces-in-england-and-wales/2011/stb-divorces-2011.html#tab-Key-findings (accessed February 2013).

O'Higgins M, St James-Roberts I & Glover V (2008) 'Postnatal depression and mother and infant outcomes after infant massage', *Journal of Affective Disord*ers, 109 (1–2), pp189–92.

Panksepp J (1998) *Affective Neuroscience: The Foundations of Human and Animal Emotions,* Oxford University Press, Oxford.

Panksepp J & Biven L (2012) *The Archaeology of Mind: Neuroevolutionary Origins of Human Emotion,* W.W. Norton & Company, New York.

Panksepp J & Watt D (2011) 'Why does depression hurt? Ancestral primary-process separation-distress and diminished brain reward seeking processes in the genesis of depressive affect', *Psychiatry,* 74 (1), pp5–13.

Pedersen LH, Henriksen TB, Vestergaard M, Olsen J & Bech BH (2009) 'Selective serotonin reuptake inhibitors in pregnancy and congenital malformations: population-based cohort study', *British Medical Journal,* 339, p3569.

Pennebaker JW & Chung CK (2011) 'Expressive writing: Connections to physical and mental health', Friedman HS (ed), *The Oxford Handbook of Health Psychology,* Oxford University Press, New York, pp417–37.

Pine DS, Klein RG, Mannuzza S, Moulton JL 3rd, Lissek S, Guardino M

& Woldehawariat G (2005) 'Face-emotion processing in offspring at risk for panic disorder', *Journal of the American Academy of Child and Adolescent Psychiatry,* 44 (7), pp664–72.

Platania-Solazzo A, Field TM, Blank J, Seligman F, Kuhn C, Schanberg S & Saab P (1992) 'Relaxation therapy reduces anxiety in child and adolescent psychiatric patients', *Acta Paedopsychiatrica*, 55, pp115–20.

Posada G & Pratt DM (2008) 'Physical aggression in the family and preschoolers' use of the mother as a secure base', *Journal of Marital and Family Therapy,* 34 (1), pp14–27.

Radke-Yarrow M, Cummings EM, Kuczynski L & Chapman M (1985) 'Patterns of attachment in two- and three-year-olds in normal families and families with parental depression', *Child Development,* 56 (4), pp884–93.

Raine A & Yang Y (2006) 'Neural foundations to moral reasoning and antisocial behavior', *Social Cognitive and Affective Neuroscience,* 1(3), pp203–13.

Reid S (1990) 'The importance of beauty in the psychoanalytic experience', *Journal of Child Psychotherapy*, 16 (1), pp29–52.

Relate (2012) online, http://www.the3ofus.org.uk (accessed February 2013).

Richardson GA, Larkby C & Goldschmidt L (2013) 'Adolescent Initiation of drug use: effects of prenatal cocaine exposure', *Journal of American Academy of Child and Adolescent Psychiatry*, 52(1) pp37–46.

Romer G, Stavenow K, Baldus C, Bruggemann A, Claus B & Riedesser P (2006) 'How children experience a parent being chronically ill: A qualitative analysis of interviews with children of hemodialysis patients', *Prax Kinderpsychology und Kinderpsychiatry,* 55 (1), pp53–72.

Rose R (2012) *Life Story Therapy with Traumatized Children: A Model for Practice*, Jessica Kingsley, London.

Rosenblum LA, Coplan JD, Friedman S, Bassoff T, Gorman JM & Andrews MW (1994) 'Adverse early experiences affect noradrenergic and serotonergic functioning in adult primates', *Biological Psychiatry,* 35 (4), pp221–7.

Sarkar P, Bergman K, O'Connor TG & Glover V (2008) 'Maternal antenatal anxiety and amniotic fluid cortisol and testosterone: Possible implications for foetal programming', *Journal of Neuroendocrinology*, 20 (4), pp489–96.

Savonlahti E, Pajulo M, Ahlqvist S, Helenius H, Korvenranta H, Tamminen T & Piha J (2005) 'Interactive skills of infants with their high-risk mothers', *Nordic Journal of Psychiatry,* 59 (2), pp139–47.

Schore AN (1999) 'Attachment and the regulation of the right brain', Steele H & Cassidy J (eds), *Attachment and Human Development*, Routledge, London.

Schore AN (2001) *Infant Mental Health Journal Special Issue: Contributions from the Decade of the Brain to Infant Mental Health*, Wiley, New York.

Schore AN (2003a) *Affect Regulation and the Repair of the Self*, W.W. Norton and Company, New York.

Schore AN (2003b) *Affect Dysregulation and Disorders of the Self*, W.W. Norton and Company, New York.

Segal J (1991) *Phantasy in Everyday Life: A Psychoanalytic Approach to Understanding Ourselves,* Karnac Books, London.

Segal J & Simkins J (1993) *My Mum Needs Me – Helping Children with Ill or Disabled Parents*, Penguin, Harmondsworth.

Simeon D, Guralnik O, Schmeidler J, Sirof B & Knutelska M (2001) 'The role of childhood interpersonal trauma in depersonalization disorder', *American Journal of Psychiatry,* 158 (7), pp1027–33.

Singleton N, Bumpstead R, O'Brien M, Lee A & Meltzer H (2000) *Psychiatric Morbidity Survey,* Office of National Statistics, London.

Smith K (ed), Osborne S, Lau I & Britton A (2012) *Homicides, Firearm Offences And Intimate Violence 2010/11: Supplementary Volume 2 to Crime in England and Wales 2010/11,* Home Office, London.

Sroufe LA, Egeland B, Carlson E & Collins AW (2005) 'The development of the person', *The Minnesota Study of Risk and Adaptation from Birth to Adulthood*, Guilford Press, London.

Sroufe LA, Egeland B & Kreutzer TP (1990) 'The fate of early experience following developmental change: Longitudinal approaches to individual adaptation in childhood', *Child Development,* 61 (5), pp1363–73.

Stanley C, Murray L & Stein A (2004) 'The effect of postnatal depression on mother-infant interaction, infant response to the still-face perturbation, and performance on an instrumental learning task', *Development and Psychopathology,* 16 (1), pp1–18.

Stolorow RD, Brandchaft B & Atwood GE (eds) (1987) 'Affects and Selfobjects', *Psychoanalytic Treatment: An Intersubjective Approach*, Vol. 8 of Psychoanalytic Inquiry series, Analytic Press, Hillsdale, NJ/London, pp. 66–87.

Straus, M and Field, C (2003) Parental Psychological Aggression: National Data on Prevalence, Chronicity, and Severity, *Journal of Marriage and Family*, p205. p.IO5.

Straus MA, Gelles RJ & Steinmetz SK (1980) *Behind Closed Doors: Violence in the American Family,* Anchor Books, Garden City, NJ.

Sulzer J (1748) 'An essay on education and instruction of children, 1748' quoted in Miller A (1983) *For your own Good: Hidden Cruelty in Child Rearing and the Roots of Violence,* Farrar Straus Giroux, New York.

Sunderland M (1997) *Draw on Your Emotions*, Speechmark Publishing Ltd, Milton Keynes.

Sunderland M (2001a) *Helping Children Who Bottle Up Their Feelings: A Guidebook*, Speechmark Publishing Ltd, Milton Keynes.

Margot Sunderland (2001b) *Using Story Telling as a Therapeutic Tool with Children*, Speechmark Publishing Ltd, Milton Keynes.

Sunderland M (2003a) *How Hattie Hated Kindness,* Speechmark, Speechmark Publishing Ltd, Milton Keynes.

Sunderland M (2003b) *Helping Children with Loss: A Guidebook*, Speechmark Publishing Ltd, Milton Keynes.

Sunderland M (2003c) *Helping Children Locked in Rage or Hate: A Guidebook*, Speechmark Publishing Ltd, Milton Keynes.

Sunderland M (2003d) *Helping Children with Fear: A Guidebook*, Speechmark Publishing Ltd, Milton Keynes.

Sunderland M (2008a) *Smasher,* Hinton House Publishers, Milton Keynes.

Sunderland M (2008b) *Draw on Your Relationships*, Speechmark Publishing Ltd, Milton Keynes.

Suomi SJ (1995) 'Influence of attachment theory on ethological studies of biobehavioural development in nonhuman primates', Goldberg S, Muir R & Kerr J (eds), *Attachment Theory: Social, Developmental and Clinical Perspectives,* Analytic Press, Hillsdale, NJ, pp185–201.

Tabibnia G, Lieberman MD & Craske MG (2008) 'The lasting effect of words on feelings: Words may facilitate exposure effects to threatening images', *Emotion*, 8 (3), pp307–17.

Taylor CA, Manganello JA, Lee SJ & Rice JC (2010) 'Mothers' spanking of 3-year-old children and subsequent risk of children's aggressive behavior', *Pediatrics*, 125 (5) pp e1057–65.

Teicher MH & Vitaliano GD (2011) 'Witnessing violence toward siblings: An understudied but potent form of early adversity' *PLUS ONE*, online 6 (12), e28852.

Teicher MH, Samson JA, Polcari A & McGreenery CE (2006) 'Sticks, stones, and hurtful words: Relative effects of various forms of childhood maltreatment', *The American Journal Of Psychiatry*, 163 (6), pp993–1000.

Teicher MH, Samson JA, Sheu YS, Polcari A & McGreenery CE (2010) 'Hurtful words: Association of exposure to peer verbal abuse with elevated psychiatric symptom scores and corpus callosum abnormalities', *American Journal of Psychiatry*, 167 (12) pp1464–71.

The Children's Society (2011) 'Include project, working with the whole family: Developing the vision for young carers', *Include Partnership Conference Report*, September [Summary Report].

The Children's Society and The Princess Royal Trust for Carers (2002) 'Making it work: Good practice with young carers and their families', online, http://www.youngcarer.com/sites/default/files/imce_user_files/Resources/Professional/making_it_work_vol_1.pdf (accessed February 2013).

The WAVE Trust Report 2005 (2005) *Violence and What to Do About It*, Wave Trust, Croydon.

Tremblay RE (2005) 'Physical aggression during early childhood: Trajectories and predictors', *Canadian Child and Adolescent Psychiatry Review*, 14 (1), pp3–9.

Tronick EZ (2004) 'Infants' moods and the chronicity of depressive symptoms: The unique creative process of being together for good or ill. Part 2: The formation of negative moods in infants and children of depressed mother', *Psychosomatic Medicine Psychotherapy*, 50 (2), pp153–70.

Troy M, Sroufe LA (1987) 'Victimisation Among Preschoolers: Role of Attachment Relationship History', *Journal of American Academy of Child and Adolescent Psychiatry*, 26, pp166–72.

Uvnas-Moberg K (2012) Birthlight Parenting Conference, Institute of Child Health, London, May.

Uvnas-Moberg K & Petersson M (2005) 'Oxytocin, a mediator of anti-stress, well-being, social interaction, growth and healing', *Zeitschrift fur Psychosomatische Medizin und Psychotherapie,* 51 (1), pp57–80.

Uvanas-Moberg, K., Arn, I., Magnusson, D. (2005) 'The psychobiology of emotion: the role of the oxytocinergic system', *International Journal of Behavioral Medicine,* 12 (2): 59–65.

Van der Kolk BA (1989) 'The compulsion to repeat the trauma: Re-enactment, revictimization, and masochism', *Psychiatric Clinics of North America,* 12 (2), pp389–411.

Van der Kolk BA (2006) 'Clinical implications of neuroscience research in PTSD', *Annals of the New York Academy of Sciences,* 1071, pp277–93.

Van der Kolk BA, Mcfarlane CA, Weisaeth L (eds) (1996) *Traumatic Stress,* The Guilford Press, New York.

Van IJzendoorn MH, Schuengel C & Bakermans-Kranenburg MJ (1999) 'Disorganized attachment in early childhood: Meta-analysis of precursors, concomitants, and sequelae', *Development and Psychopathology,* 11 (2), pp225–49.

Warren SL, Gunnar MR, Kagan J, Anders TF, Simmens SJ, Rones M, Wease S, Aron E, Dahl RE & Sroufe LA (2003) 'Maternal panic disorder: Infant temperament, neurophysiology, and parenting behaviors', *Journal of the American Academy of Child and Adolescent Psychiatry,* 42 (7), pp814–25.

Watamura SE, Donzella B, Alwin J & Gunnar MR (2003) 'Morning-to-afternoon increases in cortisol concentrations for infants and toddlers at child care: Age differences and behavioural correlates', *Child Development,* 7 (4), pp1006–20.

Whitaker RC, Orzol SM & Kahn RS (2006) 'Maternal mental health, substance use, and domestic violence in the year after delivery and subsequent behavior problems in children at age 3 years', *Archive of General Psychiatry,* 63 (5), pp551–60.

Wickes FG (1988) *The Inner World of Childhood: A Study in Analytical Psychology,* 3rd edn, Sigo Press, Boston, MA. (Original work published 1927).

Wilcox HC, Kuramoto SJ, Lichtenstein P, Långström N, Brent DA & Runeson B (2010) 'Psychiatric morbidity, violent crime, and suicide among children and adolescents exposed to parental death'. *Journal of the American Academy of Child and Adolescent Psychiatry,* 49 (5), pp514–23.

Winston's Wish (2012) http://www.winstonswish.org.uk

Woolfall K (2008) 'Addressing the needs of children of substance using parents: an evaluation of Families First's Intensive Intervention Final Report prepared for Department of Health', Centre for Public Health, Liverpool.

World Health Organisation (2001) Young people's health in context; Health Behaviour in School – aged Children (HBSC) study: international report from the 2001/2002 survey; WHO regional Office for Europe.

Yoo HI, Kim BN, Shin MS & Cho SC (2006) 'Psychopathology, parental attachment and its impact on the development of psychiatric manifestations in school-aged children', *Psychopathology,* 39 (4), pp165–74.

Zaslow J (2010) Families with a missing piece, *Wall Street Journal.*

Zimmermann LK & Stansbury K (2004) 'The influence of emotion regulation, level of shyness, and habituation on the neuroendocrine response of three-year-old children', *Psychoneuroendocrinology,* 29 (8), pp973–8.

Zolotor AJ, Robinson TW, Runyan DK, Barr RG & Murphy RA (2011) 'The emergence of spanking among a representative sample of children under 2 years of age in north Carolina', *Frontiers in Psychiatry,* 2 (36).